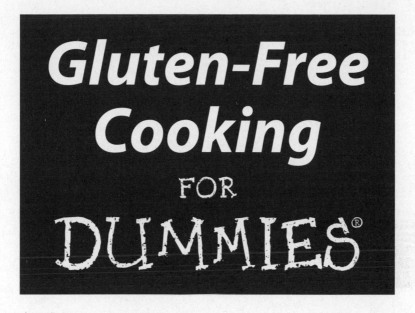

Gluten-Free Cooking FOR DUMMIES®

by Danna Korn and Connie Sarros

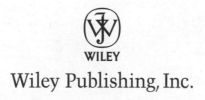

WILEY

Wiley Publishing, Inc.

Gluten-Free Cooking For Dummies®

Published by
Wiley Publishing, Inc.
111 River St.
Hoboken, NJ 07030-5774
www.wiley.com

WILEY

About the Authors

Danna Korn is also the author of *Living Gluten-Free For Dummies, Wheat-Free, Worry-Free: The Art of Happy, Healthy, Gluten-Free Living,* and *Kids with Celiac Disease: A Family Guide to Raising Happy, Healthy Gluten-Free Children.* Respected as one of the leading authorities on the gluten-free diet and the medical conditions that benefit from it, she speaks frequently to health care professionals, celiacs, parents of celiacs, parents of autistic kids involved in a gluten-free/casein-free dietary intervention program, and others on or considering a gluten-free diet. She has been invited twice to be a presenter at the International Symposium on Celiac Disease.

Danna has been researching celiac disease since her son, Tyler, was diagnosed with the condition in 1991. That same year, she founded R.O.C.K. (Raising Our Celiac Kids), a support group for families of children on a gluten-free diet. Today, Danna leads more than 100 chapters of R.O.C.K. worldwide. She is a consultant to retailers, manufacturers, testing companies, dietitians, nutritionists, and people newly diagnosed with gluten intolerance and celiac disease. She also coordinates the International Walk/Run for Celiac Disease each May in San Diego.

Connie Sarros is a pioneer in writing gluten-free cookbooks for celiacs, beginning at a time when few people had even heard of the disease. She has written five cookbooks, a "Newly Diagnosed Survival Kit," and made a DVD that covers all you need to know about gluten-free cooking. She writes weekly menus for people with additional dietary restrictions and puts out two monthly newsletters. Connie is also a staff writer for other celiac newsletters, including having a monthly "Ask the Cook" column.

In addition to being a featured speaker at national celiac conferences, Connie travels the country speaking to celiac and austistic support groups and often meets with dietitians to explain the gluten-free diet.

Authors' Acknowledgements

Danna Korn

Books are interesting. Authors get all the glory; publishers get all the money; and everyone in between gets forgotten! Well, let it be noted that I haven't forgotten anyone who has made this and my other books possible, starting first and foremost with my family.

After I finished my first book, I swore I'd never do another. And I made – and broke – that promise three more times. It's with an immense amount of gratitude that I applaud my kids, who understand that they are my highest priorities, even when I have to bury myself in front of a computer for hours on deadline. To Tyler, who is the reason I felt compelled to help others after I found myself treading in the deep end of the gluten-free pool so many years ago – and to Kelsie, my constant source of optimism and inspiration – both of you fill me with so much pride and joy, and your love and support is truly my greatest motivator. Bryan, not only are you the love of my life, but you never let me give up on this book (or anything else), in spite of what seemed to be insurmountable obstacles this past year.

Without Connie Sarros, a Real Cookbook Author, this book would be little more than zany concoctions that I made up. So thank you, Connie, not only for adding substance and validity to this real cookbook, but for your personal touches that helped make this so much more than just a book of recipes.

I'd like to offer a huge thank you to the amazing team at Wiley Publishing, starting with Mike Lewis, acquisitions editor, who got this book rolling. To senior project editor Tim Gallan, who also edited *Living Gluten-Free For Dummies,* thank you for bearing with me on yet another *For Dummies* book, and for your attention to detail and keeping me on track. To both Tim and Vicki Adang, copy editor, thank you for putting up with my retuvenantly quirky sense of humor and the overabundance of made-up words.

Connie Sarros

In January, 2007, I received a phone call from Danna Korn asking if I would like to create recipes for a new book, *Gluten-Free Cooking For Dummies.* From my heart, I thank Danna for this opportunity and for the confidence she had in me. I would be remiss if I didn't also thank her for her patience and guidance throughout this entire venture. She is absolutely amazing!

I am still awed that Wiley Publishing chose me to assist Danna with a *For Dummies* book. I am sincerely thankful to the publisher and especially to our editors, Mike Lewis, Tim Gallan, and Vicki Adang for their help and assistance throughout each phase of the book.

None of my six books would have been written at all if it hadn't been for my father, a celiac, who truly delighted in eating good food. And my dear husband: He has been so patient and understanding as, night after night, he would be my official taste-tester. Some nights we had feasts; other nights my good intentions would end up in the disposal and he would smile as he settled for eggs or a cup of soup. The support of my family has been unwavering.

A less obvious "thanks" is extended to the celiacs in the support groups across the nation. Your feedback and your shared stories gave me the needed encouragement to continue to stretch myself, creating new recipes to respond to your expressed needs. My part in the writing of this book would not have been possible without your confidence and support throughout the years.

Publisher's Acknowledgments

We're proud of this book; please send us your comments through our Dummies online registration form located at www.dummies.com/register/.

Some of the people who helped bring this book to market include the following:

Acquisitions, Editorial, and Media Development

Senior Project Editor: Tim Gallan

Acquisitions Editor: Michael Lewis

Senior Copy Editor: Vicki Adang

Editorial Manager: Michelle Hacker

Editorial Assistants: Joe Niesen, David Lutton

Photographer: T. J. Hine Photography, Inc

Food Stylist: Lisa Bishop

Art Coordinator: Alicia B. South

Cartoons: Rich Tennant
(www.the5thwave.com)

Composition Services

Project Coordinator: Katherine Key

Layout and Graphics: Carl Byers, Joyce Haughey, Stephanie D. Jumper, Julie Trippetti, Christine Williams, Erin Zeltner

Proofreaders: Laura Albert, Melanie Hoffman, Caitie Kelly, Linda Morris

Indexer: Potomac Indexing, LLC

Publishing and Editorial for Consumer Dummies

Diane Graves Steele, Vice President and Publisher, Consumer Dummies

Joyce Pepple, Acquisitions Director, Consumer Dummies

Kristin A. Cocks, Product Development Director, Consumer Dummies

Michael Spring, Vice President and Publisher, Travel

Kelly Regan, Editorial Director, Travel

Publishing for Technology Dummies

Andy Cummings, Vice President and Publisher, Dummies Technology/General User

Composition Services

Gerry Fahey, Vice President of Production Services

Debbie Stailey, Director of Composition Services

Contents at a Glance

Recipes at a Glance

Fish

Poultry

Beef and Pork

Vegetarian

Appetizers

Desserts

Table of Contents

Introduction

∙ ∙

*W*hen I was asked to write *Gluten-Free Cooking For Dummies,* I panicked. Sure, I know plenty about the gluten-free lifestyle — I've been living (and *loving*) it since 1991, and am proud to frequently be referred to as "The Gluten-Free Guru." I had already written *Living Gluten-Free For Dummies*, so I was familiar with the format of a *For Dummies* book. So why the panic?

Because although I love to cook, I'm a little — ahem — unconventional in my methods. Take measuring, for example. I don't. Oh, and recipes? Nope. I usually can't get past the list of ingredients before going my own way and modifying the recipe to suit my needs.

My ideas for recipes in this book went something like this: "Take a bunch of chicken and sauté it in butter." (Oops — forgot to tell you to cut it and heat the butter — you should have known that.) "Add a dab of whatever spices sound good to you at the moment — maybe a few globs of diced tomatoes and some veggies. When it's done, put it on the gluten-free rice noodles" (that I forgot to tell you to prepare in advance). "Voilá! You have chicken stir-fry on noodles!" That didn't go over too well.

So this book offers you a compromise. I believe in helping people figure out how to make anything gluten-free — without recipes, complicated terms, or ingredients you'll have to fly to Paris to purchase. Chapter 7 shows you how to do that using simple substitutions that you probably already have on hand.

And for those of you Real Cooks who love recipes, we have Real Recipes written by Real Cookbook Author Connie Sarros. Connie specializes in gluten-free cooking, and her recipes are easy to follow and absolutely amazing. She tends to emphasize good nutrition, which also is a passion of mine, and she introduces unique ingredients that are nutritious, delicious, and offer diverse flavors and consistencies.

Although this book focuses on *cooking* gluten-free, it also touches on medical conditions that benefit from a gluten-free lifestyle, nutritional considerations, and other practical questions and issues that you may face being gluten-free. This, though, isn't as much about lifestyle as it is about cooking. If you're interested in knowing more about living (and loving) the gluten-free lifestyle, read *Living Gluten-Free For Dummies* (Wiley).

Written in the easy-to-follow-and-incredibly-comprehensive *For Dummies* style, this book is the reference guide you need to help you create incredible gluten-free delights.

About This Book

If you've ever read a *For Dummies* book (did we mention *Living Gluten-Free For Dummies*?!?), you know they're divided into parts and chapters. Although the editors and we authors work hard to make them flow nicely from beginning to end, they're written so you can skip around if you'd like. If you get bored reading about nutrition, you can skip to shopping — or you can just dig into the recipes if you'd like.

If you're new to gluten-free cooking, I suggest you read the book in order. There are considerations that you'll want to know about for gluten-free cooking that don't relate to regular cooking, such as cross-contamination. To ensure you're making a safe gluten-free meal, make sure you read Chapter 5 before you start cooking.

Chapter 1 provides an overview of the book, so if you read nothing else, you can at least have an intelligent conversation about gluten-free cooking at the next party you attend. And by golly, won't *you* be the life of the party!

For those of you who've been cooking gluten-free for years, you're probably just dying to dig in and try Connie's amazing recipes. I encourage you to do so, but remember that rules have changed and some things that used to be off-limits on the gluten-free diet no longer are. You may want to take a look at Chapter 3 to see if something you've been avoiding is now considered safe.

By the way, I should mention that the recipes in this book have been tested by the publisher's professional recipe tester, so I'm pretty sure they all work as intended.

Conventions Used in This Book

For Dummies books are known for having consistent ground rules and conventions. Some of those used in this book include

✔ Made-up words are just part of my vocabulary — you'll get used to it, and they're not hard to figure out. For instance, a *glutenivore* is someone who eats gluten; *glutenated* means a product has been contaminated with gluten. *Glutenilicious* is a scrumptious gluten-free meal, and *glutenologism* is a made-up word having to do with gluten!

- When I refer to ingredients throughout this book, you can assume I'm referring to the gluten-free version. Soy sauce, for example — I don't say "gluten-free soy sauce" in the ingredients list. You can assume you should use a gluten-free version (please, do I really need to say that?!?).

- Recipes are designated as vegetarian by using a little tomato icon.

- Nutritional facts accompany all the recipes and are based on the actual ingredients found as the recipes appear in this book. If you make substitutions, the facts may not be valid.

- Speaking of substitutions, feel free to make them. Chapter 7 offers lots of ideas for being creative when creating your concoctions.

- A mixture of gluten-free flours works best when baking. Check out Chapter 8 for a gluten-free flour recipe and advice for storing and using gluten-free flour.

- Milk substitutes can be used in place of milk in most recipes (hence the clever name milk "substitute").

- Unless otherwise noted, all eggs are large.

- Butter and margarine are interchangeable.

- All temperatures are Fahrenheit.

- When a recipe calls for salt and/or pepper, use regular table salt and freshly ground black pepper.

- We use 90 percent lean ground beef when a recipe requires that old standby. It tastes good, has the right amount of fat for our purposes, and isn't hard on the budget.

- All Web addresses appear in `monofont`.

And follow these tips to help ensure your recipes come out tasting scrumptious:

- Read through the recipe from start to finish before you begin cooking. That way, you'll know what tools and pans you need, what ingredients to set on the counter, how the steps progress, and how much time you'll need.

- Preheat ovens and broilers at least 15 minutes before you slide the dish in.

What You're Not to Read

Well first of all, I'm impressed that you're reading this. This is the *Introduction,* folks! Aren't you just dying to dig into the good stuff?!? Because you're an introduction reader, you're likely to read all the stuff you don't need to read, but if you *want* to skip something, feel free to skip the following:

✓ **Sidebars:** Sidebars are extra bits of information you'll find in shaded boxes throughout the chapters. I think they're sometimes more interesting than the chapters themselves, but you're welcome to skip them if you'd like.

✓ **The Introduction:** Too late. You really didn't need to read it, though.

Foolish Assumptions

When we author types sit down to write a book, we make a bunch of assumptions about our readers — at the same time, you make assumptions about the author. Here are some assumptions I've made about you:

✓ You're interested in gluten-free cooking (that one was easy).

✓ You're interested because you've been diagnosed with a condition that requires a gluten-free diet, you're cooking for someone who's been diagnosed with a condition that requires a gluten-free diet, or you're interested in being gluten-free for personal interest or health reasons.

✓ You're most likely interested in the recipes, but you may also be interested in nutrition, knowing how to make your kitchen as safe as possible for cooking gluten-free foods, and cooking any food gluten-free without the aid of recipes.

✓ You're either a newbie and know very little about the gluten-free diet, or you've been at this for a while and are looking for new ideas. Either way, I've got you covered.

Likewise, while I've made assumptions about you, you can make a couple of assumptions about me and what you'll read in this book:

✓ I'm an expert on the gluten-free diet, and am known to many as "The Gluten-Free Guru." I've been researching the gluten-free lifestyle since 1991 when my son was diagnosed with celiac disease. With absolutely no resources available to me, I set out to learn everything I can — and to help others live and love the lifestyle.

✓ Unlike many authors of gluten-free cookbooks or resource materials, I *do* live the lifestyle. Granted, I didn't go gluten-free back in '91 when my son was diagnosed with celiac disease; I didn't "see the light" until 2002 when I was writing my second book and realized gluten isn't good for anyone. I've been gluten-free ever since.

✓ Connie, author of the recipes in this book, is gluten-free as well. She's the author of several gluten-free cookbooks and is a sought-after speaker, as well.

> ✔ Although this book is loaded with lots of great information about the medical conditions that benefit from a gluten-free diet, it's not intended to serve as medical advice. See your health-care professional for further guidance if you feel you need it.

How This Book Is Organized

Gluten-Free Cooking For Dummies is easy to navigate. All the parts that should go together do. The book starts out with general information about the gluten-free diet and medical conditions that it benefits; it's an overview of why you might be gluten-free or consider going gluten-free. From there, it gets into preparing to cook, which leads to the recipes. *Gluten-Free Cooking For Dummies* wraps up with the Part of Tens, familiar favorites in all *For Dummies* books.

Here's how the four parts break down:

Part 1: Preparing for Your Gluten-Free Cooking Adventures

The seven chapters in this part encompass everything but the recipes. Chapter 1 is really a brief overview of the entire book, without redundancy in reference to later chapters. The next six chapters talk about what is and isn't gluten-free, nutrition, shopping, setting up your kitchen, and figuring out how to cook anything gluten-free — without recipes.

Part II: Mouthwatering Main Courses

Part II dives right in, with recipes for main courses served up by Connie. With an emphasis on nutrition and unique ingredients, Connie's recipes are easy to follow, yet absolutely amazing.

Part III: Dishes to Enjoy Before, After, or Any Time

In this part, you'll find recipes for appetizers, salads, soups, and snacks. Desserts and baked goods round out this part, with decadent and delicious dishes you'd never guess were gluten-free.

Part IV: The Part of Tens

Without the Part of Tens, a *For Dummies* book is a *For Dum* — it's not finished. All *For Dummies* books finish with a Part of Tens, which in this book consists of two chapters, each with (get this) *ten* tips or ideas relating to gluten-free cooking. You'll find one chapter with suggestions for gluten-free comfort foods, and another with ideas for cooking gluten-free with the kids.

Icons Used in This Book

Like all *For Dummies* books, this book has icons to call out tidbits of information. Here's what the icons mean:

Can you guess what the Tip icon is for? Yep — it's for calling out *tips* that will help you with your gluten-free cooking.

You'll find friendly reminders throughout this book, marked with a Remember icon that looks like this. These are pieces of information that are important enough to have you make note of.

Text flagged with this icon can keep you out of cooking-related or diet-related trouble.

Where to Go from Here

Where to go from here is completely up to you. Like any *For Dummies* book, you can skip around if you'd like. You may want to curl up in a snuggly chair and read the first part for background information, or you may want to grab your apron (do people still wear those?) and dive into the recipes for some gluten-free cookin', good lookin'!

Part I

Preparing for Your Gluten-Free Cooking Adventures

The 5th Wave   By Rich Tennant

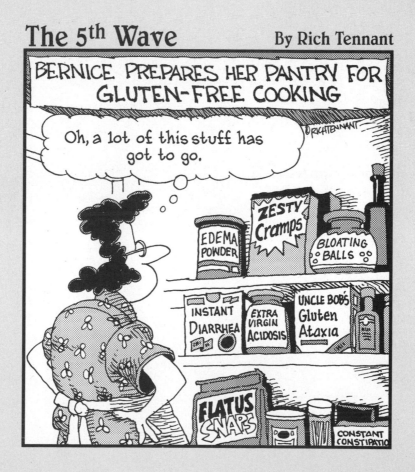

In this part . . .

You're given all of the preliminary info you need about gluten-free cooking before you dive in and try the recipes. We cover what is and isn't gluten-free, nutrition, shopping, setting up your kitchen, and figuring out how to cook anything gluten-free even when you don't have recipes.

Chapter 1

Gluten-Free: Not Just a Diet, It's a Lifestyle

In This Chapter

▶ Making long-term choices

▶ Getting the goods on gluten

*I*f you've been eating gluten (technically and in DannaSpeak that would make you a *glutenivore*) for a long time — like, oh, say, most of your life — then giving up foods as you know them like bread, pasta, pizza, cookies, crackers, and, yes, beer may seem like a tough transition at first.

You may be cooking gluten-free for one of the following reasons:

✔ You may have been diagnosed with gluten sensitivity or celiac disease.

✔ You may be cooking for someone who has been told he has to eliminate gluten from his diet.

✔ You may have read the many reasons a gluten-free diet is healthier, and you've decided to give it a try.

✔ You may have just found this book in the discount aisle of the bookstore and wondered what it's all about.

No matter why you're cooking gluten-free, you'll find that cooking gluten-free is an art form, and one that sometimes takes a little retuvenation on your part to figure out what is and isn't allowed on the diet.

Did I say diet? Because this is really more than that — it's a lifestyle. Sure, it's a diet in the sense that it concerns the things you put in your mouth — but for most people, choosing to be gluten-free is a long-term commitment, and one that affects every aspect of their lives.

Making lifestyle changes requires conscious changes in your outlook on eating. It requires long-term commitments and a great deal of education. Starting with, "What *is* gluten, anyway?!?"

Defining Gluten in Layman's Terms

There are a couple of ways to define gluten, and interestingly, the definitions actually contradict each other a little bit.

One way to define it is the scientific definition, and it involves life-of-the-party terminology like gliadin, secalin, hordein, and prolamins. This scientific definition further explains that gluten is found in all grains — yep, you heard right. All grains. Rice. Corn. All of 'em. Yet we only eliminate wheat, rye, and barley on the gluten-free diet. Well, that's why there's a layman's definition.

The layman's definition of gluten is "a protein found in wheat, rye, and barley."

Although oats don't contain gluten in and of themselves, we avoid them on the gluten-free diet because of cross-contamination issues that may arise during the production process.

So something that's gluten-free, by definition, is wheat-free. But it doesn't necessarily hold true the other way around.

Wheat worries

Gluten-free means wheat-free, but wheat-free doesn't necessarily mean gluten-free.

Something can be wheat-free but still contain gluten if it has, for instance, malt, which is usually derived from barley. In that case, the food would be wheat-free but not gluten-free because barley contains gluten.

A lot of confusion is caused by labels claiming to be "wheat-free" when the products are not. Spelt and kamut are two examples. They're definitely not wheat-free (they're actually forms of wheat), yet they're commonly marketed as being wheat-free, or being wheat alternatives. Calling spelt a wheat alternative is like calling me a human alternative. Last time I checked, I was a human, regardless of what some people might think; and spelt is, regardless of what they call it, wheat. And because spelt and kamut are forms of wheat, they are *not* gluten-free, no matter what the package says.

Common foods that contain gluten

Sometimes when I rattle off the foods that commonly contain gluten, people stare at me as though I've just recited *War and Peace* or something. It's true, the list is long. Our society has become accustomed to eating gobs and gobs of gluten; it's the most prevalent food type by far.

You can find more detail on the foods and ingredients that are okay and those that aren't in Chapter 3. As a general rule, anything with flour (white or wheat) is a no-no when you're avoiding gluten. These are some of the more obvious offenders:

✔ Bagels

✔ Baked goods (cookies, cakes, brownies, and so on)

✔ Beer

✔ Bread

✔ Cereal

✔ Crackers

✔ Malt

✔ Pasta

✔ Pizza

✔ Pretzels

✔ Soy sauce

It's important to note that there are not-so-obvious offenders, too, like natural flavorings and licorice. So you'll have to get comfortable reading labels, memorizing ingredients, and calling manufacturers to find out more details about their ingredients. (Again, Chapter 3 can help you get started.)

Don't be discouraged. Although the list may appear daunting at first, it's important to remember that the list of things you *can* eat on the gluten-free diet is a lot longer than the list of things you can't. Furthermore, for every product in this list, there's a delicious gluten-free substitution available. I talk more about specialty items and where you can find them in Chapter 6.

Deciding Whether You Should Be Gluten-Free

In the chapter opening, I pointed out that being gluten-free is a lifestyle change; that means dedication and commitment if you choose to adopt this lifestyle. So why would you do it?

Many people who go gluten-free do so not because they have any of the conditions listed in this section, but because they're striving for a healthier lifestyle.

Connie and I believe gluten isn't good for anyone (more on that in Chapter 2), especially in the highly refined form that most people know, like bread, bagels, and pasta. Cutting wheat and other gluten-containing grains out of your diet certainly isn't a bad thing and can have significant health benefits if you eat a wholesome, diverse diet. Heck, it can even be the key to maintaining your weight!

Maybe you'll find it compelling to adopt a gluten-free lifestyle when you realize that the gluten-free diet may relieve or even completely alleviate these health problems (and more):

✔ Headaches (including migraines)

✔ Fatigue

✔ Gastrointestinal distress (including gas, bloating, diarrhea, constipation, reflux)

✔ Depression and anxiety

✔ Joint pain

✔ Infertility

✔ Autistic behaviors

✔ ADD/ADHD behaviors

Wipe that look off your face; I've seen it before. I rattle off all these things that a gluten-free diet can help with, and people give me that incredulous I'm-gonna-make-her-feel-stupid-now-and-catch-her-in-her-exaggeration look, and they challenge me, "Reeeaaally? Allll those things can be helped with a gluten-free diet?" Yeah. Really.

This isn't a diet du jour. I realize that new diets pop up faster than celebrity babies with odd names, and that the diets last about as long as the celebrity marriages do. This is a lifestyle. It's a lifestyle that's perfectly in sync with the way our bodies were designed to eat — and that's why it's so effective in improving our health.

Our bodies weren't designed to eat that junk listed in the "Common foods that contain gluten" section. Bagels? Cereal? Pasta? I don't *think* so! Our bodies can rebel against those foods in ways that can sometimes severely compromise our health, and for many people, the gluten-free diet is the best — sometimes the only — treatment.

Chapter 2 explains more about gluten's effect on the body. For extensive, detailed information about the many medical conditions that benefit from a gluten-free diet, see the companion book to this one, *Living Gluten-Free For Dummies* (Wiley).

Doing Gluten-Free Nutritiously

As much as I preach about being gluten-free, I also urge people to eat a healthy diet — and the two don't always go together. I'm tempted to say there's the "right" way and the "wrong" way to do gluten-free, but that would sound a tad opinionated (who, me?!?), so I'll stick to calling them the healthy and unhealthy ways (no opinionation there, right?).

The easiest way to do gluten-free is also the unhealthiest. I call it the Simple Substitution method — you stroll through the aisles of your friendly health food store and find product after product with cute little "gluten-free" logos that make it oh-so-easy for you to identify those products as being safe on your gluten-free diet! But being gluten-free doesn't make it healthy. The fact that those products are packaged and labeled generally makes them unhealthy — albeit gluten-free.

The healthiest way to go is to stick to the "If man made it, don't eat it" rule of thumb. That means cutely labeled, processed foods aren't gonna cut it. Don't get me wrong — there are some very nutritious packaged products out there. I'm trying to generalize here, and from a bird's-eye view, the healthiest way to be gluten-free is to stick to natural, inherently gluten-free foods.

The healthiest way to eat is to follow the advice: If man made it, don't eat it.

It's pretty simple, really. Foods that fall into the "if man made it, don't eat it" allowable selections include lean meat, poultry, fish, seafood, fruits, veggies, nuts, and berries.

One pitfall people fall into when they go gluten-free is that they turn to rice, corn, and potatoes. Those would seem healthy enough, and appear to pass the "if man made it" criterion — but those foods really offer very little in the way of nutritional value, and on top of it, they're high glycemic index foods that may make you pack on the pounds. (If you didn't follow that high glycemic index part, don't worry — we talk about that more in Chapter 4.)

I encourage you to explore unique gluten-free grains-that-aren't-really-grains-but-we-call-them-grains like quinoa, millet, buckwheat, and teff. They're nutritional powerhouses loaded with vitamins, minerals, fiber, and protein — and they offer unique flavors and diverse consistencies. They're a great break from the rice, corn, and potatoes routine and pack a far more powerful nutritional punch. Chapter 3 has a lot more details on these and other gluten-free alternatives.

Getting Ready to Cook

Well, that's it. You're ready. You know why gluten-free's the way to be, and you're either committed to the gluten-free lifestyle, cooking for someone who is, or just toying with gluten-free recipes. Either way, enough chit-chat: It's time to get ready to cook!

"Getting ready to cook" means more than just donning your favorite apron, especially when you're cooking gluten-free. It usually involves a little planning, some shopping, and preparation to make sure your gluten-free food stays gluten-free.

The gluten-free lifestyle may be restricted, but it's definitely not *restrictive*.

Figuring out what to buy and where to buy it

I highly recommend planning your meals in advance. Sometimes gluten-free cooking requires ingredients you might not normally have on-hand, and you don't want to get halfway through a recipe to discover you don't happen to have any xanthan gum handy.

I also encourage you to experiment with unique, gluten-free alternatives such as quinoa, millet, buckwheat, teff, sorghum, and wild rice (more on these in Chapter 3). They're loaded with nutrition, and offer you the opportunity to think outside your usual menu plan and add new flavors, consistencies, and combinations.

Some of the unusual ingredients you may want to have on hand include xanthan gum (be prepared to sell one of your children to afford it), guar gum (when you try it for the first time, don't stray far from the potty because it can cause — ahem — "gastrointestinal distress" in some people), and unique flours like rice, tapioca, potato, and mesquite.

You can buy these specialty items online or at health food or specialty stores, co-ops, or farmers' markets; we talk more about where to find these specialty ingredients in Chapter 6.

Keep in mind that if you do gluten-free the healthiest way possible, you can find all the ingredients you need in a regular grocery store — around the perimeter. You'll just be shopping for lean meats, poultry, fish, seafood, fruits, veggies, nuts, and berries. You'll be happy, healthy, gluten-free, and relieved that you don't have to track down tapioca starch at 10 p.m.

Setting up your kitchen

Thankfully, when you decide to adopt a gluten-free lifestyle, reorganizing and setting up your kitchen is a one-time deal — and you'll pick up some habits that you'll ease into nicely. Oh, and the oven really works in your kitchen!

Setting up your kitchen just means you have to think about *cross-contamination.* Cross-contamination is when you accidentally glutenize your perfectly good gluten-free meal because you toasted your gluten-free bread in a toaster that has gluten-containing crumbs clinging on for dear life.

Crumbs can kill. Not literally, really, but they're killer in a kitchen where gluten-freebies share space with *glutenators* (people who eat gluten). Using separate utensils for cooking, and even having a few separate appliances, is a good idea. Chapter 5 covers everything you need to know about readying your kitchen and pantry for gluten-free cooking.

You don't need completely separate utensils and pots and pans for your gluten-free cooking. Washing thoroughly between preparations is fine for removing gluten left over from cooking.

Wiping away crumbs between dish preparations is crucial, and you'll find that even the order in which you cook things is altered when you're cooking gluten-free. You don't, for instance, want to fry a gluten-free grilled-cheese sandwich in the same pan you just cooked a regular sandwich in unless you thoroughly washed the skillet in between. (The easier solution is to cook the gluten-free sandwich first.) You'll get it; it's not rocket science, but it *is* crucial to keeping your kitchen as safe as it can be.

You may find it helpful to have a separate area in your pantry or kitchen to keep gluten-free products. It makes them easier to find and reduces the chances that someone's going to goof.

Cooking without Recipes (But You Can Use Them if You Like)

Connie and I believe if you give someone a recipe, you feed 'em for a meal. Teach them to make *anything* gluten-free, and you feed 'em for a lifetime. Okay, we kind of borrowed that concept from the Native American saying, "Give a man a fish and you feed him for a meal. *Teach* him to fish and you feed him for a lifetime," but you probably figured that out.

The point is, you *can* make anything gluten-free, and you're not constrained by recipes or the fact that you can't use regular flour or bread crumbs. You only need a little creativity and some basic guidelines for using gluten-free substitutions, which you'll find in Chapter 7.

If you're a die-hard recipe fan, never fear — we have them here. Real Cookbook Author Connie spent months developing the amazing recipes for this book. Most of them are super-simple to follow but leave your guests with the impression that you spent all day in the kitchen (and being thusly indebted, they're expected to do the dishes).

But I'm not a Real Cookbook Author. I don't "do" recipes. I'm more of a toss-it-in-and-see-how-it-tastes-then-modify-from-there type of cook. It stinks, because I can never make the same dish twice. I don't measure (who has the patience?), I don't *ever* have all of the specified ingredients on hand, nor do I know how to pronounce them or where I'd find them if I looked, and "proofing" to me involves finding typos or errors in my writing (turns out, that's a bread term that means "to rise"). Suffice it to say that I'm no Julia Child, but I don't have to be, and neither do you.

Connie and I believe that the most important element of cooking gluten-free is to be creative and think outside the recipe box. So I hand you a pole and say go forth and fish. May your gluten-free goodies be gastrolicious, and your fish be free of bones.

Getting Excited about the Gluten-Free Lifestyle

Most people who embark upon a gluten-free lifestyle are doing so because of health issues, and that means they have little or no choice in the matter. When people are forced to make changes in their routine, especially changes that affect what they can and can't eat, they're not always so quick to see the joy in the adjustments.

The truth is, we envision ourselves skipping merrily down a nicely paved road of life, eating what we want when we want. We don't envision ourselves having to dodge cleverly disguised gluten-laden land mines scattered about like worms after a hard rain (worms are gluten-free, in case you were wondering).

So if you're a little less than — ahem — *excited* about being gluten-free, I understand. But prepare yourself to have that frown turned upside down because there are lots of reasons to be excited about the gluten-free lifestyle.

Gluten-free doesn't mean flavor-free

People who are new to the concept of gluten-free sometimes comment that the diet is boring. When I ask what they're eating, their cuisine routine usually centers around bunny food and rice cakes. Well *duh!* Who wouldn't be bored with that?!? That type of a diet is appalling, not appealing.

I'll tell you right now I *love* food. I love the flavor, the feeling of being full, the nutritional value it provides — most of all, I love to explore new foods I've never tried before, as long as they're gluten-free, of course. There's no way I'd encourage you to endure a diet of blandiose foods that could double as packing materials.

A healthy, gluten-free diet doesn't have to be boring or restrictive. You're not constrained to eating 32 individual portions of fruits and vegetables each day, like a rabbit nibbling nervously on carrots. If you enjoy bland foods, snaps for you. But if you think gluten-free has to be flavor-free, you're in for a pleasant surprise.

Think about it. Spices are gluten-free. Onions, garlic, peppers, and other flavor-enhancing foods are gluten-free. There's really no need to languish over lackluster flavors just because you're enjoying the health benefits of being gluten-free. So slice, dice, and spice it up for a meal that's flavorful, not flavor-free.

Getting out and about

There's no reason to let the gluten-free lifestyle hold you back from doing anything you want to do. Well, okay, there are some things you can't do — like eat a Domino's pizza and Krispy Kreme donuts. But as far as your activities and lifestyle are concerned, it's important to get out and about as you always have.

I realize that for the most part it's not as easy as walking into a restaurant and asking for the gluten-free menu (a girl can dream). But eating at restaurants is definitely doable; you just need to master the art of the special order and tune in to contamination concerns. Traveling is a breeze after you're comfortable eating at restaurants *and* when you get a handle on language considerations if you're traveling abroad. Going to social events just requires a little advance planning, and holidays will barely faze you — after you get the hang of getting out and about gluten-free style.

Living your life in a bubble is for helium molecules. The gluten-free lifestyle shouldn't hold you back from doing anything (except eating gluten).

Raising kids to love the lifestyle

There are lots of things that are key in raising happy, healthy, gluten-free kids. Some of the highlights include

- Giving them control of their diet from day one
- Always having yummy gluten-free treats on hand
- Reinforcing the benefits of the gluten-free lifestyle
- Always remembering that they're learning from *you* how to feel about their lifestyle

For more inspiration and practical advice, see my book *Kids with Celiac Disease: A Family Guide to Raising Happy, Healthy, Gluten-Free Children.*

Kids are flexible and resilient. Adopting a new lifestyle like being gluten-free is usually harder for the parents than it is for the child.

Setting realistic expectations

Some people call me PollyDanna because they think I have an unrealistically optimistic view of the gluten-free lifestyle. It may be optimistic, but it's not unrealistic.

It's important to set reasonable expectations for what things will be like when you adopt a gluten-free lifestyle, because there *will* be challenges and you need to prepare to handle them well. Friends, family, and loved ones may not understand. They may not accommodate your diet when you hope or expect they will. You may find social events to be overwhelming at first; or you may get confused or frustrated and feel like giving up on the diet. There *will* be challenges — and you *will* overcome them.

Arming yourself with good information

The good news is that because the gluten-free diet is exploding in popularity, there's lots of information about it. The bad news is there's lots of information about it, and not all of it's accurate. Be leery of what you hear and read, and check the reliability of the source on everything. If you find conflicting information — and I'll warn you now that you will — dig deeper until you find out which source is right.

I cite a few good sources of information in Chapter 3, and I'm sure you'll find more on your own. Just remember to keep a skeptical eye out for the good, the bad, and the completely ludicrous.

How I got pushed into the deep end of the gluten-free pool

Here's my story about how I joined the ranks of the gluten-free.

I didn't aspire to do any of this. I was deeply involved in a successful career, and a mommy first and foremost. But today I'm an accidental author, researcher, and support group founder who was pushed into the deep end of the gluten-free pool and realized I needed to learn to swim. Fast.

Until 1991, my family and I ate a fairly typical American diet. Oh, I tried to keep it nutritious (extra cheese on the spaghetti to add protein), and I was aware of the need to limit fat and calories (scratch the extra cheese), but we didn't spend a lot of time worrying about what we ate or the long-term effects food might have on our bodies. We pretty much took eating for granted.

All of that changed in an instant when my first child, Tyler, was about 9 months old and developed what seemed to be chronic diarrhea. The pediatrician chalked it up to the antibiotics Ty was taking for ear infections and told me to call if it hadn't cleared up in a few weeks. Three weeks later, I was back in the pediatrician's office. "Yep, he still has diarrhea," the doctor

declared with confidence. "Yeah, I know. That's why I'm here," I mumbled with self-restraint worthy of the Nobel Peace Prize. "Give him foods that will plug him up like crackers and bread — and call me if it hasn't cleared up in a few weeks." *Huh?!?* That's the best you can do? My Pampers bill is higher than your paycheck, my hands are raw from washing them every six minutes, and I do eight loads of laundry a day because everything we own is covered in diarrhea, and you want me to "plug him up" and wait another three weeks? I don't *think* so!

I waited. Not patiently (patience isn't my greatest strength), but I waited. What choice did I have? Three weeks later, after another perfunctory examination of his ears, nose, and throat (did I lead you to believe this problem was *above* the waist, Doctor?!?), he made that "mmhhhmmm" noise that doctors make when they figure out the problem. Yay! We were finally going to get some answers! "Yep. He still has diarrhea." All those years of medical school had really paid off. "Don't worry about it. He's not dehydrated, and he's in the 75th percentile for height and weight. It's nothing to be concerned about." Gee, could the fact that I practically infuse him with liquids

(continued)

(continued)

have anything to do with the fact that he's not dehydrated? And does the fact that he started off in the 99th percentile and has *dropped* to the 75th mean anything? Apparently not. I was instructed not to bring him back for diarrhea, because there was nothing to be concerned about. If I was going to insist on bringing him back, I'd be fired from that pediatric office. I guess they meant it.

Doctor number two agreed with doctor number one. After a quick look in Ty's ears, nose, and throat, he declared that we had a healthy baby boy. "But what about the diarrhea?" I eeked. "Really, it's nothing to worry about. He's a healthy height and weight, he's not dehydrated, and he looks fine to me," he chirped as he raced to his next four-minute appointment. Oh, good. I'm glad he *looks* fine to you. I considered offering to give Doctor Do-Nothing a close *look* at the 22 diarrhea diapers a day that I was changing, but somehow managed to control myself.

In desperation, we changed doctors again, and — long story short — a quick look in the ears, nose, and throat turned up — you guessed it — nothing. By this time, Tyler's belly had grown hugely distended, his arms and legs were wasted to skinny little limbs, his hiney had disappeared completely, and his personality had changed. He had transformed from a lively, energetic toddler to a listless, irritable, clingy, and quiet little boy. It had been nearly a year since the diarrhea first started, and we figured we were just neurotic first-time parents with a mellow kid who pooped a lot.

Eventually, we ended up in the hands of doctor number four. By this time, "realizing" there was nothing wrong with Tyler, I thought nothing of dragging a lifeless baby with a Biafra belly into the pediatrician's office for a routine visit. After looking in Tyler's ears, nose, and throat, he laid Tyler down on his back and thumped on his belly like you might thump a honeydew melon to see if it's ripe. "My goodness," he said with that I'm-alarmed-but-I'm-a-doctor-and-don't-want-to-freak-you-out-so-I'll- talk-in-my-pediatrician—baby-talk-voice-that-will-surely-calm-you tone, "What's going on with his belly? It's very distended." I couldn't answer through the tears of relief.

After testing for cystic fibrosis, blood diseases, and cancer, we finally got the bittersweet diagnosis. "Your son has celiac disease." *Huh*? Is that anything like the flu? Surely a few weeks of antibiotics will wipe it out. "He'll need to be on a gluten-free diet for the rest of his life."

I don't have room here to give the details of the rest of the story, but you can read it in my other books or on my Web sites. Suffice it to say that the words "for the rest of his life" had a huge impact, and we realized it was time to step up to the plate and do some research and lifestyle and attitude adjustments to help ourselves — and others.

When we were told that Tyler would have to lead a gluten-free lifestyle, we had come to a fork in the road. At first, we were devastated, confused, frustrated, and grief-stricken. But we knew there was another path we could choose — a path that would have a more positive effect on Tyler's life. As we learned to live with the diet and its ramifications, we worked hard to find a way to turn the adversity into a positive force in our lives. More than a decade later, I realize that what we once interpreted as misfortune has actually been a huge blessing in our lives — and most importantly, Tyler agrees.

Chapter 2

So Why Cook Gluten-Free, Anyway?

I don't even have to renew my subscription to The Psychic Network to tell you something about you — and I've never even met you before. So what do I know? Well, I know that you're interested in whipping up some gluten-free goodies and you're looking for recipes to steer you in the right direction.

What I *don't* know is *why* you're interested in cooking gluten-free, but I can guess! Maybe you're new to the gluten-free lifestyle and you want to know what you can safely eat and how to turn it into a gluten-free gastronomic delight. Or maybe you've been gluten-free and are looking for some spice in your life and some giddyap in your gluten-free.

Maybe you suspect you have some type of gluten sensitivity, and you're trying the gluten-free diet to see if you feel better; or you're trying the gluten-free diet to help manage your weight (you'll find tons of great information about this in Chapter 4). Or maybe someone you love and cook for (or cook for and love) is going gluten-free and you're doing your best to support, encourage, and nourish your hungry guy or gal.

It doesn't really matter *why* you're cooking gluten-free, because you *are*. And that's awesome. Because the gluten-free diet can be the healthiest diet on the planet (yep, see Chapter 4 for more on that), it may dramatically improve your health, both physical and emotional.

For those of you who really want to dig into the details about the health bene-fits of a gluten-free diet, you may want to consider buying the companion to this book, *Living Gluten-Free For Dummies*. It contains everything you need to know about the medical conditions, as well as practical and emotional guidelines for living (and *loving*) a gluten-free lifestyle.

For now, we cover the basics so you know why your health may dramatically improve when you go gluten-free.

Too good to be true? Read on, my friends, read on.

Wheat May Not Be Good for Anyone

You've probably been raised to believe that wheat — especially whole wheat — is really good for you. Although wheat does offer some health benefits, the same benefits can easily be found in other foods without the unpleasant side effects that many, if not most, people experience. But here's the bottom line: I believe wheat's not good for anyone, whether you have gluten sensitivity or celiac disease or not. Move over, David Letterman — here's my top-ten list of the problems with wheat.

1. Humans don't fully digest wheat

Let's start with some basic biology. It's a simple fact that the human stomach doesn't fully digest wheat. Cows, sheep, and other ruminant animals do just fine with wheat because they have more than one stomach to complete the digestion process. When the partially digested wheat leaves their stomach, it goes to another stomach where it is further broken down, then to another and another until the process is complete.

Unlike our bovine buddies, we humans have only one stomach. When the wheat leaves our tummies, it's not fully digested. Those undigested portions begin to ferment, and do you know what the byproduct of fermentation is? Gas. Icky, belchable, fart-forming gas. For many people, this accounts for the gas and bloating they feel after they eat wheat, whether they have gluten sensitivity or not.

2. Wheat is a pro-inflammatory agent

Recently, lots of books and articles have been written on the subject of *pro-inflammatory foods*. These foods are rapidly converted to sugar, causing a rise in the body's insulin levels (read more about this in number nine on my top-ten list), causing a burst of inflammation at the cellular level. Almost everyone knows that blood sugar rises from eating sweets (cakes, cookies, and candy). But lots of foods not considered sweets have pro-inflammatory effects — foods that have wheat in them, like cereal, pasta, breads, and bagels. These foods can be high in simple starches; when these are broken down, they act the same as sweet foods, raising blood sugar levels, releasing insulin, and causing inflammation. Bear in mind that the inflammation occurs in all people, not just those with wheat or gluten sensitivities.

It turns out that inflammation, once thought to be limited to *"-itis"* conditions like arthritis, may actually be at the root of a number of serious conditions, including heart disease, Alzheimer's, and some types of cancer. And if vanity is the only way to prove a point, consider this: Dr. Nicholas Perricone, renowned author of *The Wrinkle Cure,* considers inflammation to be the "single most powerful cause of the signs of aging."

One great tool for identifying pro-inflammatory foods is the *glycemic index* (remember this term; I'm going to use it again in number nine). The glycemic index measures how fast your blood sugar rises after you eat a food that contains carbohydrates (like pasta, potatoes, and bread). It rates foods on a scale from 0 to 100, where water is 0 and table sugar is 100. The lower the glycemic index rating, the less likely the food is to be pro-inflammatory. Foods made from wheat, especially refined wheat, have a glycemic index in the 50 to 80-plus range, putting them on the high side and classifying them as pro-inflammatory.

3. Wheat can cause leaky gut syndrome

So what is leaky gut syndrome? Good question — I'm glad you asked. The simple-and-not-perfectly-correct-but-close-enough answer is that *leaky gut syndrome* is a condition whereby stuff is leaking from your gut into your bloodstream — stuff that shouldn't be there, like toxins (and large molecules like gluten!).

So how does it happen? When people eat wheat, their bodies produce extra amounts of a protein called *zonulin.*

The lining of the small intestine is basically a wall of cells that most materials can't pass through on their own. When important vitamins and minerals are present, zonulin tells the passageways in the intestinal wall to open so those nutrients can pass into the bloodstream. The blood then carries the nutrients to other parts of the body, where they can be used to nourish the body.

But when people eat wheat — not just people with celiac disease, but all people — their zonulin levels rise too high, and the passageways open too much and let things into the bloodstream that shouldn't be there. This increased permeability of the lining of the small intestine, known as *leaky gut syndrome*, can cause a variety of problems health-wise.

For people with celiac disease, leaky-gut syndrome starts the cascade of events that lead to health problems. Gluten is a large molecule that really shouldn't be able to get into the bloodstream, but it does because zonulin levels are too high, and the body allows it in. After it's in the bloodstream, the body sees the gluten molecule as an invader — a toxin — so it launches an attack, and in doing so, it damages the area around the gluten molecule, which includes the lining of the small intestine. The *villi,* which are short hair-like structures that are designed to increase the surface area of the small intestine so it can absorb more nutrients, are damaged in the attack. That's why people with celiac disease who continue to eat gluten often have serious nutritional deficiencies.

For a lot more details on how gluten affects a person who can't tolerate gluten, grab a copy of my book *Living Gluten-Free For Dummies* (Wiley).

4. Refined wheat has little nutritional value

Most of the wheat people eat is "refined." That means manufacturers take perfectly good wheat — which has some nutritional value, especially in the bran and germ — and they take the good stuff away, leaving "refined" (read "little nutritional value") wheat. Sadly, that's the form that most of our wheat-based products use — refined wheat nearly void of nutritional value, making it a high–glycemic index food that just makes you fat and messes with your insulin production.

Did you know that manufacturers actually have to *enrich* refined wheat because they've taken out all the nutrients? And even then, the wheat's not that valuable, nutritionally speaking. Whole wheat provides more nutritional value than non-whole wheat, but it's still wheat, and there are more than just a few reasons that wheat may not be good for anyone.

5. Wheat may cause wrinkles

Aha! Now *that* got your attention! Okay, so you can live with the gas, bloating, and leaky gut syndrome, but wrinkles? I think *not!* Well then put down that bagel, or buy stock in Botox, because according to some experts, the inflammatory effect of wheat — especially refined wheat — can cause wrinkles (see number two in this top-ten list for more on pro-inflammatory foods).

The most famous of these experts is Dr. Nicholas Perricone, a dermatologist and adjunct professor of medicine at Michigan State University, who maintains that inflammation contributes to accelerated aging and that through diet (and supplements and creams), you can erase scars and wrinkles, increase the production of collagen and elastin, enjoy radiance and glow, and develop a dewy, supple appearance to your skin.

Of course, this wouldn't be relevant unless the "diet" he refers to has something to do with being gluten-free. Although Dr. Perricone doesn't pinpoint gluten as a culprit per se, he does say that the pro-inflammatory response caused by wheat causes the skin to age more quickly, and he maintains that avoiding foods like wheat may help reverse the aging process.

6. Wheat may contribute to menopausal symptoms

Menopause, the time in a woman's life between about ages 45 and 55 marking the completion of her childbearing years and the end of her menstrual cycles, is often a time of marked hormonal changes. Depression, anxiety, headaches, leg cramps, varicose veins, irritability, and the famous "hot flashes" that occur are some of the more common symptoms.

But many doctors believe that lifestyle changes can minimize these symptoms, and one of those lifestyle changes is diet. Although there is some debate over wheat's role in these lifestyle changes, many experts, including Christiane Northrup, MD, author of *The Wisdom of Menopause,* believe that eliminating wheat from the diet — especially refined wheat — can help relieve menopausal symptoms.

7. Wheat is one of the top-eight allergens

Millions of people are allergic to wheat — so many, in fact, that it has made it onto the top-eight allergen list. Keep in mind that an allergy to wheat is different from celiac disease or other forms of gluten sensitivity — we'll talk more on that later in this chapter.

Allergic reactions to wheat can include gastrointestinal distress (stomach upset), eczema, hay fever, hives, asthma, and even *anaphylaxis* (a severe, whole-body allergic reaction), which is life-threatening.

Other than the anaphylaxis, these symptoms sound a lot like gluten sensitivity or celiac disease, don't they? That's why sometimes it's hard to tell the difference. That's also why sometimes people get allergy testing and find out they're *not* allergic to wheat — so they're told to go back to a normal diet of pizza, bread, and bagels. Not necessarily good advice, because they could actually have gluten sensitivity or celiac disease. So it's important to be properly tested. (Yep, you guessed it — we'll talk more about that later in this chapter, too.)

8. Wheat can mess up your blood sugar levels

Remember in number two when I talked about the glycemic index? Well, don't worry — it's not really that complicated (and there's no pop quiz). All you need to know is that some foods cause your blood sugar levels to spike, which causes your body to produce insulin. That, in turn, causes your blood sugar to fall dramatically. Basically, your blood sugar levels go from the even keel they should be on, to being the best roller coaster ride in the park. Easy, Evil Knievel. That's not a good thing in this case.

Our bodies are designed to work with stable blood sugar levels. When they're up, then down, and all around, it causes a domino effect of not-so-healthy things to occur. Lots of people talk about *hypoglycemia* — a weak, shaky feeling that usually goes away after eating, especially after eating sweet foods. Although most people don't have "true" hypoglycemia, they may feel hypoglycemic when their blood sugar drops too much. The problem with the idea of "fixing" this feeling with sugary foods is that it just continues this roller coaster of blood sugar levels that are too high, and then too low. One of the most serious conditions that can result from blood sugar whiplash is insulin resistance and diabetes.

9. Wheat can make you fat

I'm not talking about the kind of "make you fat" that you deserve if you sit around eating donuts all day. I'm talking about the kind that sneaks up on you when you think you're doing everything right, but those getting-tighter-every-day jeans say otherwise.

It could just be the wheat — especially refined wheat. That's because of what it does to your blood sugar — yeah, you can cheat and look back at number eight if you didn't read it well enough the first time — but again, it's not that complicated. Refined wheat is a high–glycemic index food that causes your blood sugar to spike. That makes your body produce insulin, which, by the way, is often referred to as the "fat-storing hormone."

Yikes. Just when you thought you were being so good by leaving the cream cheese off the bagel — you should probably ditch the bagel altogether.

10. Many people have gluten sensitivity or celiac disease and don't know it

I hear things like, "I think I'm allergic to dairy because the cheese on my pizza makes me bloat." Oh, really? What makes you think it's the *cheese?* Because more people have heard of lactose intolerance than gluten intolerance, they figure that must be what's making them feel icky.

Truth is, *most* people have no idea that they have a gluten sensitivity or celiac disease, so they usually start pointing to all the wrong culprits: cheese (dairy), tomato sauce (acids), or soy. But they're blaming the wrong foods. These people have no idea that the typical American diet comprised of bagels, pasta, pizza, cakes, cookies, and pretzels could be wreaking havoc on nearly every system in their bodies, so they continue to eat them and wonder why they don't feel good.

So how many people fall into this category? No one knows for sure. We do know that 1 in 100 people has celiac disease — but most don't know it. No one knows how many people have gluten sensitivity, but estimates are that it may be as high as 50 percent, or even 70 percent, of the population. Top that with those who have a wheat allergy, and — here, let me get my calculator out — tons of people + gobs more = an astoundingly high percentage of the population!

Recognizing Different Types of Gluten-Related Problems

Lots of people — may I dare to say *most* people?!? — have some form of gluten sensitivity (as we assert in number ten of our top-ten list in the previous section). But is it sensitivity, allergy, or celiac disease? Sometimes it's tough to tell.

I've had thousands of people tell me they're allergic to gluten. But in actuality, there's no such a thing as a gluten allergy — someone can have allergies to the foods that contain gluten: wheat, rye, and barley. In fact, wheat is one of the most common allergens, affecting millions of people (see number seven in the previous section). You could even be allergic to all three grains, and I suppose that might almost qualify for an allergy to gluten — but not really.

Allergies to gluten-containing foods

There's really no such thing as an allergy to gluten. If you happen to be allergic to all three gluten-containing grains (wheat, rye, and barley), I guess I could let it slide if you told me you were allergic to gluten — even though you're really allergic to the three grains that fall under the gluten umbrella. But most people misuse the term and say they're allergic to gluten when what they really mean to say is that they have an intolerance or sensitivity to gluten, or they have full-blown celiac disease.

Allergies to gluten-containing foods are just like other food allergies. They're all responses to a food allergen, and the reaction that someone has to those foods varies from person to person and from one food to another.

Allergic symptoms can be respiratory, causing coughing, nasal congestion, sneezing, throat tightness, and even asthma. Acute allergic reactions to food usually start in the mouth, with tingling, itching, a metallic taste, and swelling of the tongue and throat. Sometimes symptoms are farther down the intestinal tract, causing abdominal pain, muscle spasms, vomiting, and diarrhea.

Any severe and acute allergic reaction also has the potential to cause anaphylaxis, or anaphylactic shock. This life-threatening condition affects different organs, and symptoms can include a feeling of agitation, hives, breathing problems, a drop in blood pressure, and fainting. In some cases, an anaphylactic response to an allergen can be fatal unless the person having the allergic reaction receives an epinephrine (adrenaline) injection.

Distinguishing between gluten sensitivity and celiac disease

Gluten sensitivity can mean a lot of different things, and is often misused; it's a very fuzzy term. Basically, it's a sensitivity to gluten — hence the clever term, "gluten sensitivity." Often used interchangeably, the terms *sensitivity* and *intolerance* mean that your body doesn't react well to a particular food and you should avoid it. Symptoms of gluten sensitivity are usually the same as those of celiac disease, and as with celiac disease, they usually go away on a gluten-free diet.

Unlike gluten sensitivity, *celiac disease* is well-defined. It's a common, yet often misdiagnosed, genetic intolerance to gluten that can develop at any age, in people of any ethnicity. When people with celiac disease eat gluten, their immune systems respond by attacking the gluten molecule, and in so doing, the immune system also attacks the body itself. This is called an *autoimmune response,* and it results in damage to the small intestine, which can cause poor absorption of nutrients.

Although the damage occurs in the gastrointestinal tract (specifically in the small intestine), not all symptoms are gastrointestinal in nature. That's because celiac disease is *multisystemic* — the symptoms show up in many different ways and can occur in just about every organ of the body. In fact, symptoms are vast and varied, and they sometimes come and go, which makes diagnosis difficult.

Does someone who has gluten sensitivity also have celiac disease? Not necessarily. Or maybe. How's that for ambiguity? I told you it was fuzzy! Let me try to clarify.

You're told you have gluten sensitivity, but you actually have celiac disease

Some people who are told by a health-care professional that they have "gluten sensitivity" actually have celiac disease, but their testing was done improperly or was insufficient to yield conclusive results.

Say, for instance, that someone is IgA deficient (*IgA* is a special type of protein that the body produces to fight infections), and many people are. Most of the time it doesn't cause a problem. But it makes testing for celiac disease difficult, because most of the celiac tests are based on starting with a normal level of IgA. If a person doesn't have enough IgA in his body, that would make some of the celiac tests appear to be normal when actually the person's levels should have been elevated (indicating celiac disease) if he weren't IgA deficient. In other words, the person has celiac disease, but because testing was incomplete (the doctors didn't test to determine if he was IgA deficient), the results were interpreted incorrectly.

Another reason you may have celiac disease but be told you have gluten sensitivity is if the *type* of testing you undergo is specific to gluten sensitivity, not celiac disease. For instance, a stool test and a few types of saliva tests check for gluten sensitivity, but if you have celiac disease, they'll be positive. So you would, in fact, have celiac disease — but the only test you're taking in this case is for gluten sensitivity, so that's what you'll be "diagnosed" with.

If you're diagnosed as having gluten sensitivity, you may want to ask if any specific tests were done to test for celiac disease. There are antibody tests that are more specific for celiac disease, as well as genetic tests. If those tests weren't performed, you may want to get them done so you have a more definitive diagnosis.

You don't have celiac disease — YET

Sometimes in the very earliest stages of celiac disease, testing for celiac disease will be negative — but the tests for gluten sensitivity may be positive. In this case, the person has celiac disease, but it's too early to show on tests. If that person continues to eat gluten, the testing will eventually be positive (and damage will be done!).

It's important to remember that, as far as celiac testing goes, "once tested" doesn't mean "forever tested." In other words, if you're negative today, it doesn't mean you're negative forever. There's no timeline to follow in terms of how often you should have a specific test for celiac disease, but it's important to be aware that it can develop at any time.

You have gluten sensitivity, not celiac disease

Some people do, in fact, have gluten sensitivity that is not celiac disease. Symptoms are generally the same as those for celiac disease (see the very next section), and, as with the disease, health improves on a gluten-free diet.

Sorting Out the Symptoms of Gluten Intolerance

It's funny. Ask most people what the most common symptom of celiac disease or gluten sensitivity is and, if they know anything about either one (and don't look at you and say, "Huh?"), they'll most likely erupt in a loud, unabashed, confident chorus of "diarrhea, diarrhea, diarrhea!"

Yet most people with celiac disease or gluten sensitivity don't have diarrhea. In fact, they don't have any gastrointestinal symptoms at all! And if they do have gastrointestinal symptoms, they're often constipated, or they suffer reflux or gas and bloating.

Gluten sensitivity and celiac disease have hundreds of symptoms. The following sections list some of the more common ones, starting with the symptoms that are gastrointestinal in nature.

Pinpointing gastrointestinal symptoms

The gastrointestinal symptoms of gluten sensitivity and celiac disease are vast. Although most people think diarrhea is the most common symptom, gastrointestinal symptoms can include constipation, gas, bloating, reflux, and even vomiting.

These are some of the "classic" — though not the most common — symptoms of celiac disease:

- ✔ Abdominal pain and distension
- ✔ Acid reflux
- ✔ Bloating
- ✔ Constipation
- ✔ Diarrhea
- ✔ Gas and flatulence
- ✔ Greasy, foul-smelling, floating stools
- ✔ Nausea
- ✔ Vomiting
- ✔ Weight loss or weight gain

Checking out non-gastrointestinal symptoms

Celiac disease and gluten sensitivity are gastrointestinal conditions because the damage is done to the small intestine. But people more commonly have what are called *extraintestinal* (outside the intestine) symptoms. These make up an extensive list of more than 250 symptoms, including the following:

- ✔ Fatigue and weakness (due to iron-deficiency anemia)
- ✔ Vitamin and/or mineral deficiencies
- ✔ Headaches (including migraines)
- ✔ Joint or bone pain
- ✔ Depression, irritability, listlessness, and mood disorders
- ✔ "Fuzzy brain" or an inability to concentrate

✔ Infertility

✔ Abnormal menstrual cycles

✔ Dental enamel deficiencies and irregularities

✔ Seizures

✔ Ataxia (bad balance)

✔ Nerve damage (peripheral neuropathy)

✔ Respiratory problems

✔ Canker sores (aphthous ulcers)

✔ Lactose intolerance

✔ Eczema/psoriasis

✔ Rosacea (a skin disorder)

✔ Acne

✔ Hashimoto's disease, Sjögren's syndrome, lupus erythematosus, and other autoimmune disorders

✔ Early onset osteoporosis

✔ Hair loss (alopecia)

✔ Bruising easily

✔ Low blood sugar (hypoglycemia)

✔ Muscle cramping

✔ Nosebleeds

✔ Swelling and inflammation

✔ Night blindness

Watching for symptoms in kids

Kids who have celiac disease tend to have the "classic" gastrointestinal symptoms of diarrhea or constipation. They may also have some of the following symptoms that aren't gastrointestinal in nature:

✔ Inability to concentrate.

✔ Irritability.

✔ ADD/ADHD or autistic-type behaviors (I go into more detail on these behaviors and their connection to gluten later in this chapter.)

- ✔ Failure to thrive (in infants and toddlers).
- ✔ Short stature or delayed growth.
- ✔ Delayed onset of puberty.
- ✔ Weak bones or bone pain.
- ✔ Abdominal pain and distension.
- ✔ Nosebleeds.

Considering Your Options for Testing

With such an overwhelming assortment of symptoms, it's no wonder people are often misdiagnosed before finding out that they have celiac disease or gluten sensitivity. It's also no wonder so many people go undiagnosed.

A *Reader's Digest* article titled "10 Diseases Doctors Miss" cited celiac disease one of the top-ten misdiagnosed diseases. In all fairness to the medical community, it can be tough to diagnose celiac disease when you think of the myriad symptoms. Headaches, fatigue, infertility, depression — if you go to your doctor for any of those things, it's unlikely that he or she is going to say, "Hmm, you're depressed. Let's test you for celiac disease." No, it's far more likely that you'll be given an antidepressant and sent on your way.

Don't despair. There are plenty of doctors who are extremely knowledgeable about these conditions and who will do proper testing. If yours isn't one of those, keep looking until you find one who is. There are even some tests that you can order yourself without a doctor's intervention.

Looking into tests

It seems like there should be one single test you can take that would definitively determine whether you have gluten sensitivity, celiac disease, or none of the above. But alas, it's not that simple.

For one thing, there are different types of tests: blood, stool, saliva, and intestinal biopsy. In most cases, one type of test may determine whether you have celiac disease or gluten sensitivity — but most tests don't discern between the two or test for both. In other words, one test looks for gluten sensitivity but not celiac disease; another looks for celiac disease but not gluten sensitivity. And most people only get one (maybe two) of those tests, so they're rarely tested for both conditions.

So which test is best? Sounds like a simple question, but there's no simple answer. The gold standard for testing for celiac disease is a blood test followed by an intestinal biopsy. If both tests are positive, you're deemed to be confirmed as having celiac disease.

What we *can* say for certain — or close to it — is that if you test positive for celiac disease, you have celiac disease. That's because the tests for celiac disease are very specific, highly sensitive, and extremely reliable — especially when they indicate a positive outcome (diagnosis of celiac disease).

However, if the test is negative and your symptoms go away on a gluten-free diet, then you probably have some form of gluten sensitivity.

Unfortunately, there are false negatives and occasional false positives. Some people test negative yet find that they don't feel right when they eat gluten. Perhaps it was a false negative — or maybe gluten just doesn't sit right with you.

Bottom line: If it makes you feel bad, don't eat it!

Sadly, because the protocol for defining and diagnosing gluten sensitivity isn't well established and there's some disagreement about definitions of gluten sensitivity in the medical community, patients are often told to ignore inconclusive or confusing test results and to go back to eating their bagels and pizza. If you aren't sure you can trust your test results, you may want to be tested again at a later time.

For more detailed information on testing and interpreting results, see *Living Gluten-Free For Dummies* (Wiley), the companion book to this one.

Going gluten-free without testing

You may be tempted to skip the testing and jump right into a gluten-free diet. If, for instance, you highly suspect you have celiac disease or gluten sensitivity, it makes sense — going gluten-free will help you start healing the minute you start the diet. Most people begin feeling better right away, some take months to improve, but in the long-run, you can look forward to improved health — sometimes dramatically improved.

But — and I'm waving a great big caution flag here — if you plan to be tested, don't give up your gluten just yet. You have to be eating gluten for an extended length of time before getting the blood test or the intestinal biopsy.

If you don't eat gluten, or haven't eaten it for long enough, your body may not produce enough antibodies to show up on the tests, and the results *will* come back negative for gluten sensitivity or celiac disease — even if you *do* have the condition.

In other words, the gluten-free diet will "heal" you. Your body will no longer think it has celiac disease or gluten sensitivity. It will stop producing antibodies, and your intestines will heal — so the tests that determine whether you have the conditions will tell you that you don't, even if you do.

After you've gone gluten-free, you can't be properly tested for celiac disease.

No one knows for sure exactly how much gluten you need to eat to be properly tested, but if you eat the equivalent of one or two pieces of gluten-containing bread a day for at least three months, you should have enough gluten in your system to provide a measurable response.

Keep in mind, though, that you may be causing damage to your body by continuing to eat gluten! It's a conundrum, for sure!

If you decide to continue to eat gluten before testing and you have severe symptoms, talk with your doctor to decide whether you should continue to eat gluten.

Realizing the Consequences of Cheating

If you actually have gluten sensitivity and not celiac disease, you may be able to get away with eating gluten from time to time. Just make sure you remember those pesky false negatives and misdiagnoses, and make *sure* you don't have celiac disease if you're going to indulge.

Some people are told they're gluten sensitive when they really do have celiac disease. If that scenario applies to you and you continue to eat gluten, even if it's just every once in a while, you could do some serious unseen damage, not to mention you may continue to suffer unpleasant symptoms.

On the other hand, if you do have celiac disease and you want to improve your health by following a gluten-free diet, you're going to have to do it 100 percent. A "gluten-free lite" diet won't get rid of your symptoms, and it will continue to damage your body. The next few sections explain why.

Going 100 percent gluten-free is not necessarily easy. You might want to refer to *Living Gluten-Free For Dummies* (Wiley) for a more detailed manual.

Compromising your health

If you have gluten sensitivity or celiac disease and you continue to eat gluten, you *are* compromising your health, even if you don't feel any symptoms. Even the tiniest amount of gluten will cause you problems because you're still setting off autoimmune responses and your body is being robbed of important nutrients that it needs to function properly and stay strong.

When you have celiac disease, every bit of gluten you eat affects your intestinal tract adversely and keeps you from making healthy progress. That means you'll need to be extremely careful about reading labels, choosing ingredients, and avoiding contamination while cooking. (See Chapter 5 to find out more about containing contamination risks.)

Developing associated conditions

Certain conditions are associated with celiac disease. It's usually tough to tell which one developed first, but because awareness of *other* conditions is higher than that of celiac disease, people are usually diagnosed with the other one first.

It's important to understand the association between conditions for a few reasons:

✔ Someone who has one condition is more likely to have the other.

✔ If you don't give up gluten, your chances of developing an associated condition may increase.

✔ An associated condition is a red flag that you may also have gluten sensitivity or celiac disease. If you have one of these conditions, you should be tested for gluten sensitivity or celiac disease.

✔ If people in your family have an associated condition, you may want to consider urging them to be tested — and being tested yourself.

Autoimmune diseases

Several autoimmune diseases are associated with celiac disease, including

✔ Addison's disease (hypoadrenocorticism)

✔ Autoimmune chronic active hepatitis

✔ Crohn's disease

✔ Insulin-dependent diabetes mellitus (type 1 diabetes)

About 6 percent of people with type 1 diabetes have celiac disease, but many don't know it. They often find managing blood sugar levels much easier on a gluten-free diet!

- ✔ Myasthenia gravis
- ✔ Raynaud's phenomenon
- ✔ Scleroderma
- ✔ Sjögren's syndrome
- ✔ Systemic lupus erythematosus
- ✔ Thyroid disease (Graves' disease and Hashimoto's disease)
- ✔ Ulcerative colitis

Studies have shown that if you have celiac disease, the earlier in life you go on a gluten-free diet, the lower your risk of developing associated autoimmune diseases. And sometimes symptoms of other autoimmune diseases, like multiple sclerosis, improve on a gluten-free diet.

Mood disorders

Some of the mood disorders associated with gluten sensitivity and celiac disease include

- ✔ ADD (attention deficit disorder) or ADHD (attention deficit hyperactive disorder)
- ✔ Autism
- ✔ Bipolar disease
- ✔ Depression

Nutritional deficiencies

Because gluten sensitivity and celiac disease affect the small intestine, nutritional deficiencies usually develop. These can include

- ✔ Specific vitamin and mineral deficiencies
- ✔ Anemia
- ✔ Osteoporosis
- ✔ Osteopenia (low bone mineral density)
- ✔ Osteomalacia (soft bones)

Neurological conditions

Some neurological conditions are associated with gluten sensitivity and celiac disease, including

- ✔ Epilepsy and cerebral calcifications
- ✔ Brain and spinal cord defects (in newborns born to mothers with celiac disease who are eating gluten)
- ✔ Neurological problems, such as ataxia, neuropathy, tingling, seizures, and optic myopathy

Other conditions

Several other conditions are commonly associated with celiac disease, including

- ✔ Cancer (such as non-Hodgkin's lymphoma)
- ✔ Down syndrome
- ✔ Internal hemorrhaging
- ✔ Organ disorders (of the gallbladder, liver, spleen, or pancreas)
- ✔ Tooth enamel defects
- ✔ Cystic fibrosis

Understanding How Gluten Affects Behavior

You're probably not going to get too far in a court of law pleading, "The wheat bread made me do it!" But gluten is sometimes guilty when it comes to affecting behavior and moods.

Gluten can affect your behavior in many ways. Some behavioral manifestations of gluten sensitivity and celiac disease can include

- ✔ Inability to concentrate or focus
- ✔ Attention deficit disorder (ADD) and attention deficit hyperactive disorder (ADHD) type behaviors
- ✔ Autism
- ✔ Depression, bipolar disorder, schizophrenia, and mood disorders
- ✔ Irritability
- ✔ Lack of motivation

Connecting gluten and autism

Dietary interventions for developmental and behavioral disabilities have been the topic of many heated discussions for decades. One of the most remarkable (in my opinion) things about the gluten-free diet is that it seems to play a role in reversing autistic behaviors — at least in some cases.

Several credible double-blind, placebo-controlled studies are underway at reputable universities to study the relationship between gluten and autism. The results of these studies are eagerly anticipated and will most likely have a dramatic affect on the way pediatricians view the disorder.

For now, I'll summarize what we know. Gastrointestinal problems seem to be more prevalent in people with autism than in the general public — do they have a higher incidence of celiac disease? No one has studied that. Is there a connection? Maybe.

The scientific community believes that there's a genetic basis for autism. But interestingly, there seems to be a nutritional component.

The most popular diet promoted as a "cure" for autism is a gluten-free, casein-free diet (*casein* is the protein found in milk). No one claims that this works in all cases; nor do they say it's truly a cure. But *if* a dietary intervention protocol could actually improve autistic behaviors, wouldn't that be amazing? Some say it can.

Just a short time ago, the evidence was largely anecdotal, but now the "Defeat Autism Now!" protocol recommends that every autistic child be placed on a gluten-free, casein-free diet for at least three months.

In some autistic children, gluten and casein are turned into a sort of drug that the brain makes, much like morphine. Essentially, many autistic children are "drugged" on wheat and milk products, as if they were on a morphine drip.

Basically, when people with autism eat gluten and casein, they get a high off of the foods, and they become addicted. This "high" is similar to the one experienced by opiate users, and it may account for some of the typical traits found in autistic kids, such as repetitive movements like head banging and spinning, being withdrawn, and having a fascination with parts of objects (like fixating on one part of a toy rather than the toy itself).

Results on the gluten-free, casein-free diet vary. Some see improvement within a week, some within a year, and others see no improvement at all. Even in those who report behavioral changes, the changes themselves vary. Some people with autism are able to sleep through the night, others become more verbal and interactive, and some are completely "normalized" on the diet.

The gluten-free diet can be *especially* difficult for a person with autism, because these folks tend to develop food preferences, and these usually include gluten-containing foods.

Delving into depression and other mood disorders

People with celiac disease have a higher incidence of mania, seizures, and other neurological problems. In addition, clinical depression, bipolar disorder, schizophrenia, and a variety of mood disorders can sometimes be associated with or exacerbated by gluten sensitivity and celiac disease. Some journal articles even list these disorders as symptoms of celiac disease, and these conditions sometimes improve on a gluten-free diet.

Schizophrenia has been associated with celiac disease since the 1960s, when it was first noted that restricting gluten and dairy led to improvement in some institutionalized patients. Interestingly, the same opiate-like chemicals found in the urine of autistic people are often found in schizophrenics.

Some investigators have noted that the incidence of schizophrenia is higher in places where wheat is the staple grain than where people normally eat non-gluten-containing grains. In one study done in the highlands of Papua, New Guinea, where little or no grain is consumed, only two people out of 65,000 adults could be identified as chronic schizophrenics. In the coastal area, where wheat is consumed more, the prevalence of schizophrenia was about three times higher.

Chapter 3

What's Gluten-Free and What Isn't?

In This Chapter

▶ Separating the go-ahead foods from the no-nos

▶ Hunting down hidden gluten

▶ Checking out the array of gluten-free alternatives

▶ Ferreting out facts on labels and from manufacturers

*W*hen you're cooking gluten-free meals, it's crucial to ensure that your ingredients are 100 percent gluten-free. Sounds simple enough, doesn't it? Wheat = gluten; rye = gluten; barley = gluten. So a recipe minus wheat, rye, or barley is gluten-free, right? Um . . . no. Not necessarily.

Unfortunately, it's not quite that simple to figure out what's gluten-free and what's not. Picture a veggie garden with lots of healthy tomato plants. Well, gluten can be hidden, like those pesky tomato worms in your veggie garden. You can look and look; one day your tomato plants may appear to be free of the disgusting, overgrown amoebas, but when your plants are ruined, you realize you somehow missed spotting the destroyer.

Gluten can be the same way. It can hide in the ingredients you least suspect. And one little bit of it will ruin the entire plant — er, I mean meal!

The gluten-free diet may seem cumbersome at first because the *derivatives* of gluten-containing grains may contain gluten. As if that's not complicated enough, many processed foods — which contain seasonings, additives, and flavorings — can also contain questionable ingredients.

This chapter helps you find your way through the maze of grains, flours, and alternatives that you can safely use in gluten-free cooking. You're about to meet some foods that may be new to you, with exotic names like *quinoa, millet, buckwheat,* and *teff*. And you may have some surprising realizations as you discover that some of these alternatives are far more nutritious than wheat.

To help you ease into what may be unfamiliar territory, I start by separating foods into those that are definite no-nos and those that are definitely okay. Then I explain how to search out hidden gluten. Finally, I introduce you to those incredible gluten-free alternatives.

Keep in mind that the lists of foods that do and don't contain gluten vary, and they're only here to help you get started. You can find up-to-date lists of safe, forbidden, and questionable foods at www.celiac.com.

Avoiding These Definite No-Nos

I'll just get to the point. Here are the grains you need to avoid on a gluten-free diet:

- **Wheat** and almost anything with the word *wheat* in its name. Okay, we know you're thinking, "She gets her name on a book to tell me I can't eat *wheat!?*" Okay, smarty pants, I realize that staying away from this grain may seem obvious. But it's not that straightforward. Sure, it may be obvious that you'll also need to avoid hydrolyzed wheat protein, wheat starch, wheat germ, and so on, but you may not realize that you need to beware of aliases like *flour, bulgur, semolina, spelt, frumento, durum* (also spelled *duram*), *kamut, graham, einkorn, farina, couscous, seitan, matzoh, matzah, matzo,* and *cake flour.*

  Wheat grass, like all grasses, is gluten-free.

- **Wheat starch,** which is a wheat that's had the gluten washed out. In some countries, a special type of wheat starch called Codex Alimentarius wheat starch is allowed on the gluten-free diet — but standards vary from country to country. Codex Alimentarius wheat starch isn't allowed in North America because some people question whether the washing process completely removes all residual gluten.

- **Barley and its derivatives.** Besides avoiding barley in its pure form, you need to avoid malt and malt flavoring, which are usually derived from malt.

- **Triticale,** which most people have never heard of. It's a cross between wheat and rye, and was developed to combine the productivity of wheat with the ruggedness of rye.

- **Rye.** This grain isn't really hidden in any ingredients, so the pure form of rye — usually found in rye bread — is what you need to avoid.

✔ **Derivatives of gluten-containing grains.** If you thought you were done with derivatives when you finished your calculus class, you were wrong. You need to avoid derivatives of gluten-containing grains, and the most common one to watch out for is **malt,** which usually comes from barley. Malt, malt flavoring, and malt vinegar are definite no-nos. If malt is derived from another source, such as corn, it will usually say so on the label; for instance, "malt (from corn)." That's not too common, though, so if the source isn't specified, don't eat it.

Here are some foods that *usually* contain gluten. You'll need to avoid these as well:

✔ Beer

Some great new gluten-free beers are available. Not only are smaller, specialty breweries making them, but even the big boys like Budweiser have come out with a gluten-free beer that you can buy just about anywhere beer is sold.

✔ Bread, bread crumbs, biscuits

✔ Cereal

✔ Cookies, cakes, cupcakes, doughnuts, muffins, pastries, pie crusts, brownies, and other baked goods

✔ Cornbread

✔ Crackers

✔ Croutons

✔ Gravies, sauces, and roux

✔ Imitation seafood (for example, imitation crab)

✔ Licorice

✔ Marinades (such as teriyaki)

✔ Pasta

✔ Pizza crust

✔ Pretzels

✔ Soy sauce

✔ Stuffing

Now, that's not so bad, is it? And I promise you, the list of foods you *can* eat is a lot longer than this one!

Getting the Green Light: Definitely Okay Foods

Now for the good news! The list of definitely okay foods is impossibly long! There's no way we could list all the okay foods, because most *natural* foods are inherently gluten-free. So in this section, we talk about grains and starchy foods because those are the ones you may question. Some of these things may be strange sounding and new to you, but give 'em a try! You can find more information about each of the foods listed below later in the chapter.

- Amaranth
- Arrowroot
- Buckwheat/groats/kasha
- Chickpeas
- Garfava

Garfava is actually a nutritious blend of garbanzo and fava flours that Authentic Foods developed. Because it's exclusive to that one company, it's not found on many gluten-free food lists, but it has become a popular ingredient in so many cookbooks that we felt compelled to list it here.

- Job's Tears
- Mesquite (pinole)
- Millet
- Montina (Indian ricegrass)
- Quinoa (hie)
- Ragi
- Rice
- Sorghum
- Soy
- Tapioca (gari, cassava, casaba, manioc, yucca)
- Taro root
- Teff

In addition to the grains and starches listed above, plenty of other foods are naturally gluten-free. (***Note:*** These refer to plain, unseasoned foods without additives or processed products.)

✔ Beans

> Garbanzo beans by any other name are . . . well, they're still garbanzo beans. They can be called besan, cici, chana, or gram — not to be confused with graham, which *does* have gluten.

✔ Corn

✔ Dairy products

✔ Eggs

✔ Fish

✔ Fruit

✔ Legumes

✔ Meat

✔ Nuts

✔ Potatoes

✔ Poultry

✔ Seafood

✔ Vegetables

You can also find specialty products like cookies, cakes, brownies, breads, crackers, pretzels, and other products that have been made with gluten-free ingredients. Chapter 6 helps you figure out where to buy these sorts of goodies.

Snooping for Hidden Gluten

In the "olden days," the list of questionable foods and ingredients used to be really long. And it was longer than it needed to be, because it included things like vinegar, vanilla, almond extract, and sometimes, foods that were just plain ridiculous to be on the no-no list, like canola oil. For people on a gluten-free diet, staying away from these so-called questionable foods dramatically reduced their cooking and dining choices.

In the last several years, we've come a long way, baby. Thanks to new labeling laws and decades of research, there are far fewer "questionable" ingredients than there used to be. These days, manufacturers have to indicate if a product has wheat in it, and new labeling laws require manufacturers to clearly define the gluten-free status of foods. (For more on reading labels, see the section, "Labeling gluten-free: The law and what it means," later in this chapter.)

These new regulations have opened the pantry door to lots of ingredients that used to be considered off-limits. For example, we now know that regardless of the source, the distillation process eliminates all sources of gluten from vinegar. In other words, even if the vinegar started from wheat (which it usually doesn't), all the gluten is gone after distillation.

Distilled vinegar, cider vinegar, and most vinegars are okay — but malt vinegar is still off limits.

The publication *Gluten-Free Living* and its sister Web site, `www.glutenfree living.com`, are excellent sources for sorting out fact from fiction on questionable ingredients.

Ending the controversy about "questionable" ingredients

The debates will never end. You'll still see ingredients on the no-no list that shouldn't be there — and you'll still see Internet postings from people who swear grapes have gluten in them because they ate a grape and had an upset tummy the next day.

Don't believe everything you read (except in all of my books!). The Internet is loaded with bad information, and even some product guides and printed brochures can't be trusted.

Fortunately, some of the controversy has been put to rest, thanks to new labeling laws and more definitive research. The following ingredients used to be considered questionable, but are now okay on the gluten-free diet:

- ✔ Alcohol (distilled)
- ✔ Caramel color
- ✔ Citric acid
- ✔ Dextrin

  Technically, dextrin can be made from wheat, but most companies in the U.S. use corn. Again, because of labeling laws, if it's made from wheat, the ingredients list has to say so.

- ✔ Flavoring extracts
- ✔ Hydrolyzed plant protein (HPP)
- ✔ Hydrolyzed vegetable protein (HVP)

HVP can be derived from wheat. But because of the new labeling laws, if it *is,* the label has to say that. It would most likely appear on the label as "hydrolyzed wheat protein."

✔ Maltodextrin

Maltodextrin confuses people, because of the word *malt* in the name. Dextrin can be made from wheat, but maltodextrin is gluten-free unless it specifically says "wheat maltodextrin" or "maltodextrin (wheat)."

✔ Modified food starch

✔ Mono- and diglycerides

✔ Starch (in food)

✔ Vanilla and vanilla extract

✔ Vinegar (except malt vinegar)

✔ Wheat grass

✔ Yeast (except brewer's yeast)

Pharmaceuticals don't have the same labeling requirements that foods have. Some ingredients, like starch, for instance, can contain gluten, and it may not be indicated. For pharmaceuticals that have questionable ingredients listed, you'll need to call the manufacturer (I outline how to do this later in the chapter) or consult a trusted source to know whether it's gluten-free.

Gluten-free guidelines in North America might be different from those in other countries. The gluten-free status of ingredients listed in this book refers to ingredients produced in the U.S. and Canada.

Knowing which foods to question

Someday, all gluten-free foods will be clearly labeled as such, and there won't be any "questionable" foods. For now, though, you need to question some ingredients before deciding if they're safe for you to eat.

Most of these ingredients rarely contain gluten, but according to the U.S. Food and Drug Administration Code of Federal Regulations (CFR), they *can* contain gluten, which means you need to dig a little deeper to know for sure if they're okay for you to eat. Some of the ingredients you should question include

✔ Brown rice syrup

✔ Fillers

✔ Flavors and natural flavorings

✔ Seasonings and spice blends

✔ Stabilizers

✔ Starch (in pharmaceuticals)

✔ Yeast (it might be brewer's yeast)

Sometimes brewer's yeast is a byproduct of beer. In that case, it's not considered gluten-free. Nutritional supplements that have brewer's yeast in them, though, are sometimes made from sugar, in which case they're okay.

Some foods fall into the questionable category because of contamination issues. For example, oats don't have any gluten, but they're often contaminated in the manufacturing process. We recommend that you avoid them unless you can buy certified contamination-free, gluten-free oats grown in dedicated facilities with no possible risk of cross-contamination. The label will actually say "gluten-free oats." Unfortunately, only a few manufacturers produce gluten-free oats, so they're kind of hard to find, and, frankly, a little pricey. Try your local natural food stores and online sources.

Getting to Know Gluten-Free Alternatives

Even if you weren't cooking gluten-free, we'd suggest you give these gluten-free ingredients a go. Not only are they acceptable substitutes for wheat, rye, and barley, but they also offer unique flavors, textures, colors, and characteristics that you don't find in rice, corn, and other flours commonly found in the typical diet. Furthermore, many of them are loaded with nutrition, and they fill you up like a starchy wheat product might.

Lots of people call these grains, but most of them aren't actually grains. They're flowers or fruits. The following sections take a closer look at some of these alternative grains, starches, and cereals. We cover the nutritional values of these foods in Chapter 4.

Amaranth

A staple of the Aztec culture, this relative of pigweed and cockscomb is loaded with fiber, iron, calcium, other vitamins and minerals, and amino acids, including lysine, which isn't found in most grains. Amaranth is an excellent source of protein (16 percent) and has a pleasant peppery and nutty flavor. The beadlike amaranth seeds should always be cooked before eating. Amaranth can be milled, toasted, popped like popcorn, eaten like hot cereal, or used in soups and granolas. You also can cook its leaves and eat them as greens.

Separating the wheat from the gaffe: You'll make mistakes!

Because sorting out what's okay and what's not may be more difficult than you may have thought, you *will* make mistakes in the process. That's okay. You'll make mistakes from time to time not because you're lazy, dumb, or subconsciously trying to sabotage your intestines — it's because you're human, and figuring out all of the gluten-free facts can be really tough!

We're not suggesting that you slip and slide your way through the diet, but accidentally ingesting a little glob of gluten is no reason to panic, nor do you need to call 911. Gluten insensitivity isn't like a peanut allergy that can throw you into anaphylactic shock. If you accidentally have a shot of the wrong soy sauce or piece of pizza crust, learn from your mistakes and keep practicing until the diet becomes a way of life.

Arrowroot

You may remember the name *arrowroot* from the baby food aisle. Arrowroot biscuits are one of the first solid foods babies can safely eat (but beware: manufacturers usually add wheat flour to arrowroot biscuits, so they're not gluten-free). With a look and texture similar to cornstarch, arrowroot is an herb thought to soothe the stomach and have antidiarrheal effects (that's music to many people's ears when they have an intolerance to gluten and are used to — ahem — making quick trips to the bathroom). In cooking, arrowroot makes a great substitute for cornstarch and can be used to thicken soups, sauces, and confections.

Buckwheat/groats/kasha

Boy, this one causes me grief. People think I'm off my rocker when I tell them that buckwheat is gluten-free. Yeah, I know — it has the word *wheat* in its name, but buckwheat isn't even remotely related to wheat. It's a fruit, high in B vitamins, phosphorous, magnesium, iron, copper, manganese, zinc, and all eight essential amino acids (amino acids the body doesn't produce but needs to keep functioning), making it a more complete protein than many other plant sources. It's also a good source of linoleic acid, an essential fatty acid, and is the only grain known to have high levels of ruti, an antioxidant that reportedly improves circulation and prevents LDL cholesterol (the bad kind) from blocking blood vessels.

Also known as kasha and groats, buckwheat boasts a hearty, earthy flavor. Most of the time it's ground into a gritty, dark flour, and used to make soba noodles, pancakes, or other baked goods. Some people cook it like rice, boiling 1 cup of buckwheat in 2 cups of water.

Although there are pure, gluten-free soba noodles and pancake mixes made from buckwheat, read the labels! Some forms of these products also contain wheat flour.

Garfava

Garfava is the name of a commercial blend of flours made by a company called Authentic Foods. Normally I wouldn't put a specialty item in a list like this, but garfava has become such a common gluten-free flour that it's featured in many cookbooks. This mixture of chickpea (garbanzo beans) and fava bean flours is high in protein, low in fat, and rich in fiber. Its unique nutty taste adds extra flavor to quick breads, muffins, cakes, veggie burgers, and coatings for chicken and fish.

Job's Tears

Job's Tears is also referred to as coix seed, adlay, or adlai — yeah, like *that* helps at all! Job's Tears is a tall, tropical plant that produces a grain that's gluten-free.

Popular in Asia, Job's Tears is often dried and cooked as a grain like rice or barley, and it has a similar flavor to barley. People in Korea and China use it to make distilled liquors, or as a tea, sometimes by powdering the grain itself and mixing it with hot water; other times, the whole grains are simmered in water and then mixed with sugar. Job's Tears are said to have medicinal properties, helping with gastrointestinal disorders, painful joints, rheumatism, and edema.

Some Asian supermarkets sell Job's Tears as Chinese pearl barley — but it's not. And don't worry, Job's Tears isn't even closely related to barley — if it were, there might be a question about whether it's gluten-free, but there's no question at all.

Mesquite (pinole)

Mesquite — for me, it conjures images of a barbecued, smoky-sweet flavor. But it's also a tree that produces bean pods, which can be dried and ground into flour. It adds a sweet, nutty taste that bears a hint of molasses, and is even used to make jelly, wine, and juice. With soluble fibers that slow the absorption of nutrients and its low glycemic index, mesquite is helpful in controlling blood sugar levels. Its sweet pods and seeds are a good source of fiber, calcium, manganese, iron, zinc, protein, and lysine.

Millet

Some might say that millet is for the birds — that's because it's the grain found in most bird feeders. But it's good for humans, too! Millet is actually a grass — with a small seed that grows in a variety of shapes, sizes, and colors. Packed with vitamins, minerals, and other nutrients, millet is also loaded with fiber, protein, and B-complex vitamins. This easily digested, extremely nutritious seed has been a staple food in Africa and India for thousands of years. In parts of India today, millet flour is combined with sorghum flour to make a common bread called bhakri.

Millet is a small, round grain that has a mild, yet nutty flavor, especially if you toast it in a dry skillet for about three minutes. Add millet to soups for extra body, or mix it with brown rice or quinoa to add unique flavors and textures. Millet can be cooked like other grains, using 1 cup of millet to 2½ cups of water. You can use less water for a crunchier flavor or more for a consistency more like mashed potatoes.

Montina (Indian ricegrass)

Montina is actually a trademarked name by a company called Amazing Grains. Montina is a type of flour made from Indian ricegrass, which was a dietary staple of Native Americans more than 7,000 years ago and today is native to Montana. Loaded with fiber and protein, this bold-flavored grain was a good substitute when maize crops failed or game was in short supply.

Because Montina is a brand name, it comes with a recipe booklet. Because it tastes like wheat and has a hearty texture, it makes a good replacement for regular flour in baking.

Quinoa (hie)

Pronounced *keen*-wah, ancient Incas considered quinoa sacred and referred to it as "the mother of all grains" — but it's actually a fruit. Unlike other grains like wheat or rice, quinoa has a balanced set of essential amino acids and is a complete protein. It's especially high in lysine, an amino acid that most grains lack. Also high in phosphorous, calcium, iron, vitamin E, assorted B vitamins, and fiber, quinoa is exceptionally nutritious. Although quinoa is usually pale yellow, it also comes in pink, orange, red, purple, and black.

Quinoa can be cooked like rice, using 1 cup of the grain to 2 cups of water. You can also throw raw quinoa into soups to thicken and add an interesting texture, or use cooked quinoa under chili or as you would a rice dish. Quinoa flours and pastas are also available, giving you more options for gluten-free variations on gluten-containing favorites.

Quinoa has a coating called *saponin,* which is bitter. But the quinoa we buy has been processed, and the coating has been removed. By the way, that bitter coating may be what makes quinoa such a durable crop. It's likely that the birds and insects that can devastate a crop find the coating too bitter and leave it alone. Attempts to grow quinoa with less of the coating have resulted in crops that are decimated.

Ragi

Ragi is also referred to as *finger millet* and is grown as a cereal in the arid areas of Africa and Asia. It's especially valuable nutrient-wise, because it has the amino acid methionine, which is lacking in areas where poverty forces people to live on starchy staples like cassava, rice, plantain, or corn meal. Ragi is often ground and cooked into cakes, puddings, or porridge, and is made into a beer-type drink in many parts of Africa.

Rice

Rice is a common staple in the gluten-free diet because people tend to think of starches as rice, corn, potatoes, and wheat. With wheat off the menu, they turn to rice, corn, and potatoes. Not all rice is created equally, though. White rice has most of the good stuff (germ and bran), nutritionally speaking, removed. Brown rice is a whole grain and far more nutritious than white. By the way, wild rice isn't rice at all! It's the seed of an aquatic grass, grown primarily in Minnesota.

Contrary to what you might guess, glutinous rice doesn't have gluten! Made from high-starch, short-grain rice, glutinous rice thickens sauces and desserts in Asian cooking and is the rice most commonly used in sushi. (Remember, no soy sauce or fake crab in your sushi!)

Sorghum

Also known as *milo,* this gluten-free insoluble fiber is probably best known for the syrup that comes from one of its varieties. Because sorghum's protein and starch are more slowly digested than that of other cereals, it may be beneficial to diabetics. Sorghum's bland flavor and light color don't change the taste or look of foods when it's used instead of wheat flour.

Soy

Soy is actually a legume, not a grain. It's commonly used in the gluten-free diet because people know it's gluten-free and it's accessible. Usually, it's mixed with other flours — but beware: It has a strong, distinctive flavor. Either you love it or you don't, and after you've added it, there's no going back.

There are plenty of ways to incorporate soy into your diet. You can use soy milk or yogurt, flour, or tofu, each of which offers a huge variety of cooking options. For soy milk and yogurt, you can simply substitute the soy variety for dairy products. Soy flour can be mixed with other flours and used in baked goods, and tofu can be fried, baked, or grilled.

Tapioca (gari, cassava, casaba, manioc, yucca)

Think there are enough names for tapioca? Well, tapioca by any other name is still tapioca. Most people think of tapioca pudding when they think of tapioca. And, unless someone gets really freaky with their recipe, tapioca pudding is gluten-free! But the flour is used in a lot of gluten-free recipes, too. Basically, it doesn't have any flavor, which is a good thing sometimes (see the flavor description for soy!). Because it's flavorless, tapioca flour or starch makes a great thickener for sauces, gravies, soups, stews, puddings, and pies. Tapioca gives a glossy sheen and can tolerate prolonged cooking and freezing. Tapioca is native to South America, so if you visit there, you'll find lots of great tapioca (manioc) breads that are gluten-free!

Taro root

Most people know taro as the ingredient in the Hawaiian dish poi. Also called *kalo,* taro is a starchy tuber vegetable much like a potato, and it's rich in vitamins and minerals. The leaves are a good source of thiamin, riboflavin, iron, phosphorus, and zinc — and also vitamin B6, vitamin C, niacin, potassium, copper, and manganese. They're also a great source of fiber. In its raw form, taro is toxic because it has calcium oxalate, but cooking destroys the toxin, so it's safe for consumption. Like potatoes, taro roots can be fried, baked, roasted, boiled, or steamed.

Teff (tef)

This nutritional powerhouse is the smallest of the grains that aren't true cereal grains. It's actually a grass with a seed that looks (and cooks) a lot like quinoa and millet, but it's smaller. An important food in Ethiopia, teff is used to make a common bread called *injera* (but beware: Most injera has wheat flour, too). Teff packs a protein content of nearly 12 percent and is five times richer in calcium, iron, and potassium than any other grain. Its sweet, nutty flavor makes teff flour a delicious additive to baked goods, or you can cook the whole grain and serve it with sliced fruit or as a breakfast cereal.

Reading Labels and Getting Answers (Most of the Time)

It should be so simple — if a product is gluten-free, it should say so, right? Sure. It would list the ingredients, and right there in big, bold letters, it would say, "This product is 100 percent gluten-free, no ifs, ands, or buts." Fortunately, labeling laws are headed that direction, but we're not quite there yet.

The Food Allergen Labeling and Consumer Protection Act of 2004 required clear labeling of all foods that contain any of the top eight allergens — wheat, milk, eggs, fish, shellfish, tree nuts, peanuts, and soybeans. Because of this act, manufacturers must clearly identify wheat and all of its derivatives on food labels. With this act in place, knowing which foods are definitely off-limits because they contain wheat is much easier.

Although wheat and its derivatives are called out on all labels, you still need to watch for other gluten-containing grains (barley, rye, and cross-contaminated oats) and their derivatives, and realize that they can be (but often aren't) hidden in flavorings and additives. And remember that you won't see "gluten-free" on the label — at least not yet — but you don't really need to. (A new law is in the works; you'll find out more about it in the next section.)

Getting the hang of the gluten-free diet means you'll have to memorize ingredients you've never heard of. And yes, even though this is a cookbook and you'll be working with ingredients rather than prepared foods, you'll still have to read the labels on the ingredients you use.

Labeling gluten-free: The law and what it means

My friend Cynthia Kupper, Executive Director of the Gluten Intolerance Group of North America, has helped me write this section explaining the United States Food and Drug Administration's new guidelines for labeling food products gluten-free. These guidelines are still being finalized at the time of this writing and are a welcome advancement in gluten-free labeling for consumers.

Defining "gluten-free" gives consumers more information and set a standard that manufacturers will have to meet before they can label their products as such. Use of the "gluten-free" label will be voluntary, but the FDA will enforce its requirements on those who choose to use it.

Defining what a "gluten-free" label means

"Gluten-free" will most likely be defined as follows:

- A food cannot contain a prohibited grain (wheat, rye, barely, and hybrids of these grains)

  or

- If a food contains a prohibitive grains, it must show that the grain has been altered to remove the protein (generally a chemical process to remove protein and purify the starch or oil)

  and

- The finished product (as it will be sold) cannot contain more than 20 ppm (parts per million) of gluten. A company can prove this by testing for gluten in their products. Other tests can prove the lack of protein in a food. When there is no protein, there is no gluten.

If a product can meet the above criteria, it can carry the words "gluten-free" on the label.

Twenty parts per million refers to the level of gluten which is known to be very safe for persons with celiac disease. This level is generally set 3 times lower than what research shows is safe, making it virtually impossible to ever consume that amount of gluten daily from products labeled gluten-free. It is a very small amount. An example of 20 ppm is 1 tsp of cream in 65 gallons of milk.

"Wheat-free" doesn't necessarily mean "gluten-free." Remember that gluten includes wheat, rye, and barley — so something can be wheat-free and still contain malt flavoring derived from barley, for instance.

Advisory labels: Sometimes more (information) is less (helpful)

You've seen the advisory labels: "This product manufactured in a facility that produces wheat"; it's right next to the "gluten-free" designation. Or, "This product made on shared equipment that also processes wheat ingredients." What about the labels that say "gluten-free" and then say "This product may contain wheat"? Huh?

Companies are trying to be helpful (and to cover their hineys liability-wise), but sometimes the extra information adds to the confusion.

So what *do* you do if a product says it's gluten-free but manufactured in a facility that produces wheat products? There's not an easy answer.

The truth of the matter is that all manufacturers in North America have good manufacturing policies (GMPs) that require them to thoroughly clean all equipment between product lines. In other words, if they make a gluten-containing product and then the next product on the line is gluten-free, they have to clean all equipment really well before making the change.

Is there a chance that a tiny particle of gluten could get left behind on the manufacturing line? Yes. Is there a chance that you'll buy the box of cereal that contains that little bit of gluten? Sure. Is there a chance that you, the celiac in the family, will be the one to eat that little gluten particle (and the surrounding particles that have been contaminated)? Yep. Admittedly, those chances are remote.

Labeled requirements

Labeling a product gluten-free is voluntary. No manufacturer will be required to include the labeling on their products; however, if they do, they must prove the product meets the definition. The law will also include information on the following:

- ✔ If a 'naturally gluten-free product,' such as 100% orange juice, chooses to carry a gluten-free label - it must say that all 100% orange juice is gluten-free.

- ✔ Not all oats can be labeled gluten-free. They must be able to prove that they meet the definition, including containing less than 20 ppm.

Gluten-free certification

A progressive certification program with an easily recognized logo is making it easier to identify gluten-free foods. The Certified Gluten-Free logo stands for the independent verification of quality, integrity, and purity of products. Products carrying the Certified Gluten-Free logo represent unmatched reliability for meeting strict gluten-free, science-based standards.

Manufacturers requesting this gluten-free certification are inspected by the Gluten-Free Certification Organization (GFCO) (www.gfco.org), the only gluten-free certification program in the world. The GFCO, a program of the Gluten Intolerance Group (GIG), was developed in cooperation with Food Services Inc., a subsidiary of the Orthodox Union (OU), the world's largest and oldest kosher certification agency. The OU's nearly 500 field representatives, proficient in modern food-production techniques and chemical and biological processes, conduct plant inspections and review products for the GFCO.

Certification is an annual process based on ingredient review, on-site inspection, and product testing. Gluten-free certification is established for each ingredient in the final product, as well as the processing aids. The mark assures that the product contains less than 10 parts per million of gluten and similar proteins from rye and barley.

Contacting manufacturers

"Hello, does your product contain gluten?"

Don't feel awkward asking that question. Food manufacturers hear it all the time these days. Many manufacturers often voluntarily identify the ingredients in their products in very clear terms. For example, instead of saying "modified *food* starch," they're listing the specific type of starch as "modified *corn* starch." The same is true with vegetable oils. Instead of "hydrolyzed *vegetable* oil," the packaging now shows the specific type of oil, such as "hydrolyzed *corn* oil." And certainly, because of the Food Allergen Labeling and Consumer Protection Act of January 2004, if the ingredient is derived from wheat, it must clearly be identified as such.

However, if you have any doubts, don't hesitate to call the manufacturer.

People sometimes think that if they read labels they don't need to call the manufacturer, but that's not always true. If you find something questionable on a product label, or if you just want to be extra-sure that the product is gluten-free, call a manufacturer and ask. Today's manufacturers understand the gluten-free concept, and they know what you're talking about.

Contacting manufacturers is a lot easier than it used to be. Most packaging includes the manufacturer's toll-free number, or if you're having a hard time locating a manufacturer's contact information, you can always look online. Do a search on your favorite search engine, or try typing in the manufacturer's name followed by ".com" (as in www.fritolay.com).

When in doubt, leave it out. If you're not sure, don't take a chance.

Chapter 4

Making Nutrition Your Mission When You're Cooking Gluten-Free

*O*kay, I realize this is a cookbook, and you just want to dive into the recipes to start whipping up your soon-to-be-famous gluten-free gastrolicious goodies. But wouldn't you feel better about gorging down the goodies if you knew they were good for you? It's not too tough to eat a healthier diet if you know what's nutritious and what isn't. The problem is, even people who *think* they know often don't.

Nutritious food is more underappreciated than the parent of a teen. But even teenagers appreciate parents more than most people appreciate food for the value it provides. No, I'm not talking about the so-stuffed-you-can't-move feeling you get from pizza and beer. And for those of you who consider yourselves to be health food fanatics because you use skim milk on your frosted flakes, I'm not talking about that, either.

I'm talking about the valuable things food offers — taste, fulfillment, satisfaction, and — oh yeah — *nutrients*.

Food is obviously essential — without it, we'd starve to death. But the *types* of foods we eat have powerful effects on preventing disease; maintaining proper organ function, energy levels, moods, appearance, and athleticism; and even influencing our longevity and how we age. Everything about how we look and feel is directly related to the foods we eat.

You can do the gluten-free diet at least two ways — one is extremely healthy, and the other isn't quite as optimal. Either way, you're cooking gluten-free, and that's a good thing — but if you're interested in taking a more nutritious approach to being gluten-free, this chapter's for you.

In this chapter, I take a look at some foods you may have thought were nutritious but aren't — and I explore some foods you may never have heard of that pack a powerful nutritional punch. I offer tips for weight management and energy enhancement, and I give an overview of the optimal diet, which just happens to be entirely gluten-free!

Feeling Optimal Requires Optimum Nutrition

Sure, you've heard the expression, "you are what you eat." But what does that mean, really? I eat a lot of apples, and I'm not an apple. I think it really should be said that, "your quality of health is dependent upon the quality of food you eat" — but I realize that's not so catchy, and it's tough to grasp.

Few people would argue the fact that you need to eat a nutritious diet — the problem is that most people don't know what that means. And when you're eating gluten-free, there are special considerations when striving for optimal nutrition.

Fueling versus filling

Lots of people have used the car analogy to explain nutrition. They tell you that to get maximum performance from your vehicle, you have to use high-quality gas — and to get maximum performance from your body, you have to give it high-quality foods.

There are a few problems with that analogy: The first problem is that most people don't know what high-quality foods are! How can you put "good fuel" in your body when you don't really know what good fuel is? The second problem with the car-body analogy is that most people put crummy gas in their cars and their cars run just fine, so they figure they can get away with putting crummy gas in their bodies, and they'll run just fine too — albeit a little gassy from time to time.

What they don't realize is that you can get away with putting crummy gas in an average car — but our bodies aren't your average car. Our bodies are finely tuned, high-performance vehicles. You put crummy gas into a Ferrari, and you're going to find it knocks and pings (gas and bloating), doesn't start as easily (tough time getting out of bed?), doesn't go as fast (lethargic), the engine doesn't burn as cleanly (constipation), it shoots out more exhaust (fartola), and the engine wears out faster (uh oh — need I say more?).

The last problem with the analogy revolves around individual sensitivities. Imagine now that you *do* know what good fuel is, and that you have pulled into an exclusive gas station that brags of having the highest-quality gasoline from one of the world's best refineries. It should be free of anything that might cause harm to your engine, right? Not necessarily. What if you're driving a diesel-powered car? Just a few minutes running with that "high-quality" gasoline, and your diesel car would be dead. In this case, the gas is good — it's just the wrong fuel type for your car.

We should eat to *fuel,* not to *fill.*

Getting enough nutrients when you're gluten-free

Over the years, many people have claimed that the gluten-free diet is deficient in a variety of nutrients. Their reasoning comes from the fact that flour is generally enriched with vitamins. When we stop eating flour, we're missing that fortification and the supplemental nutrients it provides.

You can probably guess how I feel about that argument. If you follow the "healthy" approach to the gluten-free diet as described in this chapter, you get a nutritionally sound diet.

If you go gluten-free the unhealthy way — simply substituting gluten-free goodies for the breads, bagels, pizzas, pastas, cookies, cakes, and pretzels that you were eating before — then there's some merit to the claim that the gluten-free diet may have some nutritional deficiencies, because you won't have the advantage of the enrichment found in most products made with flour.

If you want more detail on nutrition, and specifically how it relates to the gluten-free diet, check out *Living Gluten-Free For Dummies* (Wiley). In this book, I just cover the basics — because this is, after all, a *cook*book!

Fiber

Getting enough fiber in your diet can be an issue in gluten-free diets. Gluten-free flours, such as rice and tapioca, don't offer much fiber and can cause associated problems.

The best source of fiber is fresh fruits and veggies. Broccoli, for instance, provides 25 percent of your daily fiber needs in just 1 cup. Not to mention it has 200 percent of the daily recommended dietary allowances (RDA) for vitamin C, 90 percent of the daily RDA for vitamin A in the form of beta carotene, and lots of niacin, calcium, thiamin, and phosphorus. All this for only 45 calories!

Other nutrients

People who have gluten sensitivity or celiac disease often become sick and malnourished as a result. They usually have compromised digestion and absorption that may result in nutritional deficiencies, the most common of which are iron, essential fatty acids, vitamins D and K, calcium, magnesium, and folic acid. It may be wise to seek the help of a professional to ensure adequate nutrition.

Some people believe that no matter how healthy your diet is, it's still important to take supplements. This reasoning is generally based on the fact that food isn't as nutritious as it used to be. Soils are becoming depleted of important nutrients, so the crops grown in them are less nutrient-dense than they once were. Furthermore, chemicals and genetically modified foods are changing the nutritional composition of even the most wholesome foods. For these reasons, many people believe that supplementation is key to getting all the nutrients you need, especially if you take part in athletic endeavors or exercise heavily.

If you're an athlete and are interested in learning about recommended supplementation, I recommend a book by Dr. Michael Colgan called *Sports Nutrition Guide.*

Choosing a Healthier Approach to the Gluten-Free Diet

Sometimes people do the math wrong. They know that I believe that gluten-free is the way to be. And they know I have a passion for nutrition. Therefore, they add it up and conclude, erroneously, that gluten-free must be nutritious. But that's not always true.

There are two ways to go on the gluten-free diet: one is ultra-healthy, and the other is — well, *not* — and not even close.

The unhealthy way

For simplicity sake, and to mess with my editors who like things to go in the order I've referred to them, let's start with the last category — the gluten-free diet that isn't so healthy. This is the version of being gluten-free that could be called the "substitution diet." People continue to eat all the normal foods they ate before — breads, bagels, cookies, cakes, pizza, crackers, and pretzels — but they eat the gluten-free version. Sometimes people who do this actually end up eating *more* junk than they did when they were eating gluten because they use the gluten-free goodies to help them get over their "I'm feeling deprived and restricted" thoughts.

Suffice it to say I'm not a fan of this variety of gluten-free eating. As a matter of fact, it's not just "not healthy," but it's downright *un*healthy. Those foods, with or without gluten, offer very little in the way of nutritional value — they do little more than pack on the pounds and wreak havoc with your blood-sugar levels (which we talk about later in this chapter).

The healthy way

The healthier approach to eating gluten-free is simple: If man made it, don't eat it.

In other words, stick to the natural foods that our bodies were designed to eat: lean meats, seafood and fish, fruits, veggies, nuts, and berries. These foods are healthiest for us because our bodies were designed to eat them — it's not surprising to me that they're all naturally gluten-free, as well, because our bodies weren't designed to eat gluten. Sticking to natural, healthy foods is a win-win!

I didn't "invent" this diet — in fact, there's a lot of information about this approach, which is usually referred to as the *Paleolithic diet*. That's because this diet is based on eating the foods that our hunter-gatherer ancestors ate in Paleolithic times (before the Agricultural Revolution). They didn't eat wheat — there wasn't any. They didn't eat grains or dairy — it just didn't exist. Our bodies weren't designed to eat those things, which is why so many people have intolerances to them.

By the way, it's pretty easy to see why our Paleolithic ancestors didn't do milk. First, picture them catching a wild boar — what then? It begs the question, "How many cavemen does it take to milk a wild boar?"

You may be thinking that with some scary (and hairy) exceptions, today's humans don't really resemble cavemen, so this line of reasoning about eating what our ancestors ate isn't relevant — but you'd be mistaken. DNA evidence shows that genetically, humans have hardly changed at all in the last 40,000 years.

A blast from the past for nutrition that lasts

They may have been a little stinky, but our Paleolithic ancestors were remarkably healthy. They were lean, fit, and didn't get the plethora of diseases that we get today. In fact, anthropological studies show they were lean, had good aerobic capacity, low cholesterol, low blood pressure, and better insulin metabolism. Healthwise, they rank right up there with today's elite and highly trained athletes.

In contrast, most of today's humans are a mess. We eat too much, we eat the wrong foods, we're fat, and we have lots and lots of diseases, some of which we're inventing as we go. More people are overweight than aren't, and it's killing us. Heart and blood-vessel disease is a leading killer; high blood pressure, high cholesterol, diabetes, and obesity are all epidemic.

Tip: You can find lots of detailed information about the Paleolithic diet on the Internet by doing a quick search on your favorite search engine.

Watching Your Blood Sugar

Some people figure they don't need to worry about their blood sugar levels because they don't eat sweets. Not true! For one thing, lots of foods that aren't in the sweets category at all can mess with your blood sugar levels. Potatoes, for instance — they're killers when it comes to blood sugar! We'll talk more about specific foods and how they affect your blood sugar levels later in this section, but first, what does it mean, and why does it matter?

The term *blood sugar* refers to how much glucose is in the blood. *Glucose* is the body's primary source of energy, so it's important stuff. But it has to stay in just the right range — not too high and not too low — or it can cause problems. The body uses hormones called *insulin* and *glucagon* to regulate blood sugar levels, but sometimes the body just can't keep up, often because the foods we're eating cause blood sugar levels to rise too much. Diabetes mellitus is an example of a disease related to the failure of blood sugar regulation.

Blood sugar levels also affect hunger and cravings. Foods that cause your blood sugar to go up quickly (and then come down quickly) cause you to get hungry, even when you shouldn't be. This is only one of the many reasons high glycemic index foods (I explain exactly what those are in the "Understanding the glycemic index of foods" section) result in weight gain.

For more detail on how blood sugar affects hunger and weight gain, check out *Living Gluten-Free For Dummies*.

Gluten-free fights Father Time

Can gluten-free make wrinkles flee? Possibly! According to many experts, gluten-free is the way to be if you're trying to turn back the wrinkled hands of time or stave off symptoms of menopause. Anti-aging specialists often tell patients to avoid wheat, and especially refined flours, to improve the quality of skin and erase wrinkles. One of the best known experts in his field, Dr. Nicholas Perricone, maintains that wheat and other high glycemic load foods provoke an inflammatory response that causes our skin to age more quickly. He says that avoiding foods like wheat can actually help *reverse* the aging process.

Wheat-based foods are also implicated in symptoms of menopause, such as hot flashes, night sweats, headaches, fatigue, and mood swings. Patients are often advised to give up wheat to alleviate menopausal symptoms.

Moving beyond rice, corn, and potatoes

When adopting a gluten-free lifestyle, people tend to turn to starchy, fill-me-up standbys like rice, corn, and potatoes. People seek these out partly because they *are* starchy foods, a replacement of sorts for the bread, pasta, and bagels we're accustomed to eating when we eat gluten.

So what's the problem with substituting these standbys? They're gluten-free, so they should be fine, right? Well, they're fine from a gluten-free standpoint. But they're pretty much void of nutrients, at least compared to some of the nutritional powerhouses that you *could* be eating.

See, not all carbs are created equal. Fruits and veggies are great. But rice, corn, potatoes, and refined wheat are all high glycemic load foods. High gly-huh? We'll talk more about what that means in the next section.

For now, all you need to know about high glycemic foods is that they mess with your blood sugar levels, which is especially dangerous for people with diabetes. They also can pack on the pounds almost faster than you can eat them, which is one reason many people who go gluten-free experience weight gain (to find out how to combat the gluten-free gain, check out the "Managing Your Weight When You're Gluten-Free" section later in this chapter).

Understanding the glycemic index of foods

The *glycemic index* (GI) is a way to measure how much effect a particular food will have on our blood sugar levels. The higher the glycemic index, the more quickly that food is broken down during the digestion process, and the more quickly blood glucose levels will rise. Carbohydrates that break down slowly release glucose into the blood stream more gradually and have a lower glycemic index.

Higher glycemic index isn't *always* a bad thing

Sometimes people *want* a quick rise in their blood sugar. Serious athletes often pay close attention to the glycemic index of foods they eat so they can have optimal energy available when they need it.

Usually before a competition they'll eat foods with a lower glycemic index so that energy is released more slowly.

During a competition they may try to eat a balance of high and low GI foods; the low GI foods will provide sustained energy, and the high GI foods will provide a quick burst.

When they're finished, athletes will often eat high GI foods to quickly restore depleted energy stores.

The glycemic index really just concerns foods that are high in carbohydrates. Foods that are high in fat or protein don't have as much of an effect on your blood glucose levels.

The glycemic index is sometimes categorized into three classes: low, medium, and high. Table 4-1 shows GI ranges and some examples:

Table 4-1		Glycemic Index Ranges
Classification	*GI Range*	*Examples*
Low GI	55 or less	Most fruit and vegetables (except potatoes), quinoa, and most other alternative grains
Medium GI	56–69	Orange juice, some pastas, some brown rices
High GI	70 or more	White bread, baked potato, most white rices, pizza, crackers, bagels, beer

A food's glycemic index may change depending on how it's prepared and what's eaten with it.

Unfortunately, a food's glycemic index won't be listed on the label. You can find glycemic index tables for specific foods by searching for "glycemic index (food name)" on your favorite search engine. Not all foods are listed, but many are, and it's a great start for understanding which foods cause your blood sugar to soar, and which ones don't.

A great book on the subject of blood sugar and its importance in maintaining overall health is *The New Sugar Busters!* by H. Leighton Steward (Ballantine).

Relating a gluten-free diet to the glycemic index

Gluten-containing foods like bread, bagels, pizza, pasta, cookies, cakes, and pretzels are super-high on the glycemic index. When you cut those things out of your diet, you're eliminating high GI foods that offer little in the way of nutritional value.

Now keep in mind that if you replace those things with their gluten-free counterparts — like gluten-free bread, bagels, pizza . . . you get the picture — then you're back in the high glycemic ballpark. But if you choose to eat wholesome foods like those described in this chapter as being optimal, you'll be eating gluten-free and healthfully!

People used to think that diabetics should avoid sugar — as in candy bars and table sugar. But some experts now believe that the sugar isn't as important as the effect that the food has on your blood sugar. In other words, instead of simply eliminating sugar, some experts recommend that people with diabetes should stick to a low glycemic index diet. For those people, a gluten-free diet — the kind that includes healthy meats, seafood, fruits, and veggies (but without the yummy gluten-free substitutions for the high glycemic goodies like breads and cookies) — is ideal.

Choosing healthy starches for that "fill-me-up" feeling

As we've discussed, rice, corn, and potatoes aren't your most nutritious choices, even though they *are* gluten-free. You get lots of calories and little nutrition — that's not a good thing for anyone. But let's face it — there's something to be said for that feeling of contentment you get when you eat starchy foods like that.

So what *can* you eat for that fill-me-up satisfaction when you're cooking gluten-free but you're focused on a healthier diet? Try these foods on for size. They're far more nutritious than rice, corn, and potatoes, and they're low glycemic index foods, too.

- ✔ Amaranth
- ✔ Buckwheat
- ✔ Millet
- ✔ Montina
- ✔ Quinoa

✔ Sweet potatoes (or yams)

✔ Teff

Sometimes referred to as *alternative grains,* they're not really grains at all. But they're delicious, they provide unique flavors and consistencies, and they're loaded with fiber, vitamins, minerals, and amino acids. In fact, most of them are complete proteins! (Chapter 3 gives you more information about these foods.)

The terms *sweet potato* and *yam* are often used interchangeably, yet the two are very different. It doesn't matter which one you choose, though, because both are gluten-free, loaded with nutrients and antioxidants, and quite low on the glycemic index. There are even new varieties of sweet potatoes that have purple skin and flesh! They contain *anthocyanins,* a powerful antioxidant found in berries.

 In staying consistent with the theme of this book, get creative! Try using different vegetables to replace the starchy foods you might ordinarily use. Spaghetti squash is a great alternative for pasta. You can use strips of zucchini or yellow squash instead of lasagna noodles, and you can puree cauliflower instead of using mashed potatoes.

Managing Your Weight When You're Gluten-Free

Interestingly, the gluten-free diet — when done properly — can not only be your key to better health, but it may also be the key to managing your weight. In fact, it doesn't matter if you weigh too much or too little; if you're not "just right," going gluten-free may be the answer you've been looking for.

Losing or maintaining weight

For people who need to lose weight, there's no simpler and more effective way to do it than to take the Paleolithic approach we've been talking about in this chapter (see the section, "The healthy way," for more info). Sticking to lean meats, poultry, seafood, fish, fruits, and veggies will help un-stick those unwanted pounds.

When you go gluten-free, you eliminate refined-flour products from your diet — things like bagels, bread, pasta, and of course the sweet baked goods — and that means you're cutting out high glycemic index foods that offer very little in the way of nutrition, but offer more than their fair share of calories. That's why people who go gluten-free the healthy way usually find their weight easier to maintain at healthy levels.

Syrup the saboteur

High fructose corn syrup (HFCS) may be gluten-free, but it can sabotage a weight-loss program faster than a box of old-fashioned gluten-free glazed donuts. Two main hormones signal hunger and appetite to your brain. *Ghrelin* is produced in the stomach, and increases your appetite, while *leptin* is produced by fat cells and tells your body it's full. HFCS, a sugar "substitute" (it actually is a sugar), inhibits leptin secretion so you don't get the "I'm full" message. It also never shuts off ghrelin, so even if you're stuffed, you're still getting an "I'm hungry" memo from your stomach. Beware of HFCS in foods you may not suspect, like ketchup, salad dressings, and lots of low-fat products.

Dealing with (uh-oh) weight gain

Some people find that they gain weight when they go gluten-free — and it's no wonder! Many of them are busy discovering the wonders of the gluten-free goodie world, including gluten-free brownies, cookies, cakes, pastas, and crackers. Those are foods that may as well be applied directly to the tummy or thighs — because that's where they end up pretty quickly.

These days the gluten-free goodies are delicious — and somewhat irresistible, I suppose. But for some people, eating them is strictly emotional. They tend to get carried away with these foods as a way of compensating for feelings of deprivation or restriction. They believe they're deprived because they can't eat gluten, so they "reward" themselves, or compensate, by eating extras of the goodies that they *can* eat. Before they know it, their jeans look like they belong to the neighbor's kid.

Still others experience weight gain because of the physiological changes that take place when they go gluten-free. This group of people is comprised of those who go gluten-free because they have celiac disease or gluten sensitivity. Most people with celiac disease or gluten-sensitivity don't absorb all of their nutrients, at least until they go 100 percent gluten-free. Lots of these people, while they're still eating gluten and not absorbing nutrients, become accustomed to eating far more calories than they should, because those calories aren't being absorbed, so they maintain their weight in spite of the fact that they eat far too many calories. But it's payback time after they go gluten-free. Their gut begins to heal, and they begin absorbing calories — and before they know it, they've packed on a pound (or 20).

Although I like to think of the gluten-free diet as the best diet on the planet, it's not actually the gluten-free-ness that gets the credit when we're talking about weight management on the gluten-free diet. It's the fact that you're adhering to a high-protein, low glycemic, nutrient-dense diet. And following this healthy diet provides health benefits that extend far beyond being gluten-free.

Gluten-free — indulgently!

All this talk about good nutrition is meant to provide you with guidelines for a healthy approach to the gluten-free lifestyle. Having made my point about the importance of good nutrition, I think it's also important to point out that it's okay to live a little — indulge from time to time! *Not* in gluten, of course — but in something yummy and decadent, whatever that means to you. No matter which approach you take to the gluten-free lifestyle, you need to find a balance that works for you for the long haul.

Adding some pounds if you're underweight

If you've been underweight, you're likely to find that the gluten-free diet helps you gain enough to be at a healthy weight. I know, it sounds like I'm talking out of both sides of my mouth — how can it help some people *lose* weight, and help others *gain* it?

People who are underweight are often that way because they have gluten sensitivity or celiac disease, and therefore are not absorbing important nutrients, including calories. That is, until they go gluten-free. Then their guts heal, and they begin to absorb those important nutrients again. After they start absorbing the calories they're consuming, they usually gain the weight they need to be at what's considered a healthy weight.

Chapter 5

Setting Up Your Kitchen and Pantry

I know you're the cooking type and you're eager to get started, and this *is* a cookbook after all, but it's a good idea to take some time to set up your kitchen and pantry, just to make things easier (and safer) on yourself down the road.

If your entire kitchen is already gluten-free, you're excused to skip to another chapter. But if you're going to have a shared kitchen where glutenous and gluten-free foods coexist, you'll have to take some important steps to eliminate the risk of *glutenation* (for those of you new to my books, that's DannaSpeak for gluten contamination).

Never fear, though. Although eliminating the risk of glutenation isn't a "simple" modification, it's "simply" a modification. In this chapter, I take you through the steps to ensuring a safe environment for your gluten-free cooking. You discover how to set up a shared kitchen for gluten-eaters as well as non-gluten-eaters, and how to choose appliances that can simplify your life.

To Be or Not To Be 100 Percent Gluten-Free

To clarify, I'm talking about modifying your *kitchen,* not your lifestyle. If you have celiac disease, let me make it clear that I condone a 100 percent gluten-free lifestyle. Even if you don't have celiac disease, I still believe that gluten-free is the way to be — and 100 percent is best of all.

But even if you're 100 percent gluten-free, it doesn't mean your kitchen has to be. So before you lift that ladle, touch that Tupperware, or start pulling the pantry apart, you first need to decide whether it's going to be some or none for you and your food. Will your whole house go gluten-free, or will you be mixing the fixings and cooking both ways?

In many households, when one person needs or wants to go gluten-free, the first inclination is to make the whole house gluten-free. In fact, nearly every cookbook author and expert in this field will tell you that the entire kitchen, pantry, and household should be gluten-free. With serious and sincere respect, I disagree with them, at least for the majority of people. Although going completely gluten-free certainly can make life easier, it's not only unnecessary, but sometimes it's even a bad idea.

It's pretty rare to find an entire family that needs to be gluten-free. More often than not, only one family member needs to stay away from gluten for health reasons. If you have other children or family members who don't need to be gluten-free and you force them to follow the diet anyway, you may create resentment. Yes, even among adults. I've had more than a few e-mails from despairing dads who stop for pizza and beer on the way home from work because they know they're not allowed to indulge in gluten at home.

The next couple of reasons I don't recommend an entirely gluten-free household (unless, of course, all family members need to be on a gluten-free diet) concern kids who are gluten-free.

- ✓ **Children need to learn how to make the right choices.** Kids raised in an entirely gluten-free household never have to make a choice — which means they never *learn* to make a choice: Is this food okay to eat? If all the food is gluten-free, that thought process — which really needs to become an unconscious decision later in life — is never required. As the parent of a gluten-free kid, I speak from experience when I say that I believe it's critical for kids to have gluten in the house and know how to make those decisions for themselves.

- ✓ **Kids need to learn that the world isn't a gluten-free place.** Children who grow up in an entirely gluten-free household can develop a false sense of reality, and may even assume a sense of entitlement. The child may believe that everyone else should stock his favorite foods, and everyone else should be gluten-free, too. Kids need to know that the rest of the world eats gluten. That doesn't mean people are trying to hurt their feelings or leave them out; it's just the way it is. Isn't it important for children to learn these lessons at home, in a loving and caring environment? I think so!

Unfortunately, I see the opposite decision made all the time. Someone in the family gets diagnosed with a gluten-sensitive medical condition, and the instant reaction is, "We've decided to make our whole family gluten-free!" Sadly, that decision often leads to a negative dynamic and a resentment that even adults can feel.

Having read all of this, if you're still convinced that a gluten-free house is the route you're going to take, you can skip the rest of this chapter and go straight to your favorite chapter. On the other hand, if you agree with me that it makes more sense to have gluten in the house and to prepare both glutenous and gluten-free meals, then keep on reading because the rest of this chapter shows you how to simplify the process and make it fun.

Conquering Contamination Concerns

Oh, good, you're still reading! That means I haven't scared you away and you're ready to get down to business and start thinking about the single most important challenge to maintaining your shared kitchen: containing contamination risks.

I'm not talking contamination of the my-burger-has-e-coli variety (best to avoid that, too) — I'm talking about glutenation. You know — when you have a perfectly good gluten-free meal, and somehow, someway it gets glutenated, and the entire meal is ruined. Kaput. Off limits. Dog food.

It can happen in the most innocent ways. A loving family member sticks a knife laden with gluten crumbs into the mayo jar. You accidentally use the same utensil to toss the gluten-free pasta as you used on the gluten-containing stuff. Or someone stacks the "regular" sandwiches on top of the gluten-free ones. Ugh.

When you keep gluten-containing foods in the house, you run the risk of contamination every time you prepare a meal. Contamination issues are crucial to consider when you're cooking with gluten.

Even if your house is perfectly gluten-free, remember that guests can, unknowingly, contaminate the kitchen. If they bring their own sandwich, for instance, and add it to the stack of gluten-free goodies you've prepared, the entire bunch may be ruined.

When you're sharing a kitchen with gluten, it can contaminate your food in many different ways. Crumbs seem to throw themselves off gluten-containing breads and foods, turning perfectly good gluten-free zones into danger zones in the blink of an eye. If not cleaned well, preparation surfaces, cookware, utensils, and storage containers can all contaminate food as well. Here are some tips for avoiding cross-contamination by some of the most dangerous culprits.

Keeping crumbs at bay

In a shared kitchen, crumbs are public enemy numero uno. When you're making a sandwich, buttering a piece of toast, or crumbling crackers into your soup, these tiny little crumb-culprits literally fly off the food and soar through the air.

Say you're making a regular sandwich and a gluten-free one. You can't make them both at the same time on the same cutting board. Suppose you've prepared your gluten-free sandwich, and then you set it down on a counter full of gluten-containing crumbs. What do you get? A contaminated sandwich!

From now on, you need to get into the habit of making the gluten-free version first, then making the other, and cleaning the crumbs really well in between. Going on a crumb vendetta is not so crucial if you make the gluten-free sandwich first, but it's certainly a good habit.

Protecting jars from cross-contamination

Jars are some of the most easily contaminated items in the kitchen. Say you're making a slice of toast with jelly. You dip a knife into your gluten-free jelly, then spread it on your gluten-containing toast. Then you dip the knife back into the jar for more jelly, contaminating the whole jar with those pesky crumbs. Next time you go to make gluten-free toast, those glutenous crumbs are just waiting for you.

People frequently ask, "Can I put the knife back into the jar if I used it to spread something on gluten-free bread?" No, because you'll not only end up with crumbs in the jar, but you won't know whether they were gluten-free or not and you'll end up throwing the whole jar away. I can't tell you how many times I've spent $10 on the 7-gallon size mayonnaise at my local discount shopping warehouse store and had to toss the whole thing in the trash.

Instead of using jars, I recommend getting squeezable containers for your mustard, jelly, mayonnaise, honey, and any other condiments.

Too many cooks can glutenate a meal

Ah, those wonderful holiday dinners. The house is full of people, fragrant aromas fill the air, and then Helpful Helen manages to contaminate nearly every jar in the kitchen by using the same spoon to dish up gluten-free and glutenous sauces, spreads, and condiments. Cousin Clara puts the croutons in the salad and gives it a thorough toss. Sister Susie surprises you by putting the stuffing inside the turkey. Aunt Ginny mixes the crunchy onion rings into the green bean casserole, and Uncle Sid gets crumbs in the butter after spreading some onto his roll. Last but not least, Aunt Mary spoons gravy over her stuffing, pressing down firmly to make a well, and then sticks the stuffing-crusted spoon back into the gravy boat. These wonderful, well-meaning relatives had no idea that you planned to serve everything on the side, and that they've completely ruined an entire meal for everyone eating gluten-free.

If you're having dinner guests or visitors who insist on helping in the kitchen, my advice is to tell them how much you appreciate their help, and remember that their intentions are good. Make them feel important by giving them jobs that can't possibly cause contamination, such as setting the table, pouring the drinks, and keeping small children entertained. And definitely don't pass up the opportunity to put them to work on clean-up duty.

Using utensils in food preparation

I've got a stumper for ya. You're making two types of peanut butter and jelly sandwiches — gluten-free ones and regular ones. How many knives does it take?

Answer: ten. Okay, I'm exaggerating a little, but if you want to guarantee that you won't cause contamination, you can't put the same knife back into the container after the knife has touched the bread. So here's how to make a simple peanut butter sandwich:

Dip a knife into the peanut butter and spread it on the bread. Because it touched the bread, that knife is done. Retire it to the sink. The next knife goes into the jelly, then spreads the jelly onto the bread. Whoops, you didn't get enough jelly. Because that knife also touched the bread, it too must retire to the sink, and you need yet another knife so you can add more jelly.

 Wait! I have a better solution! Do a patented maneuver I call the *gob drop!* Instead of using every knife in the house, take a huge gob of your spreadable condiment and drop it onto the bread without letting the knife touch the surface. Flick the knife so it doesn't touch the bread (or use a second knife to scrape the first one off). If you don't get enough the first time, go back for more before the knife touches the bread. A word of caution: After you get the hang of this, you'll find yourself aghast when you see people putting knives back into jars after they've touched food surfaces. Go easy on them; they don't know any better . . . yet!

Storing food

Some people worry that they can't store gluten-free foods in the same plastic containers that have held glutenous foods. They think that the plastic absorbs the gluten and will contaminate the gluten-free foods. But you can rest easy. Gluten doesn't seep into the pores, and you don't need separate containers as long as you wash everything carefully.

Some gluten-free meals are hard to make. Save time and money by making large batches, and then storing the leftovers in vacuum-sealed bags or plastic containers. Mark them well, and freeze them for later use. Here are a few tips:

- ✔ A permanent marker on aluminum foil works really well.

- ✔ If you have a plastic storage container that you don't want to mark up, use labels instead.

- ✔ You may want to a use color-coded system (red = gluten, green = gluten-free).

- ✔ Sometimes labels fall off or get dislodged. Be sure to put a label inside the container, too.

Considering cookware

Some people think they need special pots and pans to create their gluten-free meals in because they've heard that gluten can get embedded into Teflon and other cookware surfaces. This opinion is widely circulated on the Internet, but I'm here to tell you that it's nothing more than an urban legend. Gluten does not seep into Teflon or other cookware surfaces. However, scratches and cracks can harbor residue from previous cooking. The key is to thoroughly wash all cookware and utensils. My rule of thumb is that if you'd let your baby lick the pan, it's probably clean enough!

Some people use cast iron pans and "season" them, but don't wash them. If you cook gluten in cast iron pans and don't wash it with soap and water, don't use that same pan for your gluten-free cooking.

Sometimes after you drain pasta in a colander, a residue remains. I recommend that you have separate colanders for your gluten-free and glutenous foods and mark them with a permanent marker so you'll never get them confused. The same applies to those cute pasta servers with the teeth on the end (do those have a name? I digress . . .). They'll have some residue left that's iffy to remove, so again, I recommend having separate ones.

Sharing Is Caring When You're Cooking Both Ways

It goes without saying that making separate meals creates extra work for the cook (and because you're reading this book, I'm going to assume that's you!). For instance, if you're having a pasta dinner and you want to make one batch of gluten-free pasta and one regular batch, you're obviously making more work for yourself, but I still think it's the way to go when not everyone in the house has to be gluten-free.

These days, gluten-free pastas and other gluten-free foods are so delicious that it's just as yummy to make the gluten-free version for everyone. Sometimes, however, you'll want to make two versions of a meal, whether it's to save money or for personal preferences.

Having said that, I want to assure you that cooking two versions of a meal can be easier than it sounds. Getting back to that pasta dinner, you may want to make both types of pasta but keep things simple by serving one delicious gluten-free sauce that can go on both.

As the heading says, sharing is caring when you're cooking both ways, and there are plenty of foods the whole family can share. Instead of having two varieties of everything, use gluten-free versions of shared foods like sauces, spices, condiments, and salad dressings. This will certainly make your life easier and save you time in the kitchen and the grocery store.

Planning your menus for easy meal prep

It's 5 p.m., you just got home from work, and you're ready to start making dinner. You were planning to make spaghetti, but you have no gluten-free pasta in the house. Because gluten-free cooking involves special ingredients and preparation processes, you have to plan your cooking in advance and make sure you have all the ingredients on hand.

Gluten-free ingredients aren't always easy to find. For instance, if you're going to make bread and you need xanthan gum, you can't run down to the corner store and get it. And if you don't have it, you're not making bread (unless you cheat and use a mix like I do — oh, *wait* — this is a *cook*book!).

Planning your work and working your plan is essential. Make menus and lists before you head for the store (Chapter 6 has more info on where to find the items you need). Make sure you always have appropriate ingredients on hand. You may have to order some of them online, so give yourself plenty of lead time. If a holiday is coming, plan the meal several weeks in advance in case some of the ingredients are only available on the Internet.

Here's a quick list of basic ingredients to always keep in your pantry:

- ✔ All the gluten-free flours.
- ✔ Xantham gum.
- ✔ Guar gum.
- ✔ A premixed batch of the baking mix you'll find in Chapter 8.
- ✔ Quinoa (a personal favorite — great to toss into soups and other foods).
- ✔ Rice. (As you'll see in Chapter 7, brown rice is best.)
- ✔ Gluten-free bread crumbs. (You can order them online or save them from your own breads.)
- ✔ Gluten-free crackers. (You can crumble them and use them as coatings on foods, fillers in meatloaf, and in soups and salads.)
- ✔ Gluten-free snacks. (Keep them on a level that kids can easily reach. You never want to run out or leave them tempted to snack on something glutenous.)
- ✔ Your favorites. (Order a backup so you don't run out, especially with foods that are hard to get.)

Using appliances to make cooking easier

Just as you don't need separate cookware, you won't need separate appliances for cooking your gluten-free foods — with one exception. I absolutely recommend that you have two toasters, or better yet, two toaster *ovens*.

I know I've mentioned this before, but I really can't say it enough — crumbs literally fly off of bread. No matter how carefully you clean, your toaster will always be home to crumbs that can contaminate your gluten-free foods. I recommend toaster ovens over toasters because thanks to gravity, the crumbs fall down (as opposed to getting stuck on the side of the grates in a regular toaster), and you can wipe them away or put a piece of aluminum foil on the bottom of the oven and easily get rid of them.

Toaster bags are another great invention that no shared kitchen should be without. You just put your bread into the bag, put it into the toaster, and cook as usual. You can even take the bags to restaurants with you and ask the server to toast your bread in them. Use any search engine on the Internet to find toaster bags online.

Here are four appliances that can make gluten-free cooking a whole lot easier:

✔ **Bread machine:** Unless you really love the minutiae of baking, a bread machine is a must if you want fresh-baked bread. It makes the job so much easier. You'll find delicious recipes for gluten-free breads in Chapter 9, and some of them can be made in a bread machine. You can also buy mixes made especially for use in bread machines (again, I realize this is a *cook*book and that's somewhat counter to the essence of this book). The smell of fresh-baked bread in a gluten-free home is really awesome. By far, the easiest way to make homemade bread is with a machine.

Gluten-free dough is really heavy compared to regular dough. You need a bread machine with a super-strong motor, or you may catch it on fire or burn it out. (I've done both!)

✔ **Mixer:** You don't need a special mixer, but be sure to clean the beaters and the mixer thoroughly before using this appliance to whip up gluten-free foods because residuals can hang on. Have you ever noticed that film of flour on your kitchen counter after mixing up your cookie dough? That flour floats up as well as down, getting into the underside of your mixer and just waiting to drop into the next thing you make. Clean the mixer thoroughly and shake, bang, or brush it if necessary to dislodge any hidden flour.

✔ **Food processors:** These gadgets are great, but they're really hard to clean. Be especially careful if you're mixing glutenous bread crumbs. You may want to consider a high-end food-processor that comes with multiple mixing bowls. You can use one bowl for gluten-free preparation and the other for everything else.

✔ **Rice cooker:** One tool that can be invaluable is an electric rice cooker. You'll be cooking a lot of rice, and this just makes it easy.

Changing a few techniques in your two-way kitchen

To successfully share your kitchen, you don't have to change your whole life. You just have to change a few techniques:

✔ I'm a sponge person. I wash them in hot water, keep them super clean, don't use them very long, and never let them stay wet or moldy. If you keep clean sponges handy, you're more apt to wipe up the gluten crumbs that can contaminate a perfectly good gluten-free meal.

✔ If you use hand towels and dish towels to wipe up crumbs and clean countertops, make sure they're always clean.

✔ Use parchment paper or aluminum foil to cover cookie sheets, separate foods, or cover your toaster oven or broiler rack. This is a great way to make sure your gluten-free foods don't get contaminated.

✔ Teach everyone, even the littlest kids, how to do the gob drop (see the "Using utensils in food preparation" section earlier in this chapter for the skinny on this).

✔ Make gluten-free sauces and condiments that everyone can use.

✔ Dedicate a gluten-free area of the pantry.

✔ Make sure all of your spices are gluten-free.

✔ When cooking separate meals, make sure the gluten-free version is at least as yummy as the other one.

✔ Cleanliness is next to godliness. Crumbs are a no-no.

✔ When making two varieties of a meal, make the gluten-free version first.

✔ Use brightly colored labels to distinguish gluten-free foods. This is especially helpful when you have baby sitters or other people in the house who may grab the wrong food.

Chapter 6

Shopping for the Gluten-Free Stuff You Need

My first gluten-free shopping experience was harrowing. It was the summer of 1991, and my then-toddler son Tyler had just been diagnosed with celiac disease. The hospital dietitian was no help at all, sending me home with a tattered list of 7,498 things that Tyler would never again be able to eat, and three things he could: rice, corn, and potatoes. Great. Toddlers love rice, corn, and potatoes.

Keep in mind this was ages ago — there was no Internet; there were no books on the subject, and there weren't any support groups. I was on my own to figure out the intricacies of the gluten-free diet — toddler-style.

Mustering all the strength a good mommy feels she needs to have, I faked a smile and asked Tyler, "What sounds good for a snack?" "Kwackers," he said. I didn't remember crackers being on the "forbidden" side of the tattered sheet, so off to our local grocery store we went. That's where the strong-mommy act ended and reality set in.

The cracker aisle isn't the best place to start if you're gluten-free because it's an exercise in futility. Row after row of varieties I had never noticed before seemed to be screaming a sing-songy taunt, "You can't eat us, ha ha ha ha ha ha." "But you're whole grain! Aren't you nutritious?!?" I wondered. The crackers didn't answer. They just continued to mock.

Three hours, five rows, and gallons of tears later, I ended up in the chips aisle. As I continued to read labels and compare ingredient after ingredient to the 7,498 things Tyler couldn't eat, I stumbled onto a bag of Fritos. You know — normal-every-day-food-that-comes-in-a-normal-looking-package Fritos. Normal-looking packages are important to kids. I couldn't believe my eyes — I reread the label 14 times, before crying with joy, "You can *eat* these, Baby, you can *eat* them!" People in the store stared. I hugged passersby and didn't care. There was something he could eat.

So if you find shopping for gluten-free foods to be a bit of a challenge, let me tell you I feel your pain. But thankfully, you shouldn't have to endure what I experienced. Today not only are foods labeled "gluten-free," or at least "wheat-free," but some stores conveniently stock all the gluten-free items together. It's a whole new world.

In this chapter, I reveal where to find all the ingredients you'll need for gluten-free cooking, whether you're throwing together a quick gluten-free snack, or creating gluten-free greatness.

Coming Up with a Shopping Strategy

The grocery store is filled with all kinds of wonderful foods, even for those who need to live gluten-free. You just have to know what you want to shop for and where you need to shop within the store.

I advocate sticking to natural foods as much as possible, as discussed in the next section. But that doesn't mean you're restricted to a diet of plain meats, fruits, and vegetables for the rest of your life. After all, this is a cookbook, and it's filled with fantastic ideas for turning basic, natural, healthy foods into culinary delights.

Sticking to natural foods: It's so much easier

Shopping for your gluten-free creations can be just as easy as shopping for *any* type of cooking. It's even easier if you follow my mantra for optimal nutrition: *If man made it, don't eat it.*

If you think about it, that makes shopping pretty easy. For the most part, if you avoid packaging, you're set! The best part about this healthy formula for eating is that natural foods are generally gluten-free. Foods like plain meats, poultry, fish, seafood, fruits, and vegetables — they're all gluten-free, and in the long-run, they cost less, too.

From a shopping standpoint, using all-natural ingredients means you get to avoid the middle aisles of the grocery store and only shop the perimeter. That's because the perimeter is where they keep the good stuff like meats (keep 'em lean), fish, poultry, fruits, veggies, nuts, berries . . . you get the picture. The inner aisles of grocery stores are typically loaded with the processed stuff stores want you to buy because their profit margins are higher — foods like cereals, crackers, cookies, chips, breads, and other foods that aren't allowed on the gluten-free diet.

If you want to save time and money and eat more nutritiously, shop the perimeter of the grocery store.

Buying the occasional man-made item

You'll have to venture into the center aisles of the grocery store to gather basic necessities like spices (most are gluten-free) and household products. You may be lucky enough to have a local grocery store that carries specialty items, like gluten-free pastas or mixes. They'll be in the center aisles, too.

I must confess that I think everyone needs to give in to indulgences from time to time (not gluten-containing ones, though!). However, if you must buy man-made foods, read the labels carefully and don't be taken in by the marketing claims on the front of the package.

Words like *wholesome, nutritious,* and *organic* don't mean gluten-free. I have a girlfriend who still can't understand, even after knowing my son for many years, why it's not okay to give him certain products when they say *organic* on the front. Remember, foods can be organic and still contain gluten.

Before you go shopping and start reading labels, make sure you know which ingredients are and are not gluten free. You might want to print out a list such as the one you can find on www.celiac.com. Click on the "Safe Gluten-Free Food List/Unsafe Foods & Ingredients" link.

Scouting Out the Best Stores

The ingredients you need for your gluten-free goodies can run the gamut from specialty pastas to gluten-free soy sauce to baking mixes, flours, and wacky ingredients like xanthan gum. People have told me they refuse to make gluten-free meals because some of this stuff is just too hard to find. But you're in luck, because I have some ideas! And they won't take a lot of time, cost a small fortune, or require a trek to the far reaches of the continent. This section outlines where you'll have the best luck finding these specialty ingredients.

Visiting your neighborhood grocery stores

These days, many of the ingredients you need for your gluten-free concoctions can be found at regular grocery stores. You may have to search through the specialty aisles or the natural foods section, if the store has one, but give your local grocery store a try before you begin your hunt in other types of stores. If your grocery store *does* carry what you need, you'll save time, money, and the frustration of driving all around town.

Don't forget to check out your nearby "superstore." Although I can't name names, the one that rhymes with "hall cart" is so dedicated to the gluten-free world that it carries more than 1,000 private-label products that are labeled gluten-free. This is a huge signal to the world that gluten-free living is a very big deal.

Talk to the store manager

One of the first steps to take when embarking on a gluten-free lifestyle is to get to know your grocery store manager. In fact, this person should become your new best friend! Not only can store managers help you find the products you love, but if you bug them enough, they'll start carrying more gluten-free items and maybe even make them easier to find in the store. If you've been mail-ordering these products, you'll be delighted to save on shipping and let the store take care of that. The squeaky wheel definitely gets the grease when it comes to gluten-free shopping.

Your store manager can be one of your best resources for gluten-free foods. Start by asking a few simple questions, such as

- ✓ Does your store have a gluten-free aisle, or do you mix the gluten-free products in with everything else?

- ✓ Would you be willing to start carrying certain products or brands? (This simple request can save you from paying for shipping if you've been ordering online.)

- ✓ Do you have a list of your gluten-free products and where they can be found?

Years ago, one of my favorite gluten-free product lines was very hard to find and available only by mail order. I asked the manager of a natural foods store I frequented to consider carrying the product, and he eagerly said yes. At my local grocery store, where I'd also shopped for many years, I once mentioned that it would be really cool if the store would carry some gluten-free products I wanted. The store manager quickly said, "Just name it and we'll carry it." Today, with gluten-free diets enjoying far more recognition and popularity, I'm sure almost any store would be happy to oblige.

Look for info within the store

Many stores post specialty product lists, including gluten-free, near the main entrance. Look around when you walk inside, or ask your new best friend, the store manager, if he has a gluten-free list. Like fat-free, dairy-free, and other similar lists, it will tell you which products the store carries and where to find them.

Get on the Web

Another excellent source of information is your store's Web site. While doing the research for this book, I logged onto the Web sites of several major grocery chains in various parts of the country. Most offered visitors the ability to search the site, and when I searched for "gluten-free," the sites yielded impressive results. I quickly found all sorts of goodies, ranging from bread, brownie, and pancake mixes to cereals, pizza crusts, tortillas, and seasonings.

Shopping at specialty stores

Specialty stores include natural food stores, gluten-free stores (yep, they exist!), farmers' markets, kosher stores, and co-ops. You'll normally pay more to shop at these places, but the convenience and the fact that you probably can pick up everything you need in one spot often makes them worth it.

Here's a closer look at the different types of specialty stores and what they have to offer.

- ✔ **Natural food stores:** Growing in popularity, these stores can be found almost anywhere in the country, and in some areas, they're everywhere you look. Some have end-caps or kiosks that showcase their gluten-free products, and many have developed their own little gluten-free logos that they put on the products or on the shelf tags. Some of these stores are so committed to the gluten-free market that they've even created their own line of gluten-free products.

✓ **Gluten-free stores:** An online search will reveal any stores in your area that are dedicated to gluten-free products. Try using key words like "gluten-free store" and "gluten-free grocery store." I know of several throughout the country.

✓ **Farmers' markets:** These markets are not only full of the "If man made it, don't eat it" products I talk so much about, but they often have alternative grains like quinoa, millet, buckwheat, and others, and many even carry gluten-free breads. You can usually find good prices, and you can even get fresh flowers while you're there!

✓ **Kosher stores:** Kosher stores (or the kosher aisles of your local grocery store) hold an abundance of gluten-free items. Again, try searching online for key words like "kosher stores" and "gluten-free kosher." Now, not all kosher foods are gluten-free, but some are; you still have to read labels. It's important to note that some kosher foods are made differently during Passover; the Passover versions may *not* contain gluten when the non-Passover version does, and vice versa. Again, be sure to read your labels carefully. Any products that contain cake flour or matzo flour also contain gluten because both types of flour have gluten in them.

✓ **Co-ops:** Some parts of the country have co-op stores where buyers band together to take advantage of quantity pricing. An online search for "gluten-free co-op" revealed many different options, including online co-ops with extensive lists of gluten-free products.

Do an online search for "gluten-free coupon" and see what you can find. A lot of gluten-free manufacturers offer discounts on their products with coupons you can print at home and take to any store that carries those products.

Buying online

Online gluten-free stores abound. To find a specific product or brand, do an online search for the product you want, either by brand name or product type (such as brownies, cake, and so on). To find an online store, try searching for "gluten-free online shopping" or "gluten-free online store."

One significant advantage with online shopping is that some online stores warehouse their products. That's great news for shoppers because it means lower shipping costs (because all products come from the same source) and faster delivery time. The alternative — ordering products from different manufacturers — can result in higher shipping costs and a bigger investment of your time.

International online shopping can add a whole new dimension to your gluten-free meals. Some international brands are delicious and easily available online. Be careful, though. Some European manufacturers use Codex Alimentarius wheat starch, which is approved as gluten-free in some countries but not in the United States. Always read the ingredient lists carefully.

Saving Money on Ridiculously Expensive Ingredients

If you're going to buy specialty items, try small quantities first to make sure you like them. After you find items you like, buy in bulk and freeze what you're not going to use right away. If you're ordering by mail, you'll save on both quantity orders and the shipping costs. If you're ordering from a store, don't be afraid to ask for a quantity discount.

Don't be swindled into buying "specialty" items that are already gluten-free. Online and specialty stores sometimes sell high-priced gluten-free condiments and spices, but these things are naturally gluten-free, and there's no need to spend the extra money for a label. You can pick up these types of items in your neighborhood grocery store.

People complain about the high cost of eating gluten-free, but those people usually are eating a lot of the specialty items — breads, crackers, cakes, cookies, brownies, and pretzels. But you don't have to buy specialty items. When you stick with wholesome ingredients like fresh fruits, vegetables, meats, fish, and poultry, you eat healthier and save money. (See the "Sticking to natural foods: It's so much easier" section earlier in the chapter for more on this.)

Even if you stick to my "if man made it, don't eat it" philosophy, you'll still need to keep some gluten-free products on hand. And when you need them, you need them badly. One way to save money and always be prepared is to buy in bulk and freeze items. While you're at it, you may as well cook in bulk and freeze the dishes. Ask your store manager if you can get better pricing by ordering larger quantities (such as by the case).

Buying generic is a money-saver, and lots of generic products are gluten-free. Most companies' customer-service representatives can tell you whether the products contain gluten; just call the toll-free number listed on the packaging, or visit the company's Web site to see if you can find a list of generic gluten-free products. If you can't, the manufacturer can probably send you one. (See Chapter 3 for more information about calling manufacturers to get information on a product's gluten content.)

Chapter 7

You Don't Always Need Recipes

. . . .

In This Chapter

▶ Making ingredient substitutions

▶ Serving naturally gluten-free foods

▶ Transforming standard recipes into gluten-free masterpieces

▶ Seeing the benefits of mixes

. . . .

I'll let you in on a little secret about me: Patience isn't my strong suit. So give me a recipe, and the first thing I do is size up the list of ingredients. If there are more than about three things on the list, I'm outta there. It's not that I don't *use* a lot of ingredients — I do. In fact, I probably use far more than what a normal recipe calls for because I tend to get carried away once my creative juices get flowing. But that *list* can be so daunting, and often, I've never even heard of some of the ingredients — seriously, "tragacanth gum powder"?!? And then there's this measuring thing you have to do. Who has all the fancy spoons and cups — and who has the time? A glob, a dopple, and a smidge are fine forms of measurement for me.

I know, people love recipes, and this *is,* after all, a cookbook. You get recipes in the chapters ahead, and better yet, they're created by a real live recipe inventor, so you don't have to worry that I made them up.

But before we start slicing, dicing, mixing, and measuring, I need to point out that you don't always *need* recipes. With a glob, a dopple, and a smidge of creativity, you can turn any meal into a gluten-free favorite. That's right, *any* meal. Even flour-filled favorites like pastas, pastries, and Mom's apple pie. And you don't need complicated instructions, tons of time, or hard-to-find ingredients you have to order from France.

Gluten-free cooking doesn't have to be complicated. This chapter points you toward convenient mixes, simple substitutes, and fabulous foods that don't require all that mixing, measuring, and sorting of ingredients. And if you have a gluten-filled recipe to start with, this chapter shows you how to alter it and make it work so you can still enjoy all your favorite foods.

Transforming Any Meal into a Gluten-Free Delight

Transform *any* meal? That's a pretty big promise, but that's exactly what I'm talking about doing. Just because a recipe doesn't say "gluten-free" doesn't mean you can't use it. I'm going to teach you to make some awesome alterations!

I always love it when someone tells me they miss their favorite foods. I look at that as a challenge to find a way to make that food available in a gluten-free form. And with the tips in this chapter, you discover that there's nothing you can't make gluten-free and there are no boundaries. At first, it may seem hard to believe. Like many people, you may be thinking that saying hello to a gluten-free lifestyle means saying good-bye to rolls, gravies, lasagnas, and sauces. Well, say hello again because all those foods are back on the menu.

The key to making the transformation is creativity. Forget the ingredients list. Forget the measuring spoons and cups. Whether you're working from a recipe that isn't gluten-free and converting it to a gluten-free goodie, or making it up on the fly, the most important ingredient is creativity. Having good gluten-free substitutions in mind and on hand is important, too.

Finding fun substitutions

With more and more people adopting wheat-free and gluten-free lifestyles, and with recent improvements in product labeling laws, it's easier than ever to find gluten substitutions. Grocery stores and specialty stores offer a wide variety of ingredients, from bean flours and xanthan gum (prepare to take out a second mortgage when you buy xanthan gum) to buckwheat, quinoa, and amaranth. Chapter 6 gives you ideas of where to shop and how to save money on those ingredients, some of which are ridiculously expensive.

As you may already know, a little flexibility goes a long way when you're living a gluten-free lifestyle. Start flexing — here are some savvy substitutions for some of your favorite ingredients:

✔ **Flour:** Start with the most obvious and mostly commonly used ingredient. If your recipe calls for flour, consider using cornstarch or a gluten-free flour or mix. I talk more about buying and making your own baking mixes in the "Messing with Mixes" section at the end of this chapter. Experiment with the many new flours available, like bean flours, sorghum, and amaranth. They're nutritious and add flavor, and oh yeah — they're gluten-free!

✓ **Breading and coatings:** If a recipe calls for breading, bread crumbs, flour coating, or a similar preparation, consider using a wheat- or gluten-free mix (either homemade or store bought). Bread and muffin mixes work well for coatings on chicken and other fried goodies. Seasoned cornmeal or corn flour (masa) and crushed potato chips (my favorite chips for coatings are barbecue flavor) are also excellent alternatives.

✓ **Thickeners:** Cornstarch, arrowroot flour, and tapioca starch make great substitutes for flour and other thickeners. Dry pudding mix works well for sweet recipes, and bread or baking mixes work well for just about anything.

✓ **Binders:** Whoa. That's one of those ingredient categories that would make me put away the cookbook, and I personally wouldn't use a recipe if it called for binders. But if you're more culinarily courageous, consider using gelatin, xanthan gum, or guar gum.

✓ **Pie crust:** People think that if something calls for a pie crust — say a quiche or — well, say a *pie* — then it's off limits unless they make a really complicated crust from a really complicated recipe. I say think again! First, consider making the dish *without* the crust. Seriously — a quiche without a crust is still a quiche. And admit it — when you eat a pie, you just eat the crust to be polite, right? The crust is really just a means to get to the gushy stuff inside. Okay, if you really want to make a gluten-free crust without a schmancy recipe, crush a couple of handfuls of gluten-free cookies or a sugary gluten-free cereal, add some butter or margarine (a glob or a dopple, whichever you prefer), and press the stuff into a greased pie pan. Then follow the baking instructions for a regular pie. You'll probably just eat the good stuff out of the middle, anyway.

✓ **Bread crumbs:** Many gluten-free breads turn to crumbs when you look at them. And certainly, there are always plenty of crumbs in the bag; just use them as extras for cooking. Or crumble some bread slices and toast or broil the crumbs to make them crunch.

✓ **Croutons:** Cut fresh, gluten-free bread into cubes, deep fry, and then roll in Parmesan cheese and spices. Some people suggest letting the bread get just a tad stale (not moldy) before making croutons this way.

✓ **Granola:** If you can find gluten-free oats, you're set. But if you can't, you can still make granola. Toss together toasted nuts and seeds, and then mix them with gluten-free cereal, honey, vanilla, a tiny bit of oil, and spices or seasonings. How much spices and seasonings? A smidge or so, till it tastes like you like it. Bake at 300 degrees for an hour, stirring every 15 minutes. Add dried fruit that's first been soaked in water for 10 minutes, let cool, and then refrigerate or vacuum seal and freeze.

✓ **Trail mix:** Lots of trail mixes that are available at the stores are already gluten-free, but if you like to make your own, mix some peanuts, raisins, dried fruit, and gluten-free chocolate candies or chips.

Dates and some other dried fruits are often dusted with oat flour. Be sure to check the labels. If they've been dusted with oat flour, the ingredients label will say so.

✔ **Oatmeal/hot breakfast:** Try corn grits. Prepare them like oatmeal and top with butter, cinnamon, and sugar, or fry them. Hot cereals also are available from the producers of gluten-free flours. Some new amaranth and quinoa hot cereals that are nutritional powerhouses are also available.

✔ **Buns and flour tortillas:** Substitute lettuce, gluten-free bread, corn tortillas, or rice wraps (found in Asian markets and often used in Thai cooking). If you like *nori* (the seaweed wrap on sushi), you can use it as a wrap with anything stuffed inside.

✔ **Soy and teriyaki sauce:** Asian markets carry some absolutely amazing Asian sauces that are gluten-free, but you have to read labels carefully (and sometimes that requires a crash course in another language). If you can't find a gluten-free soy sauce, you can substitute Bragg Liquid Aminos. You can find Bragg in the health-food aisle of your grocery store or at a natural-foods retailer. To make your own teriyaki, add equal parts of sugar and wine to your favorite soy sauce substitute.

When in doubt, leave it out. And really, what's the harm in leaving it out, anyway? If your soup recipe calls for a tablespoon or two of flour, try leaving it out and see what you think.

Putting mindless meals on the menu

Sometimes we get so caught up in "how to do the diet" that we forget how easy cooking can be. I love to experiment and play in the kitchen, but there are plenty of days when I just don't have the time. That's where mindless meals come in. These are easy meals that don't require a recipe. Here are some ideas to get you started.

When starting a gluten-free diet, people often forget they can eat normal, everyday foods like the ones I list below. Just make sure to read the labels and use substitutions for specific ingredients, if needed.

Breakfast

Most people start their day with a bowl of cereal, bagel, toast, pancakes, or waffles, and those things, unless they're a special gluten-free variety, are definitely not allowed on the gluten-free diet. But that's okay! There are healthier options for starting your day off gluten-free style, and they're quick and easy, too:

- Yogurt or cottage cheese topped with fruit, trail mix, or cereal
- Corn grits with a glob of butter and a little mix of cinnamon and sugar on top
- Eggs, any style, with sausage or bacon
- Fruit and cheese
- Fruit smoothie (I'd add some extra protein powder myself)
- Toast or French toast (made from gluten-free bread, of course)
- Quesadillas on a corn tortilla
- Leftovers from dinner the night before (my personal favorite)

Lunch or dinner

No need to scramble for cookbooks and recipes when you're putting together your gluten-free lunch or dinner. You can make plenty of quick and easy meals using easy-to-find ingredients.

- Hot dogs or burgers, plain or wrapped in a lettuce "bun" or corn tortilla
- Deli meats on a lettuce wrap or corn tortilla, or just plain or rolled up with condiments
- Caesar salad with chicken
- Roast beef, chicken, or turkey
- Premarinated or grilled chicken or turkey (add veggies and you have fajitas!)
- Chili
- Seafood
- Shish kebabs
- Frozen tamales
- Frozen taquitos

Side dishes and snacks

Whether you want simple or snazzy, you can prepare endless gluten-free side dishes and snacks without a recipe. The key is to think about what you would eat that has gluten in it, and use the substitution ideas in this book to help you modify the meal. If you're out of ideas, use this list as a starter:

- Fruit (fresh or dried)
- Vegetables (fresh or cooked)

✔ Quinoa (you can eat it hot or cold — use it as rice or even tabbouleh)

✔ Rice (I recommend brown rice if you're going to eat rice)

✔ Potatoes (sweet potatoes and yams are far more nutritious than other types)

✔ Potato skins (yeah, a little decadent if you goop 'em up with cheese and sour cream, but yummy nonetheless)

✔ Deviled or hard-boiled eggs

✔ Tuna

✔ Nachos or chips

✔ Cheese squares (you can get all sorts of gluten-free crackers if you want cheese and crackers)

✔ Cream cheese wrapped in ham or salami

✔ Rice cakes or popcorn

✔ Nuts

✔ Baked beans

✔ Sloppy Joes (on gluten-free bread, of course)

✔ Soup (you do have to check labels on commercial brands, but you can find gluten-free soups out there; consider making a super simple version of your own by using a premade stock and tossing in some veggies and gluten-free pasta)

✔ Celery with peanut butter or cream cheese

✔ Ice cream (stay away from varieties that contain the cookies, brownies, pretzels, and other gluten-containing treats)

Converting a Gluten-Filled Recipe into a Gluten-Free Recipe

Like rules, some recipes are meant to be broken. I know, I know, this is a *recipe* book, and you *will* get your recipes, I promise. But stay with me for a little bit, and think about breaking a few rules and bending a few recipes.

With gluten-free cooking, it's especially important to think outside the recipe box because you may not be able to find recipes for everything you want to make. You don't have to follow recipes to a T. With a little creativity and a willingness to bend, break, or bury the rules, you can transform any recipe into a gluten-free masterpiece, whether you found it in your great-grandma's recipe box, saw it on the hottest new cooking show, or ran across it on the Internet.

In this section, I show you exactly how to transform a recipe, or at least how I do it.

For this example, I chose a recipe that's gushing with gluten for dramatic effect. It's called "Fried Broccoli Florets with Soy Curry Sauce." Yikes. The title alone should sound warning bells in your head because "fried" usually means breading, and "soy" is usually followed by the word "sauce."

Here's the recipe as it appears online:

Fried Broccoli Florets with Soy Curry Sauce

This dish can be served as an appetizer or a first course.

Preparation time: 40 minutes

Cooking time: 5 minutes

Yield: 2 servings

¼ cup all-purpose flour	¾ teaspoon dark brown sugar
¼ cup plus 1 teaspoon beer	1½ teaspoons red wine vinegar
1 garlic clove, peeled	1 teaspoon fresh lemon juice
1 pinch kosher salt	½ teaspoon soy sauce
1 teaspoon butter	oil (for deep frying)
¼ teaspoon curry powder	12 broccoli florets

1 In a small bowl, whisk together the flour and the beer and let the batter stand for 30 minutes.

2 Finely mince the garlic, and on your cutting board, mix in the salt. Mash the garlic and salt together with the blade of a knife until it's a paste.

3 In a pan, melt the butter over moderately low heat and cook the curry powder, stirring for 1 minute.

4 Stir in the garlic paste, brown sugar, vinegar, lemon juice, and soy sauce, and transfer the sauce to a small dish.

5 In a deep, heavy skillet, heat 1 inch of oil to 375 degrees.

6 Whisk the beer batter, dip the broccoli florets into it, tossing off the excess batter, and fry them in the oil for 1½ to 2 minutes or until golden.

7 Transfer the broccoli to paper towels to drain, and serve it while warm with the curry sauce.

Per serving: Calories 117; Total fat 2g; Saturated fat 1g; Cholesterol 5mg; Sodium 190mg; Carbohydrate 19g; Fiber 1g; Protein 4g.

Converting the ingredients

Okay, so we have all-purpose flour, beer, *more* beer (Why do they do that? Is that one extra teaspoon *really* going to make a difference?!? But I digress . . .), and soy sauce. No go, no go, and no go. *Not* on a gluten-free diet.

So how do I transform this into a gluten-free goodie? Well, first I get rid of the measurements, because this is cooking Danna-style. Table 7-1 shows you what the new ingredients list can look like. (I included the original ingredients list in the left-hand column of the table so you don't have to keep flipping back and forth, only to give up after five or six flips. You're welcome!)

Table 7-1	Comparison of Original and Converted Ingredients Lists	
Original Ingredient and Measurement	*My Converted Measurement*	*Gluten-Free Ingredient*
¼ cup all-purpose flour	A fist-full of	any gluten-free mix you happen to have lying around. All you have is muffin mix, and it's a little sweet? No problem! It might make it even better!
¼ cup beer, plus	A glug of	gluten-free beer would be the obvious ingredient here, and there are excellent ones on the market now, even available at regular grocery stores. If you don't have access to gluten-free beer, try using chicken broth, ginger ale, or white grape juice.

Original Ingredient and Measurement	My Converted Measurement	Gluten-Free Ingredient
1 teaspoon beer	Another splash of	beer substitute (see above).
1 garlic clove, peeled	A bunch of	garlic. (Personally, I'm a fan of the sliced, diced, and otherwise-ready-to-go variety in a jar.)
1 pinch kosher salt	A pinch of	kosher salt. (Okay, seriously, does it need to be kosher?)
¼ teaspoon curry powder	A dash or splash of	curry powder. (This borders on being a little chichi for my taste, but I'll let it slide.)
¾ teaspoon dark brown sugar	A glob of	dark brown sugar (or light brown — do you really think it's going to make a difference?).
1½ teaspoons red wine vinegar	A glob of	red wine vinegar.
1 teaspoon fresh lemon juice	A bunch of squeezes of	fresh lemon juice. (I like my foods extra lemony, so I upped the amount.)
½ teaspoon soy sauce	A few splashes of	gluten-free soy sauce. (If you don't like or don't have access to soy sauce, try Bragg Liquid Aminos or an Asian sauce [check the label carefully for gluten].)
oil (for deep frying)	Lots of	oil (for deep frying).
12 broccoli florets	As many as you want	broccoli florets.

When you deep-fry glutenous foods, like "regular" breaded items, the oil becomes contaminated with gluten. You can't use that same oil for your gluten-free goodies, or you're defeating the purpose of cooking gluten-free. Always use fresh, non-contaminated oil for frying or deep-frying.

Interpreting the instructions

Okay, so now it's time for the instruction part of the recipe. In the "real" recipe, the beer and flour have to hang out together for a half hour or so to do their thing: thicken, bubble, yeastify. That borders on being a little schmancy for my type of cooking, but I'll let it slide. Check out Table 7-2 to see how the original steps compare to what I would do.

Table 7-2	Formal Instructions versus Danna-Style Instructions
Original Steps	*My Version of the Steps*
1. In a small bowl, whisk together the flour and the beer and let the batter stand for 30 minutes.	1. Mix the gluten-free flour mixture and gluten-free beer together and set it aside while you figure out what else you have to do to prepare this dish.
2. Finely mince the garlic, and on your cutting board, mix in the salt. Mash the garlic and salt together with the blade of a knife until it's a paste.	2. Dump all of the rest of the ingredients *except the broccoli* into a frying pan and heat them up. Swish everything around a little so it's all mixed together. This is going to be your dipping sauce, so when it's finished heating, you can put it into a dipping bowl (if you *have* a dipping bowl, you're far too advanced for these instructions).
3. In a pan, melt the butter over moderately low heat and cook the curry powder, stirring for 1 minute.	3. Dunk the broccoli into the flour-and-beer mixture. How you do this without getting the mixture all over your fingers is up to you.
4. Stir in the garlic paste, brown sugar, vinegar, lemon juice, and soy sauce and transfer the sauce to a small dish.	4. Put the coated broccoli into the hot oil (if I really had to tell you to heat the oil when you knew you were going to *deep-fry* something, skip ahead to the real recipes that call out each step). Deep-fry until it's done. (If I have to tell you when it's done, creative cooking is not for you.)
5. In a deep, heavy skillet, heat 1 inch of oil to 375 degrees.	
6. Whisk the beer batter, dip the broccoli florets into it, tossing off the excess batter, and fry them in the oil for 1½ to 2 minutes or until golden.	
7. Transfer the broccoli to paper towels to drain, and serve it while warm with the curry sauce.	

Beer is less acidic than wine, vinegar, or citrus juices, so it tenderizes meats without breaking down the texture as fast. That's why you can use it to tenderize and marinate raw fish, or add it to dishes that call for vinegar. And of course, I don't have to remind you to make sure it's of the gluten-free variety!

Keep in mind that the whole point of this chapter is to be creative and think outside the recipe box. So the example I've given you here is just that — an example. Feel free to modify it however you'd like to suit your fancy.

Messing with Mixes

Bear with me while I whine for a moment, will you? When I first started "doing gluten-free" in 1991, there weren't any mixes — at least not that I found. Remember, that was before Al Gore invented the Internet, before there were any books on the subject, and even before support groups were widely available.

The first gluten-free mixes to hit the streets were basically a little rice flour with a lot of sugar. And hey — I'm the first to admit that a little sugar can go a long way in making up for lost flavor, but they were lacking something. Flavor . . . nutrition . . . the ability to stick together.

We've come a long way, baby. Today you can easily find gluten-free mixes for brownies, cookies, breads, pizza crust, muffins, cakes — you name it. For those who don't want to explore recipes and worry about all the ingredients they involve, mixes are a great alternative.

Even if you're a pro in the kitchen, mixes can be a valuable addition to your pantry shelf. Keep them on hand to use when you're in a hurry or as a ready-made substitute for gluten-containing ingredients. For instance, if your recipe calls for dredging chicken in flour, and you obviously can't use regular white flour, just use a gluten-free bread or muffin mix in its place.

One of my favorite mixes is a blend of several different kinds of flour. You can use flour mixtures like this in recipes that call for regular flour. In Chapter 8, I give you a recipe you can use to make your own flour mixtures, but you can buy them premixed, too. The mixes actually work better than individual flours alone, because each flour adds a cooking characteristic of its own. When you combine different varieties, such as rice, potato, tapioca, quinoa, buckwheat, amaranth, and other flours, they rise better, cook better, and offer more nutritional value than each individual flour alone.

Add some flaxseed to your favorite mix for some extra fiber and omega-3 fatty acids. Omega-3s are important building blocks for our cell membranes, and are essential for good health. Among other things, they play an important role in heart health and in lowering cholesterol.

Don't let the price tag fool you

Besides the obvious convenience factor, one of the best things about mixes is that although they may *seem* prohibitively expensive, they can actually save you money in the long run.

Personally, I've spent exorbitant sums of money on ingredients for my home-made concoctions (seriously, have you priced xanthan gum?), not to mention hours putting them together, only to end up with inedible bricks of bread, or cookies that crumble when you have the audacity to attempt to remove them from the baking sheet. Sometimes even my dogs couldn't stomach the mixture mishaps.

Mixes today are a sure bet. Not only are they edible (a plus for food products), but they taste great and are often loaded with extra nutrients thanks to the more widespread use of alternative flours such as amaranth, quinoa, and buckwheat. Investing in a sure thing can beat experimentation and save you money in the long run.

They're easy to find

You can find these incredible mixes in many grocery stores and specialty stores. Even some of the larger grocery stores have gluten-free sections, or they carry these types of products in their health food sections.

You can also find a large assortment of mixes and other products online. For a general assortment, search for keywords like "gluten-free products" and "gluten-free mixes." If you know what you're looking for, make your search criteria more specific, like "gluten-free brownie mix" or "gluten-free cookie mix."

Part II

Mouthwatering Main Courses

The 5th Wave   By Rich Tennant

"I think my family's finally accepted my new way of cooking. I've eliminated all of the gluten, some of the fat, and most of the sarcasm."

In this part . . .

Everyone has a busy life anymore. We're rushing around trying to meet work deadlines, taking the kids to their soccer games, completing a volunteer project that we didn't want to do in the first place but didn't know how to say "no" to. So how are we supposed to have time to prepare meals, too? With just a little forethought and planning, you can actually have a balanced, gluten-free meal at home. Honest. Just try a few of the recipes in this part. We provide recipes for the three main meals you eat (or should eat) each day: breakfast, lunch, and dinner.

Chapter 8

Gluten-Free Flours: Your Foundation for Great Breads and Pastries

In This Chapter

▶ Wheat flour? Who needs it!

▶ Getting to know the alternative flours

▶ Creating your own gluten-free flour mixture

▶ Reviewing some general baking tips

Yes, you are a celiac (or you've decided to avoid foods containing gluten). Yes, you must give up all products containing wheat, rye, and barley. And *yes,* you can still enjoy eating *all* of your favorite foods. If this sounds contradictory, read on.

This first chapter in the recipe section of this book is devoted to setting your mind at ease by explaining how to use alternative flours successfully. Let's be honest. We all love bread, cakes, pizza, and pasta. Celiacs, especially those who are newly diagnosed, have nightmares of never being able to eat these processed carbohydrates again. None of these foods is traditionally gluten-free — but they can be!

After you understand the basics of baking gluten-free and realize that your food selections aren't limited, you can then peruse the rest of the recipes in this book with peace of mind, knowing that you won't be deprived of any of your favorite foods.

Baking Decent Bread without Wheat Flour: It's No Joke

If you're living the gluten-free life, you certainly know that you can't go to the store, buy a bag of wheat flour, bring it home, dip your measuring cup into the bag, and begin baking. The properties in wheat are difficult to duplicate, so you need a variety of alternative flours to attain the results you would get from wheat flour. Even then, you're dealing with gluten-free flours that have no, well, no gluten. Gluten gives bread its light, spongy consistency and cakes their airy lift. In a few recipes, you can get away with substituting cornstarch in place of wheat flour, but those instances are rare.

Don't despair. There are viable ways to imitate the texture and taste of wheat flour. When you use the right combination of alternative flours, add some additional flavoring and include something acidic to help the product rise. Your cookies, cakes, and pie crusts will taste every bit as good as their wheat counterparts.

You may have noticed that breads weren't included in the ". . . will taste every bit as good as . . ." list above. Breads are some of the most difficult recipes to convert to gluten-free, and converting them takes a little more understanding. After you've mastered the art of this conversion (I give you some hints a few paragraphs below), you'll have a loaf of bread that is gorgeous to look at, heavenly to smell, and delectable to eat. But it's not quite as simple as that.

Surviving a gluten-free bread disaster

If you do end up with a disastrous loaf of bread at some point, *do not* throw it out! Gluten-free ingredients are far too expensive to simply toss in the trash can, and you put too much effort into your creation. Instead, cut the loaf into slices and lay them on a baking sheet. Bake the slices at 200 degrees for 1 hour, or until the bread is crisp. (The baking time will vary considerably depending on the thickness of the slices and the texture of bread.) Let the slices cool, and then put them into a blender with seasonings to make your own bread crumbs.

If the loaf is semi-salvageable, first cut slices, and then cut those slices into cubes. Toss the bread cubes in a bowl with a little oil and seasonings, and then spread the cubes out on a baking sheet. Bake the cubes at 200 degrees until they're crisp (but not jaw-breaker crisp). Use these cubes as croutons in salads, or freeze them until you're ready to make bread dressing or bread pudding.

The first time you try to convert a wheat yeast bread recipe to gluten-free, you'll most likely end up with a glob that is raw in the center, has a crust that requires a jackhammer to cut through it, and an aftertaste that redefines the word "bitter." If the loaf actually bakes all the way through, then the slices may crumble beyond recognition when you attempt to cut it.

Fortunately, you have this book in your hands. It contains excellent bread recipes with all the necessary adjustments, so you don't have to worry about converting your Grandma's homemade bread recipe immediately. Be aware that if you use a different flour mixture with the recipes in this book, you may get different results.

To create a loaf of gluten-free bread that is a masterpiece, the proportion of yeast to salt and sugar has to be correct. Adding an extra egg white to the mix usually results in a lighter texture. Adding a little light flaxseed meal helps the yeast rise. Adding something acidic (usually cider vinegar) also helps with the rising. Additional flavoring is beneficial. Again, the recipes in this book have already had these adjustments made. The finished product may not be as airy as the commercial, non-nutritional, touch-it-and-it-smooshes white bread, but the texture will be light and the taste divine. Some of the ready-made loaves of gluten-free breads that you find at health food stores are edible (that's a generous summation), so seriously consider baking some homemade bread. You deserve to eat a slice of bread that actually tastes great!

A Brief Overview of Alternative Flours

If you tour a health food store, and even some grocery stores, you'll be amazed at the variety of alternative flours available. If you're health-conscious, use three-fourths of the basic gluten-free flour mixture in a recipe, and add up to one-fourth of a different kind of flour so the mixture has more fiber and protein. Experiment with almond flour, light flaxseed meal, light teff, chestnut flour, mesquite flour, or lentil flour.

Where to purchase your flours may be an issue. You can buy some of these alternative flours at Asian markets. The advantage to buying them from Asia is that they are usually less expensive and the flours are ground finer, yielding better baking results. The disadvantage is that you're rarely able to confirm that the flours are processed in a gluten-free facility. If you prefer to stay away from Asian markets or you don't have one nearby, alternative flours are readily available at health food stores, and many mainstream grocery stores now have gluten-free sections that offer a large variety of flours.

✔ You can choose between **white rice flour** and **brown rice flour.**

- • *Brown rice flour* still has the bran layer, so it offers more vitamins, minerals, and fiber than its white counterpart, but the finished product will be slightly darker in color and just a bit nuttier tasting. Even though brown rice flour still has the bran layer, this kind of bran is gluten-free.

- • There is *white rice flour* and *glutinous white rice flour;* the two are not interchangeable. White rice flour is used in the flour mixture for baking. Glutinous white rice flour is *glutinous* (sticky) and is used like cornstarch to thicken gravies. Don't let the name "glutinous" confuse you. *Rice gluten* (which is safe for celiacs) is not the same as *wheat gluten* (which is not safe for celiacs). If you are a *newbie* (an affectionate reference to someone who is newly diagnosed), all this flour stuff does make sense after a while.

✔ **Potato starch flour** shouldn't be confused with potato flour. Potato flour is used as a thickener for gravies; potato starch flour is used as a base for baked goods. The powdery texture helps keep baked foods light in texture and helps with the expansion during baking. It also helps maintain moisture in baked goods.

✔ **Tapioca** (or **cassava**) **flour** is a thickening agent that helps prevent breads and cakes from crumbling. It also lightens baked goods while adding a chewiness (perfect for cookies), and it helps gluten-free products to brown. It's very easily digested.

✔ There are two main bean flours on the market — **garbanzo bean (chickpea) flour** and **garfava bean flour** (a combination of garbanzo beans and fava beans). Both of these flours are slightly yellow in color, and they're excellent sources of protein. A little more challenging to locate are **lentil, mung bean,** and **pea flours.** The bean flours add extra nutrition to the mix, and they also help make the product lighter, so it's beneficial to add a *little* bean flour to your flour mixture. Adding too much bean flour may give your product a potent aftertaste and may also cause flatulence (yup — gas).

✔ **Cornstarch,** although it has no nutritional value, is used to lighten the texture of baked goods.

✔ **Sorghum** (or **milo**) **flour** offers more nutritional value (protein and fiber) than the rice flours. It's neutral tasting, and it helps keep your baked goods from shrinking.

✔ **White sweet potato flour** is difficult to find, but it adds a delicious flavor to cookies and cakes, and is also higher in fiber than most other flours.

✔ **Amaranth** is sweeter than most alternative flours with an almost nutty taste. Although the taste is good, the texture tends to be very sticky, so no more than 10 percent of your flour mixture should be amaranth. The advantage to including it is that it's more nutritious than most of the alternative flours. It's high in fiber, iron, and calcium.

✔ **Soy flour** is an option, but it tends to leave a distinctive aftertaste, as do **teff** and **buckwheat.** (No, buckwheat does not have wheat in it.)

You'll have a slight glitch if you bake gluten-free products and wheat products in your home (for the celiac and non-celiac members of your family). You'll need to bake the gluten-free baked goods first, and then cover them securely. Flour particles can stay in the air for up to 24 hours, so no matter how careful you are to clean your mixer, baking sheets, and countertops, the gluten-free food may still become contaminated with wheat flour if you bake the wheat product first.

Creating the Gluten-Free Flour Mixture

Setting out all the different alternative flours, the xanthan gum, the cornstarch . . . this can create quite a mess in your kitchen. You'll undoubtedly find flour powder lightly dusting your kitchen counters when you're through with the measuring and sifting.

Yes, gum is involved

If you are new to gluten-free baking, you may have panicked when you saw the word *xanthan gum* (pronounced *zan*-thun). It's just a fancy name for a gum (sticky stuff) that will help hold your baked product together. Point of clarification — the *result* of using the gum is sticky, not the gum itself. Xanthan gum is available at most health food stores and even at some mainline grocery stores. It's a cream-colored powder that comes packaged either in a pouch or a jar. Adding just a little of this gum to your flour mixture helps prevent your baked goods from crumbling.

Guar gum is sometimes used in place of xanthan gum. It accomplishes the same thing as the xanthan gum (preventing crumbling). Although guar gum is gluten-free, it may cause distress of the lower intestinal tract in some people (that's the politically correct way to say diarrhea). Another alternative to using xanthan gum is to use twice the amount of unflavored gelatin. If the recipe calls for 1 teaspoon of xanthan gum, use 2 teaspoons of unflavored gelatin.

Precisely because of the mess that occurs when you assemble the flour mixture, we only use one flour mixture throughout this book. Why? Because you can measure and sift once, and then spoon the combined flours into a self-seal plastic bag and freeze it. When you're ready to bake, you don't have to drag out all the different bags of flour — one flour mixture will suffice for all the recipes in this book. Just take the bag out of the freezer, measure the amount you need, and begin baking. It doesn't get much easier than that. It should be noted that in a few of the bread recipes, sorghum flour or flaxseed meal is added to the basic flour mixture to get the right consistency.

When making more than one batch of the flour mixture, measure and sift each batch separately to be certain that the ingredients combine evenly. After one recipe has been sifted into a bowl, stir the mixture with a whisk to guarantee that everything is well blended. Place it in a freezer bag, and then begin mixing up the second batch.

Why should you freeze the flour mixture? The alternative flours don't have the shelf life of wheat flour. By keeping the mixture in the freezer, it will stay fresh for months. After you measure the amount of the gluten-free flour mixture you need for a recipe, let it set out on the kitchen counter for about 15 minutes to reach room temperature before mixing it with other ingredients.

♉ Gluten-Free Flour Mixture

This recipe is the magical gluten-free flour mixture that is used in the recipes throughout this book. Although many other suitable combinations of flours are available, cooking and baking is so much simpler when you use only one flour mixture. When making a double batch of this flour mixture, sift together one recipe at a time, and then stir together the batches of flour mixture.

Preparation time: *5 minutes*

Yield: *5 cups*

2½ cups rice flour	¼ cup garbanzo bean flour
1 cup potato starch flour	¼ cup cornstarch
1 cup tapioca flour	2½ tablespoons xanthan gum

1 Sift all the ingredients into a large bowl, and then stir them together with a whisk.

2 Spoon the mixture into a self-seal freezer bag and freeze until needed.

Per ¼ cup: Calories: 138; Total fat: 0g; Saturated fat: 0g; Cholesterol: 0mg; Sodium: 1mg; Carbohydrates: 32g; Fiber: 2g; Sugar: 0g; Protein: 1g.

Recipe for Success: A Few Baking Tips

Baking is just as much a science as it is an art. You can't play around with a bread or cake recipe like you can a soup recipe. You have to know what you're doing, which takes practice. Here are some general baking tips that should help as you develop your skills:

- Eggs should be at room temperature when making baked goods. If you forget to take the eggs out of the refrigerator ahead of time, place the eggs (still in their shells) in a bowl of warm water for 5 minutes. Eggs that are cracked or leaking should not be used. Because of the risk of salmonella, none of the recipes in this book contain raw eggs.

- If a recipe calls for softened butter and your butter is still in the refrigerator, cut off the needed amount. Cut that block into 1-tablespoon chunks, set the chunks on a plate, and put the dish in the microwave for 14 seconds to soften.

- If you substitute margarine for butter, only use margarine made with 80 percent fat. Products with a lower fat content may affect the quality and texture of the end product.

- Periodically test your cornstarch for freshness by mixing 1 teaspoon of vinegar with 1 teaspoon of cornstarch. The mixture will bubble if the cornstarch is fresh.

- If sifting is called for in a recipe, instead of sifting, you can place all the dry ingredients in a bowl and mix them with a wire whisk or mixer. Or you can place the dry ingredients in the bowl of your food processor and give them a couple of quick pulses.

- For baked goods that call for oil, you can replace half of the oil with applesauce to produce a low-fat version of the recipe. You'll need to reduce the baking time just slightly to prevent the product from becoming too dry.

- When mayonnaise is called for in a cake recipe, use real mayonnaise (not reduced-calorie, fat-free, or imitation). Anything other than real mayo will break down under the heat of the oven and leave a metallic taste.

- When measurements are given, they are level (not heaping) measures. When measuring honey, molasses, or anything sticky, spray the measuring spoon or measuring cup with nonstick cooking spray first so the sticky stuff slides out easily.

Chapter 9

Breakfast: Don't Leave Home Without It

*I*f you eat dinner at 6 p.m. and wake up at 7 a.m., you'll have fasted for more than 13 hours before you sit down to breakfast. At that point, your body's blood sugar levels are screaming for nourishment. If you're weight conscious, eating breakfast jump-starts your metabolism so it works harder and more efficiently all day. Simply put, never skip breakfast.

Forget the excuse, "I don't have time for breakfast." There are foods that you can take in the car and eat as you commute to work. At the very least, you can grab a piece of fruit, a container of gluten-free yogurt, and a gluten-free health bar. Some foods can be prepared the night before so that, in the morning, you can put them in the oven while you shower, and they're ready by the time you're dressed. Now, did that cover all the "I don't have time for breakfast" excuses? Besides, after making the recipes in this chapter, you'll wake up each morning anticipating your first meal of the day.

Many of the recipes in this chapter call for a gluten-free flour mixture. See Chapter 8 for our no-fail recipe.

Starting the Day the Gluten-Free Way

Most people climb out of bed, shuffle into the kitchen, and pop some bread into the toaster or pour a bowl of cereal — you can too. You just have to make sure your bread and cereal are gluten-free.

If you have non-celiacs in the house, you need to be certain that your toast is not contaminated by their toast crumbs. The easiest way to do this is to have two toasters or to use Toast-It! Bags. With these bags, you insert the bread into the bag, and then insert the bag into the toaster. The bag allows heat to penetrate so the bread will toast, but no crumbs or essence of crumbs can cling to the bread. These bags are great to take with you when you're traveling so you can have toast on the road without fear of cross-contamination.

But you are about to realize that breakfast is so much more than mere bread and cereal.

☞ *Cinnamon Breakfast Cereal*

Think outside of the box. This is a terrific warm-your-tummy hot rice cereal. To speed things up in the morning, cook the rice the night before or use leftover dinner rice. If you prefer a more liquid cereal, add more warmed milk.

Tools: *Double boiler*

Preparation time: *4 minutes*

Cooking time: *5 minutes*

Yield: *2 servings*

2 cups cooked brown rice	2 tablespoons maple syrup
1 cup milk	1 tablespoon butter
2 tablespoons brown sugar	2 tablespoons raisins
⅛ teaspoon cinnamon	⅓ cup toasted pecan pieces
¾ teaspoon vanilla	

1 Place all the ingredients in the top of a double boiler over boiling water, stirring frequently, for about 5 minutes.

2 When the cereal is thoroughly warmed, spoon it into 2 serving bowls.

Per serving: Calories: 605; Total fat: 25g; Saturated fat: 7g; Cholesterol: 27mg; Sodium: 108mg; Carbohydrates: 88g; Fiber: 6g; Sugar: 39g; Protein: 11g.

Raspberry Smoothie

This may not be a typical breakfast, but you're still getting your dairy and fruit. In just a few minutes, you have a filling drink you can take with you and sip on the way to work.

Tools: *Blender*

Preparation time: *3 minutes*

Cooking time: *None*

Yield: *4 servings*

1 cup frozen raspberries

12-ounce can frozen lemonade concentrate

2 cups 1 percent low-fat milk

1 cup frozen vanilla yogurt

1 Place all the ingredients in a blender.

2 Blend on "puree" for 20 seconds.

3 Pour the smoothie into 4 glasses.

Vary It! *For a thicker smoothie, add a banana.*

Per serving: Calories: 354; Total fat: 4g; Saturated fat: 2g; Cholesterol: 6mg; Sodium: 72mg; Carbohydrates: 77g; Fiber: 2g; Sugar: 64g; Protein: 7g.

☞ *Homemade Cereal*

Make up a big batch of this and keep it stored in self-seal bags or a large plastic container. Kids will love to munch on the dry cereal, too. Be very careful to bake it enough the first time so the cereal is crunchy, and be equally as careful *not* to over-bake it on the second baking or it becomes too hard and won't soften in milk. After you get the timing of the baking down pat, you'll want to keep an ample supply of this cereal on hand.

Tools: *Food processor*

STAGE 1

Preparation time: *10 minutes*

Cooking time: *30 minutes*

STAGE 2

Preparation time: *5 minutes*

Cooking time: *10-plus minutes*

Yield: *10 cups*

Nonstick cooking spray	*1 teaspoon salt*
3 cups gluten-free flour mixture	*1 teaspoon baking soda*
½ cup coconut flour	*2 cups buttermilk*
¼ cup flaxseed meal	*2 teaspoons vanilla*
1¼ teaspoon cinnamon	*½ cup slivered almonds*
¼ teaspoon nutmeg	*½ cup dried cranberries*
1 cup brown sugar	

Stage 1

1 Preheat the oven to 350 degrees. Spray a large baking sheet with cooking spray.

2 In a large bowl, whisk together the flours, flaxseed meal, cinnamon, nutmeg, brown sugar, salt, and baking soda.

3 In a small bowl, stir together the buttermilk and vanilla.

4 Stir the wet ingredients into the dry mixture until they're well blended.

5 Spread the soft, cookie-like dough evenly in the prepared baking sheet.

6 Bake the dough at 350 degrees for 15 minutes, and then turn it over (so both sides brown evenly). It's okay if the dough breaks into pieces. Continue to bake the dough for 10 to 15 more minutes until it's golden brown and crisp.

7 Place the pan on a wire rack to cool. Let the cereal dough stand, uncovered, for several hours or overnight in a cool place to completely dry out.

Stage 2

1 Preheat the oven to 300 degrees.

2 When the cereal dough is dry, break it into small pieces and chop it in a food processor (a blender works, but not quite as well) until the pieces are the size of dried peas.

3 Spread the cereal on two baking sheets.

4 Bake the cereal at 300 degrees for 10 to 15 minutes until it's crisp and lightly browned. Stir the cereal often during baking. Do not over-bake (or the cereal will turn into rocks!)

5 When the cereal has cooled, stir in the almonds and cranberries and store it in a sealed container.

Tip: This cereal makes an excellent topping for yogurt, frozen yogurt, or ice cream.

Per serving: Calories: 369; Total fat: 6g; Saturated fat: 1g; Cholesterol: 2mg; Sodium: 423mg; Carbohydrates: 73g; Fiber: 6g; Sugar: 28g; Protein: 6g.

Adding Some Sizzle to Your Morning with Eggs, Omelets, and Breakfast Wraps

It is amazing what a little whipping can do for an egg. I like to think of egg preparations in terms of the height of the finished product. Here's what I mean:

- Fried eggs aren't beaten at all; scrambled eggs are just stirred up. When cooked, neither rises much at all.

- Omelets, whose eggs are given a quick beating, rise a little bit.

- Frittatas have even more lift.

- One step above the frittata is the quiche.

- And the ultimate elevation results in a soufflé.

And you thought cooking eggs for breakfast was going to be simple!

Now take that same egg, scramble it, lay it in a gluten-free flour or corn tortilla, spoon on your choice of toppings, and you've just created a breakfast wrap. Kids love wraps because they're fun to eat and a welcome reprieve from the usual bowl of gluten-free cereal.

Farmer's Skillet Eggs

Scrambled eggs are fine, but mundane. An omelet takes very little additional effort and cooking time, yet the final product is so much more rewarding, both to the eye and to the tummy. Children often won't eat zucchini — but they won't even taste it in this gorgeous omelet.

Preparation time: *8 minutes*

Cooking time: *8 minutes*

Yield: *4 servings*

½ cup sliced mushrooms	4 large eggs
1 green onion, sliced	⅛ teaspoon dried thyme
2 teaspoons butter	¼ teaspoon dried dill
1 teaspoon olive oil	⅛ teaspoon salt
½ small zucchini, finely chopped (about ⅓ cup)	¼ teaspoon pepper
3 slices deli ham (sliced, not shaved), cut into ¼-inch cubes	¼ cup (1 ounce) shredded Swiss cheese

1 Preheat the broiler. Wrap the handle of a 10-inch skillet with foil.

2 In the skillet, sauté the mushrooms and onions in the butter and oil over medium-high heat, stirring frequently, until the vegetables are tender but not browned.

3 Stir in the zucchini; cook the vegetables 2 to 3 minutes until the zucchini is tender.

4 Stir in the ham.

5 In a medium bowl, whisk the eggs until the whites and yolk are blended but not foamy. Stir in the thyme, dill, salt, and pepper. Stir in the cheese.

6 Pour the egg mixture over the ham and vegetables. Cook over medium-low heat, without stirring, until the mixture begins to set on the bottom and around the edges. As the eggs set, run a rubber spatula around the edge of the skillet, lifting the egg mixture to allow the uncooked portion to flow underneath. Continue doing this until the eggs are almost set.

7 Set the skillet under the broiler and broil for 2 minutes, or until the eggs are just set.

8 To serve, cut the omelet in wedges.

Per serving: *Calories: 163; Total fat: 12g; Saturated fat: 5g; Cholesterol: 236mg; Sodium: 439mg; Carbohydrates: 2g; Fiber: 0g; Sugar: 1g; Protein: 12g.*

Pepperoni Frittata

Think of a frittata as the midpoint between an omelet and a soufflé. Customize this masterpiece to your liking. You can use cooked, crumbled sausage in place of the pepperoni. Instead of the broccoli, try asparagus tips. You can substitute cheddar or mozzarella cheese for the Swiss cheese. Try different combinations — variety is the spice of life!

Preparation time: *10 minutes*

Cooking time: *5 minutes*

Yield: *6 servings*

1 tablespoon olive oil	*¼ teaspoon dried dill*
1½ cups thinly sliced broccoli florets	*1 tablespoon snipped fresh parsley*
¼ cup sliced green onion	*6 eggs*
¼ teaspoon salt	*3 tablespoons cornstarch*
¼ teaspoon pepper	*1½ tablespoons milk*
½ teaspoon dried Italian seasoning	*10 slices pizza pepperoni, chopped*
¼ teaspoon dried thyme	*¾ cup shredded Swiss cheese*

1 Preheat the broiler. Wrap the handle of a 10-inch nonstick skillet with foil.

2 Heat the oil in the skillet. Add the broccoli, green onion, salt, pepper, Italian seasoning, thyme, dill, and parsley. Cook the vegetables and seasonings over medium-high heat, stirring, until the broccoli florets are tender-crisp. Sprinkle pepperoni over broccoli.

3 In a small bowl, whisk together the eggs, cornstarch, and milk until they're very light. Pour the mixture over the vegetables.

4 As the eggs begin to set, run a rubber spatula around the edge of the skillet, lifting the egg mixture to allow the uncooked portions to flow underneath. Continue cooking and lifting the edges until the eggs are nearly set. (The top surface will still be moist.)

5 Sprinkle the top of the frittata with cheese.

6 Place the skillet under the broiler and broil the frittata for 1 to 2 minutes until the top is set and the cheese has melted. Cut the frittata into wedges to serve.

Per serving: Calories: 197; Total fat: 13g; Saturated fat: 5g; Cholesterol: 229mg; Sodium: 261mg; Carbohydrates: 10g; Fiber: 1g; Sugar: 1g; Protein: 12g.

Crab Quiche

You can make a gluten-free pie crust for this quiche, but it isn't needed. The taste, sans crust, is absolutely exquisite.

Preparation time: *10 minutes*

Cooking time: *20 minutes*

Yield: *6 servings*

Nonstick cooking spray

3 eggs

2 green onions, chopped

¼ cup plain low-fat yogurt

2 teaspoons cornstarch

¼ teaspoon dried basil

½ teaspoon dried dill

2 tablespoons fresh parsley, minced

⅛ teaspoon salt

⅛ teaspoon pepper

¾ cup (½ of a 10-ounce box) chopped broccoli, thawed

4.25-ounce can flaked crabmeat, drained

2 tablespoons grated Romano cheese

¼ cup (1 ounce) shredded Swiss cheese

2 plum tomatoes, sliced thin

¼ cup gluten-free bread crumbs

1 Preheat the oven to 375 degrees. Spray a 9-inch pie plate with cooking spray.

2 In a large bowl, whisk together the eggs, green onions, yogurt, cornstarch, basil, dill, parsley, salt, and pepper until they're thoroughly blended.

3 Stir in the broccoli, crabmeat, and Romano and Swiss cheeses.

4 Spread the mixture evenly in the prepared pie plate.

5 Lay the tomato slices neatly across the top of the quiche and then sprinkle them with breadcrumbs.

6 Bake the quiche, uncovered, at 375 degrees for 20 minutes, or until a knife inserted in the center comes out clean. Let the quiche stand for 5 minutes before cutting.

Vary It! *You can use a 6-ounce can of salmon in place of the crabmeat with equally excellent results.*

Per serving: Calories: 123; Total fat: 6g; Saturated fat: 3g; Cholesterol: 133mg; Sodium: 299mg; Carbohydrates: 7g; Fiber: 1g; Sugar: 2g; Protein: 12g.

☕ Maple Soufflé

This most definitely is not your run-of-the-mill soufflé! This creation is the lightest, puffiest, airiest egg soufflé you've ever experienced. Drizzle a little maple syrup over the top of each piece for a perfect presentation.

Tools: *Electric mixer*

Preparation time: *10 minutes*

Cooking time: *40 minutes*

Yield: *4 servings*

6 large eggs, separated	*¼ cup small-curd cottage cheese*
6 tablespoons maple syrup	*2 tablespoons butter, melted*
¼ teaspoon cinnamon	*⅓ cup sliced almonds*
⅛ teaspoon salt	

1 Preheat the oven to 350 degrees.

2 In a small mixing bowl, use the mixer to whip the egg whites on high speed until soft peaks form. Set the bowl aside.

3 In a large mixing bowl, use the mixer to whip the egg yolks about 3 minutes until they're thick. Whip in the maple syrup, cinnamon, salt, and cottage cheese until blended.

4 Fold the egg whites into the egg yolk mixture.

5 Brush the melted butter on the bottom and sides of a 9-x-1½-inch round straight-sided soufflé dish. Pour the egg mixture into the prepared pan. Sprinkle the top with almonds.

6 Bake for 40 minutes at 350 degrees, or until the top is puffed and lightly browned.

7 Cut into wedges to serve.

Per serving: *Calories: 240; Total fat: 13g; Saturated fat: 5g; Cholesterol: 60mg; Sodium: 123mg; Carbohydrates: 16g; Fiber: 1g; Sugar: 13g; Protein: 7g.*

Egg Burrito

When was the last time you surprised your family by serving them a really fun breakfast? Kids, as well as adults, will love this burrito. Wrap it in wax paper and you transform the burrito into a to-go breakfast sandwich that you can eat in the car on the way to work or school. One can of refried beans makes 10 servings.

Preparation time: *10 minutes*

Cooking time: *5 minutes*

Yield: *1 serving*

10-inch gluten-free tortilla	*2 tablespoons refried beans*
2 strips bacon	*2 tablespoons shredded cheddar cheese*
1 egg	*1 tablespoon salsa*

1 Preheat the oven to 350 degrees.

2 Wrap the tortilla in foil and warm it in the oven for 4 minutes.

3 Cook the bacon in a large skillet over medium-low heat until it's crisp. Remove the bacon and drain it on a paper towel. Pour out the bacon grease but don't wipe out the pan.

4 Break the egg into the same skillet and scramble it with a fork as it cooks over medium heat. Cook the egg until it's firm but not dry.

5 In a small saucepan, warm the beans.

6 Top the tortilla with the beans, bacon, egg, cheese, and salsa. Roll the tortilla into a burrito.

Per serving: *Calories: 468; Total fat: 22g; Saturated fat: 8g; Cholesterol: 248mg; Sodium: 1,158mg; Carbohydrates: 42g; Fiber: 4g; Sugar: 3g; Protein: 24g.*

Breakfast Enchilada

This dish is fancy enough to serve to company, but easy enough to serve for breakfast to the family. For ultimate enjoyment, top off the enchiladas with salsa and sour cream. Breakfast doesn't get any better than this!

Preparation time: *40 minutes*

Refrigeration time: *1 hour*

Cooking time: *40 minutes*

Yield: *2 servings*

½ cup finely minced cooked ham

2 sliced green onions

⅓ cup finely chopped green pepper

1 tablespoon olive oil

Two 8-inch gluten-free tortillas

6 tablespoons shredded cheddar cheese

3 eggs

⅓ cup half-and-half

2 teaspoons gluten-free flour mixture

⅛ teaspoon garlic powder

3 drops hot pepper sauce

Salsa

Sour cream

1 In a medium skillet, sauté the ham, green onions, and green pepper in the oil over medium heat, stirring occasionally, until the vegetables are tender, about 10 minutes.

2 Lay out the tortillas. Spoon the ham mixture down the center of each tortilla, dividing the mixture evenly. Sprinkle the cheese on top of the ham mixture.

3 Roll up the tortillas and place them in a greased 9-x-6-inch baking dish.

4 In a medium bowl, whisk the eggs until they're frothy. Add the half-and-half and whisk until the ingredients are blended.

5 Add the flour, garlic powder, and hot pepper sauce to the eggs and mix well.

6 Pour the egg mixture over the tortillas. Cover the pan with plastic wrap and chill for at least 1 hour.

7 Remove the baking dish from the refrigerator 30 minutes before baking.

8 Preheat the oven to 350 degrees.

9 Bake the enchiladas, uncovered, at 350 degrees for 40 minutes, or until the eggs are set and the top is very lightly browned. Serve the enchiladas with salsa and sour cream.

Per serving: *Calories: 514; Total fat: 31g; Saturated fat: 12g; Cholesterol: 372mg; Sodium: 979mg; Carbohydrates: 30.7g; Fiber: 3g; Sugar:32g; Protein: 3g.*

Rise and Shine! Breads and Bagels

Ah, bread. Bread is probably the most difficult item to convert successfully to gluten-free. It's challenging but conquerable! The sweet breads and those that depend on baking soda and baking powder for leavening aren't the problem. They taste every bit as good as their wheat counterparts. The yeast breads, however, get us exasperated at times. Fortunately, you can play tricks with the dough to achieve a delicious loaf of bread.

In Chapter 8, we emphasize that only one gluten-free flour mixture is used throughout this book to make it easier for the baker. You may notice that the bread recipes that follow use the gluten-free flour mixture and then call for additional flours to be used. Here's the reason: Adding cornstarch and/or sorghum flour changes the consistency of the bread for the better. Occasionally coconut flour is used for flavor. You can use just the gluten-free flour mixture, but your breads won't turn out as well. Light flaxseed meal is also added frequently. Flax not only adds fiber to the bread, but it helps to activate the yeast so your bread is lighter. The light flaxseed meal has virtually no taste, so it doesn't affect the taste of the bread.

Choosing and prepping yeast

Quick-rising yeast is very effective in some instances, but active dry yeast tends to work better with the alternative flours. Sometimes people *proof* yeast (let it rise) in warm water before adding it to other ingredients to make sure it will work, but most times you can simply mix it in with the dry ingredients.

It's vital when working with yeast that the water (or other liquid) temperature be between 110 to 120 degrees. If the liquid is cooler than that, it may not activate the yeast. If the liquid is warmer than that, it may kill the yeast. When running warm water on your wrist, 115 degrees feels comfortably warm but not hot.

Make sure that all the ingredients are at room temperature before beginning. Adding cold eggs or other cold liquid may keep the yeast from fermenting.

Working the dough: You don't need Popeye arms

Kneading is an important step in making bread, but not with gluten-free breads. The process of turning the dough on a board activates the gluten in wheat so the bread will rise. Because wheat gluten is absent in the alternative flours, kneading is only done long enough to form a smooth ball from the dough. However, many gluten-free bread doughs are more like the consistency of cake batter, so they usually need no kneading at all.

Instead of depending on wheat gluten to help the bread rise, you add additional ingredients (something acidic like vinegar) to trick the dough into rising. If you find large holes in the baked loaf of bread, you have added too much *leavening*.

In regular bread preparation, you let the bread rise, punch it down, and then let it rise again. No can-do with gluten-free dough. Because the alternative flours are heavier than wheat flour, gluten-free bread dough only rises once, so after mixing the dough, place it in the container in which you intend to bake it and let it rise.

As bread rises, it shouldn't be exposed to drafts. A trick that works well is to heat your oven to 200 degrees. When it reaches that temperature, turn off the oven and wait 5 minutes, and then place your bread pans in the oven to rise and close the oven door. Usually your dough will only need to rise between 30 to 45 minutes with this method, depending on the kind of yeast used and the size of the loaf.

Creating the crust

You can get the desired type of crust on your bread by doing one of the following:

- For a **shiny crust,** warm 1 tablespoon of sugar with 5 tablespoons of milk just to a simmer, and then brush the liquid on the hot loaves as soon as they come out of the oven.

- For a **soft crust,** brush melted butter on the hot, baked loaves of bread, and then cover them with a clean towel to retain the heat.

- If you want a **thin, light crust,** place a pan of hot water on the bottom rack of your oven to create moist heat as your bread bakes.

- For a **medium crust,** brush milk over the loaves before placing them in the oven, and then brush them again with milk when the bread is about halfway through baking.

- **Crunchy crusts** are also possible. Whip an egg white with 1 tablespoon of water until it's frothy, and then brush this on top of the loaves before baking.

- Finally, if you like a **hard crust** on your bread, mix together ½ cup of water with 1 teaspoon of salt and brush it on the loaves before placing them in the oven, and then again about halfway through the baking time.

Troubleshooting breads

It may take several attempts at bread making to get it right, so don't get discouraged if your first try isn't perfect. Here are a few troubleshooting points to keep in mind:

- If your baked loaf of bread isn't fully cooked inside, the easiest remedy is to bake the dough in two smaller pans next time. If your bread is still mushy inside, often the cause may be due to the oven temperature. Gluten-free products frequently need to be baked at a lower temperature for a longer period of time. If you lower the oven temperature by 25 degrees, that may solve the problem. If the loaf starts to get too dark, cover it with foil halfway through baking. And don't use dark or Teflon-coated baking pans. They may cause the bottom of the bread to burn before the inside is completely baked.

✔ Periodically you'll bake a loaf of bread that may suffer from the crumbles. It looks pretty and smells divine, but when you go to cut it, it falls apart. First, do *not* throw out the crumbs. Dry them out and add seasonings to make bread crumbs. The cause of the crumbles may be that the dough was too dry. Next time, slightly reduce the amount of flour used. Add a teaspoon of unflavored gelatin to the dry ingredients to help bind the bread (in addition to the xanthan gum called for in a recipe). Before even trying to cut the loaf, refrigerate it and then slice it with a serrated knife while it's cold.

✔ Finally, let's address the taste of the bread. Without some precautions, gluten-free bread can easily taste like cardboard. Fortunately, you can add all sorts of things to the dough to avoid this from happening. Substitute some of the water with a liquid that has flavor, like cold brewed coffee, honey, maple syrup, molasses, or fruit juice (pineapple, lemon, orange, or apple). Add extra flavoring (more vanilla or almond flavoring, cinnamon, Italian seasoning, Parmesan, or cheddar cheese). You can add toasted seeds (sesame, poppy, caraway, or sunflower) as well as toasted nuts of all kinds. Toasted coconut or mini chocolate chips are also optional stir-ins, as are minced dried fruits. Try using dark brown sugar in place of granulated sugar. And finally, think about substituting a portion of the gluten-free flour mixture with a flour that has more flavor, such as cornmeal, almond flour, coconut flour, or sweet potato flour.

We've made these adjustments to the recipes that follow. When you convert a wheat bread recipe, experiment several times with the options above until you get a loaf of bread that rises, tastes fantastic, has the ideal crust, and doesn't crumble. You can do it!

◌ *French Baguettes*

When was the last time you bit into a piece of really good French bread? We're talking a light, soft, airy center and a crunchy crust! This bread is perfect for making French toast, bread pudding, and stuffing mix because the center is porous. If you like, sprinkle sesame seeds on top of the dough before baking.

Tools: *Electric mixer*

Preparation time: *15 minutes*

Rising time: *40 minutes*

Cooking time: *40 minutes*

Yield: *2 baguettes (10 slices per loaf)*

¾ cup cornstarch

¼ cup sorghum flour

1⅓ cups gluten-free flour mixture

2 tablespoons light flaxseed meal

1 teaspoon salt

½ teaspoon garlic powder

1 teaspoon dried onion flakes

2 tablespoons granulated sugar

1½ teaspoons active dry yeast

1 teaspoon cider vinegar

1 tablespoon honey

2½ tablespoons olive oil

1 egg, at room temperature

2 egg whites, at room temperature

¾ cup warm water (110 degrees)

Nonstick cooking spray

1 Preheat the oven to 200 degrees. When the oven reaches that temperature, turn it off.

2 Place the cornstarch, sorghum flour, gluten-free flour mixture, flaxseed meal, salt, garlic powder, onion flakes, sugar, and yeast in a large mixing bowl. Blend the ingredients together with a whisk.

3 Stir in the vinegar, honey, oil, egg, and egg whites.

4 Stir in the warm water last.

5 Turn on the mixer and slowly increase the speed to high. Beat the ingredients for 4 minutes.

6 Spray the cooking spray on a large baking sheet.

7 Divide the dough in half. Place half of the dough on one side of the baking sheet. The dough will be very sticky.

8 With wet hands, form the dough into a long, thin loaf approximately 11 inches long and 2½ inches wide.

9 Repeat Step 8 with the remaining dough, placing it on the other side of the baking sheet.

10 Cover the loaves with a sheet of wax paper that has been sprayed with cooking spray.

11 Place the baking sheet in the oven and let the dough rise for 40 minutes.

12 Remove the baking sheet from the oven. Preheat the oven to 350 degrees.

13 If you want a crisp crust, stir ½ teaspoon of salt into ¼ cup of water and brush it on top of the loaves. For a hard crust, brush the loaves again with this mixture halfway through baking.

14 Bake the loaves at 350 degrees for 40 minutes, or until golden and baked through.

Per slice: *Calories: 94; Total fat: 2g; Saturated fat: 0g; Cholesterol: 11mg; Sodium: 126mg; Carbohydrates: 17g; Fiber: 1g; Sugar: 2g; Protein: 2g.*

☙ Breakfast Biscuit Bread

We're talking "real" bread here. It looks, smells, cuts, toasts, and tastes like actual bread should. Whether you slice it thin to make sandwiches, toast it and spread it with peanut butter and jam, or use it as a base for French toast, the outcome will be the same — fabulous!

Tools: *Electric mixer*

Preparation time: *15 minutes*

Rising time: *40 minute*

Cooking time: *35 minutes*

Yield: *1 loaf (12 slices)*

Nonstick cooking spray	*¾ teaspoon active dry yeast*
¼ cup cornstarch	*½ teaspoon cider vinegar*
¼ cup sorghum flour	*1 tablespoon honey*
½ cup plus 2 tablespoons gluten-free flour mixture	*4 teaspoons melted butter, cooled*
1 tablespoon light flaxseed meal	*1 egg, at room temperature*
½ teaspoon salt	*2 egg whites, at room temperature*
¾ teaspoon cinnamon	*2 tablespoons buttermilk, at room temperature*
2½ tablespoons granulated sugar	*¼ cup warm water (110 degrees)*

1 Preheat the oven to 200 degrees. When the oven reaches that temperature, turn it off. Spray a 4-x-8-inch baking pan with cooking spray.

2 Place the cornstarch, sorghum flour, gluten-free flour mixture, flaxseed meal, salt, cinnamon, sugar, and yeast in a medium mixing bowl. With a whisk, stir the ingredients to blend thoroughly.

3 With a rubber spatula, stir in the vinegar, honey, melted butter, egg, egg whites, and buttermilk.

4 Stir in the warm water last.

5 Turn on the mixer and slowly increase the speed to high. Beat the batter for 3 minutes. (It will be more of a batter than a dough consistency.)

6 Spoon the batter into the prepared baking pan.

7 Cover the pan with wax paper that has been sprayed with cooking spray.

8 Place the pan in the oven to rise for 40 minutes.

9 Remove the pan from the oven and preheat the oven to 350 degrees. When the oven reaches that temperature, remove the wax paper from the bread.

10 Bake the bread at 350 degrees for 35 to 40 minutes, or until baked through.

11 Let the bread set for 5 minutes. Then remove the bread from the pan and allow it to cool on a wire rack.

Per slice: Calories: 93; Total fat: 2g; Saturated fat: 1g; Cholesterol: 21mg; Sodium: 125mg; Carbohydrates: 17g; Fiber: 1g; Sugar: 4g; Protein: 2g.

⌓ Olive Oil Bread

This loaf makes absolutely perfect sandwich bread. Or better yet, pour a little extra-virgin olive oil in small bowl, and then add some freshly ground pepper and a little grated Parmesan cheese to the oil. Now tear off a chunk of the olive oil bread and dip. *Oh,* but that's good!

Tools: *Electric mixer*

Preparation time: *15 minutes*

Rising time: *40 minute*

Cooking time: *40 minutes*

Yield: *1 loaf (12 slices)*

Nonstick cooking spray

½ cup gluten-free flour mixture

¼ cup sorghum flour

¼ cup cornstarch

2 tablespoons light flaxseed meal

2 tablespoons dry milk powder

2½ tablespoons granulated sugar

¾ teaspoon Italian seasoning

½ teaspoon garlic powder

½ teaspoon salt

¾ teaspoon active dry yeast

½ teaspoon cider vinegar

1 egg, at room temperature

2 egg whites, at room temperature, plus 1 egg white

2 tablespoons olive oil

2 tablespoons buttermilk, at room temperature

¼ cup warm water (110 degrees), plus 1 tablespoon water

1 Preheat the oven to 200 degrees. When the oven reaches that temperature, turn it off. Spray a 4-x-8-inch baking pan with cooking spray.

(continued)

2 Place the gluten-free flour mixture, sorghum flour, cornstarch, flaxseed meal, milk powder, sugar, Italian seasoning, garlic powder, salt, and yeast in a medium mixing bowl. With a whisk, stir the ingredients to blend thoroughly.

3 With a rubber spatula, stir in the vinegar, egg, 2 egg whites, olive oil, and buttermilk. (If you forgot to bring the buttermilk to room temperature, warm it in a glass bowl in the microwave for 10 seconds.)

4 Stir in the warm water last.

5 Turn on the mixer and slowly increase the speed to high. Beat the batter for 3 minutes. (It will be more of a batter than a dough consistency.)

6 Spoon the batter into the prepared baking pan and cover the pan with wax paper that has been sprayed with cooking spray.

7 Place the pan in the oven to rise for 40 minutes.

8 Remove the pan from the oven and preheat the oven to 350 degrees. When the oven reaches that temperature, remove the wax paper.

9 In a small bowl, whisk together the remaining egg white with 1 tablespoon of water. Brush the mixture on top of the loaf. Place the loaf in the oven and bake for 20 minutes.

10 Brush the top of the loaf again with egg white, and then continue to bake the bread for 15 to 20 minutes longer, or until baked through.

11 Let the bread set for 5 minutes, and then remove the loaf from the pan and cool the bread on a wire rack.

Per slice: Calories: 95; Total fat: 3g; Saturated fat: 1g; Cholesterol: 18mg; Sodium: 122mg; Carbohydrates: 14g; Fiber: 1g; Sugar: 3g; Protein: 3g.

Bagels (or Pretzels)

How great is this! You can make up one batch of dough, divide it, and then make bagels from one half and pretzels from the other half! Sprinkle sesame seeds or cinnamon sugar on the bagels before baking and kosher salt on the pretzels. The dough is the same but the preparation is just a tad different. For bagels, follow the recipe below. For pretzels, roll the balls of dough into long, thin ropes, and then fold like a pretzel, sealing the edges of dough securely, and then continue with the raising, boiling, and baking directions given below.

Tools: *Electric mixer*

Preparation time: *15 minutes*

Rising time: *40 minutes*

Cooking time: *20 minutes*

Yield: *8 bagels (or 8 soft pretzels)*

2⅓ cups gluten-free flour mixture

3 tablespoons dry milk powder

½ teaspoon salt

1½ tablespoons plus 2 teaspoons granulated sugar

¼ teaspoon cinnamon

2¼ teaspoons (1 packet) instant rise yeast

2 tablespoons butter, melted and cooled

1 egg, at room temperature

2 egg whites, at room temperature, plus 1 egg white

½ cup warm water (110 degrees), plus 1 teaspoon water

Nonstick cooking spray

1 Preheat the oven to 200 degrees. When the oven reaches that temperature, turn the oven off.

2 Place the flour mixture, milk powder, salt, 1½ tablespoons of sugar, cinnamon, and yeast in a medium mixing bowl. With the mixer on low, blend the ingredients.

3 Add the butter, egg, and two egg whites to the dry mixture. Whip on low speed until blended.

4 Add the water. Beat for 3½ minutes.

5 Remove the dough from the mixing bowl and divide it into 8 balls.

6 Roll each ball into a 7-inch rope and then connect the ends of the rope to form a circle, sealing the ends securely.

7 Lightly grease a baking sheet with corn or olive oil. Place each bagel on the baking sheet. Cover the bagels with wax paper that has been lightly oiled.

8 Set the baking sheet in the oven for 40 minutes to allow the dough to rise. (It won't double in bulk.)

9 Remove the baking sheet from the oven and preheat the oven to 400 degrees.

10 Fill a large saucepan with water (about 4 inches deep) and add the remaining 2 teaspoons of sugar. Bring the water to a boil.

11 Place 4 bagels at a time in the boiling water and boil for 1 minute, turning each bagel over after 30 seconds.

12 Cover the baking sheet with wax paper or parchment paper and spray the paper lightly with cooking spray. (The bagels tend to brown too much on the bottom without the paper.)

13 Remove the bagels from the water with a slotted spoon and lay them on the paper.

14 Repeat Steps 11 and 13 with the remaining 4 bagels.

(continued)

15 In a small bowl, whip the remaining egg white with 1 teaspoon of water until frothy. Brush the mixture on top of the bagels. If desired, sprinkle tops with cinnamon sugar or sesame seeds.

16 Bake the bagels for 20 minutes.

Vary it! Customize the flavoring of these bagels or pretzels to your own personal taste. In place of the cinnamon, add ½ teaspoon dried onion flakes. Fold raisins into the dough. Or fold shredded cheese into the dough. Your options are only limited by your imagination!

Per serving: Calories: 212; Total fat: 9g; Saturated fat: 2g; Cholesterol: 34mg; Sodium: 199mg; Carbohydrates: 39g; Fiber: 2g; Sugar: 4g; Protein: 3.g.

Flatbread Wrap

Aren't you tired of the bland, blah, commercial gluten-free tortilla wraps? Do you miss pita bread? Although this wrap won't replace pita bread, it's *so* easy to make and it's pliable and tastes wonderful. You can make the wraps ahead and freeze them between sheets of wax paper. To thaw and reheat, merely place the wraps between sheets of damp paper towels and microwave them for a few moments. Fold the wrap in half to create a gyro, or fill and roll for a traditional wrap. This flatbread is *very* flat so that it will be pliable.

Tools: *Rolling pin*

Preparation time: *15 minutes*

Cooking time: *15 minutes*

Yield: *4 wraps*

1 cup plus 2 tablespoons gluten-free flour mixture

½ teaspoon baking powder

½ (heaping) teaspoon salt

½ teaspoon granulated sugar

½ teaspoon Italian seasoning

¼ teaspoon garlic powder

½ teaspoon gluten-free chicken bouillon granules

¼ cup warm water (110 degrees)

Nonstick cooking spray

1 In a medium bowl, whisk together 1 cup of the flour mixture, the baking powder, salt, sugar, Italian seasoning, and garlic powder.

2 In a small bowl, dissolve the chicken bouillon in the warm water.

3 With a rubber spatula, blend the water mixture into the flour mixture until a dough forms.

4 Divide the dough into four sections. Roll each section into a ball.

5 Sprinkle a sheet of plastic wrap with ¼ teaspoon of the remaining flour mixture, place one of the balls of dough on the plastic wrap, and cover it with a second sheet of plastic wrap. Using a rolling pin, roll the ball into a flat, 7-inch round about ⅛ inch thick. Repeat with the remaining balls of dough.

6 Heat an 8-inch skillet over medium heat and spray it very lightly with the cooking spray.

7 Place one of the circles of dough in the pan and cook, turning once, for about 3 minutes total, or until it just begins to brown on each side. (If you overcook these, they won't be pliable.) Repeat with the remaining circles of dough.

Per serving: Calories: 145; Total fat: 0g; Saturated fat: 0g; Cholesterol: 0mg; Sodium: 395mg; Carbohydrates: 33g; Fiber: 2g; Sugar: 1g; Protein: 1g.

☙ Zucchini Bread

This bread is an all-time favorite, whether you toast it for breakfast, slather it with gluten-free cream cheese for a snack, or eat a slice with a salad for lunch. When you have too many zucchinis maturing in your garden, make a slew of these breads and freeze them for gift-giving during the holidays. And no, kids won't taste the zucchini.

Tools: *Electric mixer*

Preparation time: *20 minutes*

Cooking time: *55 minutes*

Yield: *1 loaf (10 slices)*

Nonstick cooking spray	*1½ teaspoons cinnamon*
2 eggs	*1½ cups gluten-free flour mixture*
1 cup granulated sugar	*¼ teaspoon salt*
1 cup grated unpeeled zucchini, squeezed dry	*1 teaspoon baking soda*
½ cup corn oil	*1 teaspoon baking powder*
1½ teaspoons vanilla	*½ cup chopped walnuts*
1 tablespoon mayonnaise	

1 Preheat the oven to 325 degrees. Spray an 8-x-4-inch baking pan with cooking spray.

2 In a medium mixing bowl, use the mixer to whip together the eggs, sugar, zucchini, oil, vanilla, and mayonnaise. Beat for 3 minutes.

3 In a small bowl, whisk together the cinnamon, flour mixture, salt, baking soda, and baking powder.

(continued)

4 Whisk the dry ingredients into the egg mixture, and then stir in the walnuts until everything is blended.

5 Pour the batter into the prepared pan.

6 Bake the batter at 325 degrees for 55 minutes, or until a toothpick inserted in the center comes out clean.

7 Let the hot loaf set in the pan for 5 minutes, and then remove the bread and let it cool on a wire rack.

Per serving: Calories: 322; Total fat: 17g; Saturated fat: 2g; Cholesterol: 43mg; Sodium: 247mg; Carbohydrates: 41g; Fiber: 2g; Sugar: 21g; Protein: 3g.

What a Sweet Idea! Pastries and Muffins

Nature provides us with fresh fruits and vegetables to keep us healthy. But pastries and muffins were created to keep us happy.

Because these items are derived primarily from a gluten-free flour base, if you are converting a wheat recipe, you'll need to add extra flavoring in the form of stir-ins (nuts, coconut, fresh, canned, or dried fruit, shredded carrots or zucchini, mashed bananas, applesauce or jars of baby fruit, chocolate chips, or even liqueurs) or added flavoring (extra vanilla, almond, or other liquid flavoring plus additional or increased amounts of spices). Add an extra egg and 1 tablespoon of mayonnaise to help the pastry rise. It also helps to substitute some of the liquid called for in the recipe with something more flavorful, like brewed coffee, juice, or sweetened condensed milk. The recipes in this section already have these adjustments made, so start baking!

☙ Breakfast Bread Pudding

Now how great is this? A dessert for breakfast! Try to select porous gluten-free bread for this recipe. Because of the soaking time required, it's best to assemble this the night before. You can use orange juice in place of the rum. This is best served warm from the oven.

Preparation time: *10 minutes*

Refrigeration time: *At least 2 hours*

Cooking time: 20 minutes

Yield: 9 servings

4 eggs

⅔ cup whole milk

½ teaspoon cinnamon

4 teaspoons vanilla

½ cup plus 1 tablespoon brown sugar

¼ teaspoon baking powder

6 slices gluten-free bread

¾ cup raisins

2 tablespoons dark rum

Nonstick cooking spray

1 banana, sliced thinly

2 teaspoons cinnamon sugar

3 tablespoons maple syrup

1 In a large bowl, whisk together the eggs, whole milk, cinnamon, vanilla, ½ cup of the brown sugar, and baking powder.

2 Cut the bread slices into small cubes, and then stir them into the egg mixture. Cover the mixture and refrigerate it for at least 2 hours.

3 In a small bowl, stir the raisins into the rum. Cover the mixture and let it cure at room temperature for at least 2 hours.

4 Preheat the oven to 400 degrees. Spray a 9-x-9-inch baking pan with cooking spray.

5 Stir the raisins into the bread mixture.

6 Spoon half of the soaked bread into the prepared pan. Slice the banana on top of the bread and sprinkle with remaining 1 tablespoon brown sugar. Spoon the remaining bread over the banana slices, pouring any remaining egg mixture on top. Press down gently on the bread cubes to even out the top.

7 Sprinkle the top of the pudding with cinnamon sugar.

8 Bake the pudding at 400 degrees for 20 minutes, or until the top is lightly browned. Remove the pudding from the oven and drizzle it with maple syrup. Cool the pudding for 10 minutes before cutting.

Per serving: Calories: 239; Total fat: 5g; Saturated fat: 1g; Cholesterol: 96mg; Sodium: 72mg; Carbohydrates: 43g; Fiber: 2g; Sugar: 29g; Protein: 4g.

🍎 Cream Cheese Coffeecake

If you peek through the oven window while this breakfast delight is baking, don't panic if you see it rising above the edge of your pan — it will shrink back down to normal size after you remove it from the oven. Broil the topping until it's bubbling all over. If you overbroil it, the topping will burn. If you underbroil it, the topping will be too loose, so keep a close eye on it.

Tools: *Electric mixer*

Preparation time: *25 minutes*

Cooking time: *35 minutes*

Yield: *9 servings*

Nonstick cooking spray

¼ cup plus ½ cup plus 2 tablespoons granulated sugar

8 ounces cream cheese, softened

2 eggs plus 2 eggs

1 teaspoon plus 1 teaspoon vanilla

1 cup gluten-free flour mixture

½ teaspoon baking soda

1½ teaspoons baking powder

¼ teaspoon salt

½ teaspoon cinnamon

½ cup butter, softened

½ cup sour cream

¼ cup milk

1 Preheat the oven to 350 degrees. Spray a 9-x-9-inch baking pan with cooking spray.

2 In a small mixing bowl, use the mixer to whip together ¼ cup of sugar, cream cheese, 2 eggs, and 1 teaspoon of vanilla for 2 minutes, or until the mixture is smooth. Set aside.

3 In a medium bowl, sift together the flour mixture, baking soda, baking powder, salt, and cinnamon. Set aside.

4 Cream the butter and the remaining ½ cup plus 2 tablespoons of sugar in a large bowl until it's fluffy.

5 Add the 2 remaining eggs and the remaining 1 teaspoon of vanilla to the butter mixture.

6 Add the sour cream and the milk, and then blend in the flour mixture.

7 Pour half of the batter into the prepared pan. Spoon the cream cheese mixture over the batter. Use the back of wet spoon to smooth the filling. Pour the remaining batter over the filling, using the back of a wet spoon to spread the batter evenly.

8 Bake the batter at 350 degrees for 35 minutes, or until a toothpick inserted in the center comes out clean.

9 While the coffeecake bakes, prepare the topping.

10 When the coffeecake is done, remove it from the oven and turn on the broiler.

11 Spoon the pecan topping evenly over the top of the cake.

12 Broil the coffeecake for 2 minutes, or until the topping bubbles. Watch carefully so the topping doesn't burn.

13 Cool the coffeecake completely before cutting.

Topping

3 tablespoons butter

3 tablespoons milk

¼ cup brown sugar

½ cup finely chopped pecans

1 In a small saucepan, melt the butter.

2 Add the milk, brown sugar, and pecans. Cook over medium heat, stirring frequently, for 1 to 2 minutes.

Per serving: *Calories: 484; Total fat: 33g; Saturated fat: 17g; Cholesterol: 166mg; Sodium: 435mg; Carbohydrates: 43g; Fiber: 1g; Sugar: 27g; Protein: 7g.*

Cranberry Cornmeal Muffins

These muffins are the perfect breakfast accompaniment to scrambled eggs. They also go well with salads or warmed for a snack. With wheat flour muffins, the directions usually say, "Stir the ingredients just until blended." With the gluten-free flours, it's advisable to whip the liquid ingredients first to incorporate air so the finished product will be lighter.

Tools: *Electric mixer*

Preparation time: *15 minutes*

Cooking time: *20 minutes*

Yield: *16 large muffins*

(continued)

Nonstick cooking spray

¾ cup 2 percent milk

1 tablespoon lemon juice

2 eggs

1 egg white

⅓ cup granulated sugar

¼ cup olive oil

1½ teaspoons vanilla

½ teaspoon almond extract

1 tablespoon mayonnaise (not low-fat version)

¾ cup gluten-free flour mixture

¼ cup coconut flour

¾ cup cornmeal

3 teaspoons baking powder

¼ teaspoon salt

1⅓ cups dried cranberries

½ cup chopped, toasted pecans

1 Preheat the oven to 400 degrees. Spray muffin tins with cooking spray.

2 In a small bowl, stir together the milk and lemon juice; set the mixture aside for a few minutes to thicken.

3 In a mixing bowl, use the mixer to whip the eggs and egg white for 1 minute.

4 Add the thickened milk, sugar, oil, vanilla, almond extract, and mayonnaise, and continue to whip for another minute.

5 In a medium bowl, stir together the flour mixture, coconut flour, cornmeal, baking powder, and salt.

6 Add the flour mixture to the egg mixture; blend the dry ingredients in thoroughly using a whisk.

7 Fold in the cranberries and pecans.

8 Spoon the batter into the prepared muffin tins.

9 Bake the batter at 400 degrees for 15 minutes, or until a toothpick inserted in the center comes out clean.

10 Cool the muffins slightly, and then remove them to a wire rack.

Tip: Keep leftover muffins stored in the freezer to keep them from drying out. To thaw, wrap a muffin in wax paper and pop it into the microwave or wrap it in foil and bake at 300 degrees for 15 minutes.

Per serving: Calories: 183; Total fat: 8g; Saturated fat: 1g; Cholesterol: 28mg; Sodium: 185mg; Carbohydrates: 27g; Fiber: 2g; Sugar: 12g; Protein: 3g.

Banana Chocolate Chip Muffins

Everyone loves muffins, and these are some of the best. They will stay moist and fresh for several days if you store them in an airtight container or in a self-seal plastic bag. Use very ripe bananas for this recipe. Fair warning — make a double batch because these have a habit of disappearing quickly!

Preparation time: *15 minutes*

Cooking time: *17 minutes*

Yield: *18 muffins*

Nonstick cooking spray	*2 medium ripe bananas, mashed*
2 eggs	*1¼ cups gluten-free flour mixture*
½ cup milk	*½ teaspoon salt*
¼ cup vegetable oil	*½ teaspoon baking powder*
½ cup granulated sugar	*½ teaspoon baking soda*
1 teaspoon vanilla	*½ cup mini semisweet chocolate chips*

1 Preheat the oven to 350 degrees. Grease the muffin tins with cooking spray.

2 In a large bowl, beat the eggs slightly with a whisk.

3 Whisk in the milk and oil.

4 Whisk in the sugar, vanilla, and bananas.

5 Sift the flour mixture, salt, baking powder, and baking soda into a small bowl.

6 Slowly stir the mixture into the egg mix until everything is blended.

7 Stir in the chocolate chips.

8 Fill the greased muffin tins ¾ full with batter.

9 Bake the muffins at 350 degrees for 17 minutes, or until a toothpick inserted in the center comes out clean.

Per serving: Calories: 143; Total fat: 6g; Saturated fat: 2g; Cholesterol: 24mg; Sodium: 121mg; Carbohydrates: 22g; Fiber: 1g; Sugar: 11g; Protein: 2g.

❀ Corn Muffins

Unlike some gluten-free muffins you've had, these muffins may take some getting used to because they taste fantastic and they won't crumble. Imagine that!

Preparation time: *8 minutes*

Cooking time: *12 to 15 minutes*

Yield: *16 muffins*

Nonstick cooking spray	*½ teaspoon salt*
1 cup cornmeal	*2 eggs*
1 cup gluten-free flour mixture	*1¼ cups buttermilk*
⅓ cup brown sugar	*¾ cup corn oil*
½ cup granulated sugar	*1 tablespoon mayonnaise*
2 teaspoons baking soda	*½ teaspoon vanilla*

1 Preheat the oven to 400 degrees. Spray the muffin tins with cooking spray.

2 In a medium bowl, whisk together the cornmeal, flour mixture, brown sugar, granulated sugar, baking soda, and salt.

3 In a second medium bowl, whisk together the eggs, buttermilk, oil, mayonnaise, and vanilla.

4 Stir the egg mixture into the flour mixture until the two are thoroughly combined.

5 Spoon the batter into the prepared muffin tins.

6 Bake the muffins at 400 degrees for 12 to 15 minutes, or until a toothpick inserted in the center comes out clean.

7 Cool the muffins in the pan for 3 minutes, and then remove them to a wire rack.

Per serving: Calories: 227; Total fat: 12g; Saturated fat: 2g; Cholesterol: 28mg; Sodium: 264mg; Carbohydrates: 27g; Fiber: 1g; Sugar: 12g; Protein: 3g.

Whipping Up Pancakes and Waffles

Nothing warms the tummy on a cold morning like hot pancakes fresh off the griddle. The next time you mix up a bowl of pancake batter, brainstorm and add something new. Shredded apples, pears, or zucchini are great add-ins to the batter, as are chopped walnuts or pecans, mashed bananas, miniature chocolate chips, or a tablespoon of peanut butter (or all four if you're daring). Substitute brown sugar for the white sugar or coconut milk for the whole milk. If you always serve maple syrup for a topping, surprise your family with new toppings like cherry or strawberry sauce, cinnamon maple butter, blueberry syrup, apple cinnamon syrup, or maple rum syrup.

When cooking pancakes, use just enough butter to keep the batter from sticking. Too much butter causes the pancakes to brown before they are cooked through. Or you can lightly brush the pan with a little bit of corn oil instead of using butter.

Creating perfect gluten-free waffles is both an art and a science. Resist the urge to overbeat the batter. Spray both sides of the iron generously with gluten-free nonstick spray. Batter needs room to expand, so only pour in enough batter to just cover the lower cooking grid — too much batter will result in a waffle that has a soggy middle. Cook the waffle at a medium-high setting; too low of a setting results in moisture condensation, and you'll end up with a mushy mess. Despite the temptation, wait at least 3 minutes before opening the iron to check for doneness. When breakfast is over, wash the iron grates, and then season them with a very light coat of corn oil.

✑ Baked Apple Pancake

This definitely is not your traditional pancake. You won't need syrup — just spoon some of the apple syrup from the bottom of the pan onto the top of each slice of pancake. Breakfast was never meant to taste this fantastic. The edges of the pancake will rise during baking and then sink to the level of the pancake after you remove it from the oven.

Preparation time: *20 minutes*

Cooking time: *30 minutes*

Yield: *6 servings*

Nonstick cooking spray	*2 eggs*
3 tablespoons plus 2 tablespoon butter	*⅓ cup milk*
¼ cup plus 1 tablespoon granulated sugar	*⅓ cup gluten-free flour mixture*
¼ cup brown sugar	*½ teaspoon baking powder*
1 teaspoon plus ¼ teaspoon cinnamon	*⅛ teaspoon salt*
1 large McIntosh apple, peeled, cored, and sliced thin	*¼ teaspoon vanilla*

1 Preheat the oven to 350 degrees. Spray a 9-inch pie plate with cooking spray.

2 Melt 3 tablespoons of butter in a large nonstick skillet.

3 Add ¼ cup of granulated sugar, the brown sugar, and 1 teaspoon of cinnamon. Stir constantly until the sugars melt.

(continued)

4 Add the apples and sauté, stirring frequently, until the apples are softened (about 15 minutes).

5 Spoon the apples and sauce into the prepared pie pan.

6 In a small mixing bowl, whisk the eggs until they're frothy. Add the milk and whisk until the eggs and milk are blended.

7 Add the flour mixture, the remaining 1 tablespoon of granulated sugar, the baking powder, the remaining ¼ teaspoon of cinnamon, the salt, the remaining 2 tablespoons of butter, and the vanilla to the egg mixture and continue to whisk until blended.

8 Pour the batter over the apples.

9 Bake the pancake at 350 degrees for 30 minutes, or until the pancake is cooked through. Cut the pancake into wedges to serve, spooning the sauce and apples over the top of each individual pancake.

Per serving: *Calories: 242; Total fat: 12g; Saturated fat: 7g; Cholesterol: 146mg; Sodium: 121mg; Carbohydrates: 32g; Fiber: 2g; Sugar: 24g; Protein: 3g.*

Crepe magic

Crepes are versatile and delicious. A few tips can help you enjoy them more often:

To cook crepes ahead, layer the unfilled crepes with wax paper between each crepe. You can wrap them in plastic wrap or slide them into a self-seal bag and refrigerate them for up to three days.

To freeze crepes for up to two months, stack the unfilled crepes between sheets of wax paper. Wrap the stack in foil and then place the stack in a self-seal freezer bag. When you're ready to use the crepes, thaw them in the refrigerator overnight.

To reheat thawed crepes in the oven, remove the stack of crepes from the freezer bag, and while they're still wrapped in foil, place the stack on a baking sheet. Bake the crepes in a preheated 350 degree oven for 10 minutes or until they're heated through. To reheat the crepes in the microwave, remove the crepes from the freezer bag and foil. Then place a stack of 4 crepes, separated with wax paper, on a microwave-safe plate. Cover the stack with a damp paper towel and heat on a medium setting for 1½ minutes.

To make dessert crepes, work with the Feather-Light Crepes recipe in this chapter and use one or more of the following substitutions or additions:

- ✔ Replace ¾ cup of the milk with coconut milk.
- ✔ Replace the granulated sugar with brown sugar.
- ✔ Add 3 tablespoons of chocolate syrup to the batter.
- ✔ Add 1 tablespoon of rum or brandy to the batter.

🍑 Feather-Light Crepes

Making crepes that are paper thin yet hold up when rolled with a filling isn't an easy task. But follow this recipe and you'll be okay.

Preparation time: *5 minutes*

Cooking time: *10 minutes*

Yield: *8 crepes*

2 eggs	*½ teaspoon vanilla*
1¼ cups whole milk or half-and-half	*¼ teaspoon almond flavoring*
2 tablespoons granulated sugar	*Dash salt*
½ cup gluten-free flour mixture	*3 tablespoons stick butter*
1 tablespoon melted butter	

1 Preheat the broiler.

2 In a medium bowl, whisk together the eggs and milk (or half-and-half).

3 Add the sugar and whisk to blend it in.

4 Stir in the flour mixture until the batter is smooth.

5 Add the melted butter, vanilla, almond flavoring, and salt, stirring with a whisk just until blended. The batter should be the consistency of thin cream. If it's too thick, slowly add more milk as needed.

6 Wrap the handle of an 8-inch nonstick skillet with heavy-duty foil. Heat the skillet over medium-low heat on the stove.

7 Holding the stick of butter with a paper towel, rub the butter over the entire surface of the skillet (do not overgrease the pan).

8 Remove the pan from the stove and pour in about 3 tablespoons of batter (a gravy ladle usually works perfectly for this).

9 Tilt the pan quickly so the batter is evenly distributed.

10 Return the pan to the stovetop and cook the batter for about 1 minute. Lift the edge of the crepe with a rubber spatula to see when the underside is just beginning to brown.

11 Place the pan under the broiler for 40 seconds, or until the top of the crepe is just beginning to brown.

12 Remove the crepe from the pan to wax paper and repeat the process from Step 8 with the remaining batter. It may be necessary to re-butter the pan after the first four crepes.

Per serving: Calories: 139; Total fat: 8g; Saturated fat: 5g; Cholesterol: 72mg; Sodium: 93mg; Carbohydrates: 13g; Fiber: 0g; Sugar: 5g; Protein: 3g.

⌒ *Pumpkin Waffles*

The waffles we made using this recipe were made on a 7-inch waffle iron that forms 4 small waffles. One 4-piece, 7-inch waffle determines one serving. You may need to adjust the serving portions in accordance to the size of your waffle iron. And if you think it's a bit odd that the cooking time is listed as 24 minutes, wonder no longer. It takes an average cooking time of 4 minutes per waffle, or a total of 24 minutes to cook 6 waffles. You may opt to feed your family in shifts as the waffles come hot off the iron . . . or not. A better option may be to make the waffles ahead and warm them in the oven or in a toaster just before you call the family in for breakfast.

Preparation time: *10 minutes*

Cooking time: *24 minutes (4 minutes per waffle)*

Yield: *6 servings*

Nonstick cooking spray	*2 teaspoons baking powder*
2 eggs	*1 teaspoon baking soda*
2 egg whites	*¼ teaspoon salt*
3 tablespoons brown sugar	*1½ teaspoons cinnamon*
1¾ cups milk	*½ teaspoon nutmeg*
½ cup canned pumpkin	*¼ teaspoon ginger*
2 teaspoons vanilla	*¼ teaspoon ground cloves*
1 cup gluten-free flour mixture	*⅓ cup toasted finely chopped walnuts*

1 Preheat the waffle iron to the medium-high setting.

2 Spray the waffle iron grates with cooking spray.

3 In a large bowl, whisk together the eggs and egg whites.

4 Add the brown sugar, milk, pumpkin, and vanilla, and whisk until the ingredients are completely blended.

5 Sift the flour mixture, baking powder, baking soda, salt, cinnamon, nutmeg, ginger, and cloves over the egg mixture. Whisk the mixture together just until everything is combined.

6 Stir in the walnuts.

7 Pour ¾ cup of batter onto the waffle iron. Cook for 3 minutes, or until the waffle is cooked through and the outside is crisp. Repeat with the remaining batter, remembering to spray the waffle iron with cooking spray each time.

Note: The exact number of waffles will depend on the size of your waffle iron.

Per serving: Calories: 247; Total fat: 12g; Saturated fat: 7g; Cholesterol: 146mg; Sodium: 121mg; Carbohydrates: 32g; Fiber: 2g; Sugar: 24g; Protein: 3g.

⌖ Cheese Waffles

Wow! Are these waffles ever versatile! Add some bacon crumbles to the batter and you have a breakfast. Make them as directed below, and you have the perfect "bed" for sloppy joes. (This may come as a shock, but sloppy joes don't *have* to be served on a bun.) The cheese, onion, green pepper, and even the cornmeal complement the taste of sloppy joes. Lay a slice of cheese on top of a waffle and stick it in a toaster oven for a luscious toasted cheese sandwich. Or add a little cumin and cayenne to the batter, then spread 1 waffle with refried beans, sprinkle it with a little cheese and a dollop of salsa, and top with a second waffle — tacos were never like this! Try it, you'll like it!

Preparation time: *12 minutes*

Cooking time: *12 minutes (3 minutes per waffle)*

Yield: *4 servings*

Nonstick cooking spray	*⅓ cup sorghum flour*
2 green onions, minced	*2 tablespoons cornmeal*
3 tablespoons minced green pepper	*1 tablespoon baking powder*
¼ cup corn oil, plus some for sautéing	*2 teaspoons granulated sugar*
2 eggs	*¼ teaspoon salt*
1 cup milk	*⅛ teaspoon pepper*
½ cup gluten-free flour mixture	*¼ cup grated Monterey Jack cheese*

1 Preheat the waffle iron to its medium setting.

2 Spray the waffle iron grates with cooking spray.

3 In a small skillet over medium-high heat, sauté the onion and green pepper in oil until they're tender but not browned. Remove the pan from heat and let the vegetables cool slightly.

(continued)

4 In a medium bowl, whisk together the veggies, ¼ cup of oil, the eggs, and milk. Add the flour mixture, sorghum flour, cornmeal, baking powder, sugar, salt, and pepper, and whisk until the ingredients are thoroughly blended. (Add a little more milk if the mixture is too thick.)

5 Stir in the cheese.

6 Pour ¾ cup of batter onto the waffle iron. Cook for 3 minutes, or until the waffle is cooked through and the outside is crisp. Repeat with the remaining batter, remembering to spray the waffle iron with cooking spray each time.

Note: The exact number of waffles will depend on the size of your waffle iron.

Per serving: *Calories: 308; Total fat: 21g; Saturated fat: 5g; Cholesterol: 118mg; Sodium: 517mg; Carbohydrates: 38g; Fiber: 2g; Sugar: 6g; Protein: 10g.*

⌒ Peachy French Toast

French toast always tastes good, but this version is a real winner. Keep the cap on the bottle of maple syrup because you won't need it. The peach syrup that goes over the French toast is two steps up from sublime! You need to have porous gluten-free bread to make this recipe. The Breakfast Biscuit Bread in this chapter is ideal.

Preparation time: *8 minutes*

Cooking time: *10 minutes*

Yield: *4 servings*

15-ounce can sliced peaches with syrup	*2 teaspoons cornstarch*
1 tablespoon honey	*1 tablespoon water*
1 tablespoon plus 4 teaspoons butter	*6 eggs*
1 tablespoon brown sugar	*1 teaspoon vanilla*
¼ teaspoon maple flavoring	*¾ cup milk*
¼ teaspoon plus ¼ teaspoon cinnamon	*8 slices gluten-free white bread*

1 Coarsely chop the peaches into a small saucepan. Add the syrup from the peaches to the pan.

2 Stir in the honey, 1 tablespoon of butter, brown sugar, maple flavoring, and ¼ teaspoon of cinnamon. Heat over medium heat until the butter has melted.

3 In a small bowl, stir together the cornstarch and water until the cornstarch is dissolved. Stir this into the peach mixture.

4 Cook over medium heat, stirring constantly, until the mixture thickens (about 4 to 5 minutes).

5 In a medium shallow bowl, whisk together the eggs, vanilla, ¼ teaspoon of cinnamon, and milk.

6 Melt 2 teaspoons of butter in a large skillet over medium heat.

7 Dip 4 slices of bread, one slice at a time, into the egg mixture. Drain for a moment, and then cook the slices in a skillet, turning once, until they're browned on both sides.

8 Melt the remaining 2 teaspoons of butter in the skillet and repeat Step 7 with the remaining 4 slices of bread.

9 To serve, spoon the warm peach syrup over slices of French toast.

Per serving: *Calories: 470; Total fat: 20g; Saturated fat: 9g; Cholesterol: 381mg; Sodium: 430mg; Carbohydrates: 58g; Fiber: 3g; Sugar: 32g; Protein: 15g.*

Chapter 10

Brilliant Brunches, Luscious Lunches

....

In This Chapter

▶ Splitting the difference and serving brunch

▶ Fixing foods that travel well

▶ Savoring hot and cold sandwiches with *bread!*

▶ Getting the inside scoop on wraps, pitas, and pizzas

▶ Changing the pace with casseroles

....

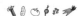

*I*t's hard to even say the word *brunch* without emoting an audible sigh of satisfaction and conjuring images of luxury and overindulgence. Brunch is usually a feast of fancy drawn out over a ridiculously long and relaxing time frame, with far too many calories for normal human consumption.

Certainly not limited to the Sunday variety, brunch and its same-idea-but-just-a-little-later cousin, lunch, present the perfect opportunity to decompress with a midday meal to give you that boost you need before launching into the rest of your day.

With just a few tweaks and twists, you can enjoy a gluten-free brunch or lunch that's every bit as decadent (or not!) and delicious as those that aren't gluten-free.

Breaking for Brunches

Overslept, didja? Or is it just a lazy day and you're getting a late start? Either way, you missed breakfast time, and that means it's not breakfast — it's not lunch — it's cleverly combined to make the word *brunch*.

Breakfast may consist of a bowl of fruit or gluten-free cereal. But brunch — ah, that's *so* much more. Brunch invokes the anticipation of fancier foods that will amuse and arouse your appetite. Brunches are for cultivated connoisseurs and aficionados with refined tastes (that's us — people who like to eat good food). Just mentioning brunch denotes a wow factor.

You're likely to find most any concoction offered at a brunch. Sometimes the fare consists primarily of breakfast foods, but often there are lunch-type offerings, such as beef, chicken, or seafood with a side of rice, and even dessert. The plethora of choices is what makes brunches fun.

Make-Ahead Brunch Casserole

Avoid the hassle of having to make all the food the morning of your brunch. Assemble this dish the day before, and just pop it in the oven before your friends arrive. Then sit back and listen to the raves! This recipe is for a 9-x-9-inch dish, but you can easily double the ingredients to fit a 9-x-13-inch pan for a larger crowd.

Preparation time: *20 minutes*

Cooking time: *35 minutes*

Yield: *6 servings*

Nonstick cooking spray

3 large Idaho potatoes, boiled, peeled, and diced

5 hard-boiled eggs, peeled and diced

¾ pound low-salt ham, cut into ½-inch cubes

¼ green pepper, minced

½ medium onion, minced

2 tablespoons chopped fresh parsley

¼ teaspoon pepper

1 cup plus 2 tablespoons grated sharp cheddar cheese

2 tablespoons butter, melted

2½ tablespoons cornstarch

8-ounce container sour cream

Paprika

1 Preheat the oven to 375 degrees. Lightly spray a 9-x-9-inch baking dish with cooking spray.

2 Place the diced potatoes, eggs, ham, green pepper, and onion in the baking dish.

3 Sprinkle the parsley, pepper, and 1 cup of cheese on top; using a spoon, toss the ingredients lightly to distribute the cheese evenly.

4 In a small bowl, stir together the melted butter, cornstarch, and sour cream (the mixture will be thick). Spoon tablespoonfuls of the mixture on top of the casserole. With the back of the spoon, smooth the topping to cover the casserole evenly.

5 Sprinkle the top with the remaining 2 tablespoons of cheese and paprika.

6 Bake the casserole at 375 degrees for 35 minutes. Let the dish set for 5 minutes before serving.

Per serving: *Calories: 524; Total fat: 28g; Saturated fat: 10g; Cholesterol: 281mg; Sodium: 722mg; Carbohydrates: 42g; Fiber: 4g; Sugar: 8g; Protein: 26g.*

Filet and Eggs a la Béarnaise

This is the ultimate in brunch offerings. The sauce transforms a piece of beef and an egg into an elegant presentation and yields a taste sensation that will be savored and long remembered. If you don't have poaching rings or a poaching pan, break each egg, one at a time, into a small dish, and then carefully slide the egg into the boiling water.

Tools: *Double boiler*

Preparation time: *20 minutes*

Cooking time: *10 minutes*

Yield: *4 servings*

Four 3-ounce filet mignons	*¼ teaspoon thyme*
¼ teaspoon plus ⅛ teaspoon salt	*⅛ teaspoon cayenne pepper*
¼ teaspoon plus ⅛ teaspoon pepper	*4 egg yolks*
2 green onions, minced	*½ cup butter, melted*
¾ cup sherry	*2 teaspoons white vinegar*
1 tablespoon fresh lemon juice	*4 eggs*

1 Preheat the broiler.

2 Lay the filets on a broiler pan. Season both sides with ¼ teaspoon of salt and ¼ teaspoon of pepper. Set the meat aside so it can reach room temperature.

3 In a medium skillet, combine the green onions, sherry, lemon juice, thyme, cayenne pepper, ⅛ teaspoon of salt, and ⅛ teaspoon of pepper. Cook over medium heat, stirring constantly, until the liquid is reduced by half (about 7 minutes). Remove the sherry mixture from the heat, pour it into a small bowl, and let it cool. Then strain the mixture into a small bowl and discard the solids.

4 Put the egg yolks in the top pan of the double boiler. (The water in the bottom pan should not be touching the top pan.) With a wire whisk, beat the egg yolks over medium heat until they're light and lemon colored (about 1 minute). Do not let the eggs begin to cook.

5 While beating the eggs, slowly add the melted butter, and then immediately stir in the reserved sherry mixture. Continue stirring and cooking the sauce over medium-low heat until the sauce starts to thicken. Remove from the heat.

6 Broil the filets to the desired doneness (about 7 minutes for medium), turning once. Remove the filets from the oven and place them on breakfast plates.

7 Fill a 10-inch skillet half full with water. Add the vinegar (this helps cook the egg white faster so it doesn't spread). Bring the water to a slow boil.

8 Break one egg at a time into a shallow dish, and then gently slide the egg into the water, taking care not to break the yolk. (If you do break the yolk, use a spoon to remove the egg and start over with a fresh egg.) Reduce the heat to a gentle simmer and cook the eggs

3 minutes, or until the egg whites are set but the yolks remain soft. Remove the eggs with a slotted spoon, allowing the edges to drain.

9 Place 1 poached egg on top of each filet. Spoon béarnaise sauce over the eggs.

Per serving: Calories: 555; Total fat: 42g; Saturated fat: 21g; Cholesterol: 554mg; Sodium: 510mg; Carbohydrates: 3g; Fiber: 0g; Sugar: 1g; Protein: 33g.

Ham with Glazed Bananas

If you like Bananas Foster, you're going to love this new rendition with ham. Select fairly firm bananas so they don't get too soft when cooked. If the ham you select has skin or rind encircling it, it's best to cut it off before preparing this dish.

Preparation time: 5 minutes

Cooking time: 5 minutes

Yield: 4 servings

3 tablespoons plus 1 tablespoon butter	½ teaspoon cinnamon
3 tablespoons brown sugar	2 large bananas, peeled
¼ cup dark corn syrup	8-ounce ham steak, cut into 4 pieces

1 Melt 3 tablespoons of butter in a nonstick medium skillet. Stir in the sugar until it melts.

2 Stir in the corn syrup and cinnamon and bring it to a gentle simmer. Slice the bananas into the syrup and simmer for 2 minutes.

3 In a medium skillet, melt 1 tablespoon of butter. Add the ham pieces and brown quickly on each side, turning once.

4 Place the ham slices on a serving dish and top with the banana glaze.

Per serving: Calories: 335; Total fat: 14g; Saturated fat: 8g; Cholesterol: 53mg; Sodium: 786mg; Carbohydrates: 43g; Fiber: 2g; Sugar: 25g; Protein: 13g.

Potato Tomato Pie

It's far too messy and time consuming to make hash brown potatoes for a crowd. Besides, hash browns are ordinary. Not only is this pie delicious, but it looks impressive. You can serve it at a brunch, as a side dish for dinner, and even as a main entrée with a tossed salad.

Preparation time: *15 minutes*

Cooking time: *65 minutes*

Yield: *8 servings*

Nonstick cooking spray

2 cups firmly packed grated raw potatoes

¼ teaspoon salt

2 eggs

¼ cup grated onion

3 or 4 medium tomatoes, sliced ⅛-inch thick

½ teaspoon oregano

¼ teaspoon pepper

1 teaspoon Italian seasoning

8 slices bacon, cooked crisp and crumbled

¾ cup grated Parmesan cheese

¾ cup mayonnaise

⅓ cup gluten-free seasoned bread crumbs

1 Preheat the oven to 400 degrees. Spray a 9-inch pie plate with cooking spray.

2 Place the raw potatoes in a colander or sieve. Sprinkle them with salt and let them set for 5 minutes.

3 In a medium bowl, whisk the eggs. Squeeze out the excess water from the potatoes and add them to the eggs. Stir in the onion.

4 Put the mixture into the prepared pie plate. Using the back of a spoon, pat the mixture onto the bottom and sides of the pan.

5 Bake the crust at 400 degrees for 35 minutes. Remove the pan from the oven and reduce the oven temperature to 350 degrees.

6 Layer half of the tomato slices onto the bottom of the baked crust. Sprinkle with half of the pepper and Italian seasoning and half of the bacon. Repeat the layer with the remaining tomatoes, pepper, Italian seasoning, and bacon.

7 In a small bowl, stir together the cheese and mayonnaise. Drop this mixture in dollops on top of the tomatoes and then spread it carefully to cover the top of the pie.

8 Sprinkle the bread crumbs on top of the pie. Bake the pie uncovered at 350 degrees for 30 minutes, or until the bread crumbs begin to brown.

Per serving: *Calories: 222; Total fat: 15g; Saturated fat: 4g; Cholesterol: 76mg; Sodium: 645mg; Carbohydrates: 14g; Fiber: 1g; Sugar: 3g; Protein: 9g.*

Potato Nests with Shrimp

We have five senses. Obviously, when we're hungry, taste is key. However, the sense of sight also plays a role. If food is presented in an appealing, enticing manner, we begin to anticipate how absolutely wonderful it will taste. These potato nests are the perfect presentation for this shrimp dish.

Preparation time: *20 minutes*

Cooking time: *20 minutes*

Yield: *8 servings*

Nonstick cooking spray	*¼ cup whole milk*
4 medium russet potatoes, shredded	*8 ounces cream cheese, cubed*
¼ teaspoon plus ¼ teaspoon salt	*2 tablespoons dried parsley flakes*
3 tablespoons melted butter	*⅛ teaspoon pepper*
1 tablespoon olive oil	*2 tablespoons chopped pimento*
¼ cup chopped onion	*1 pound small cooked shrimp*
¾ cup sliced fresh mushrooms	*¼ cup dry white wine*

1 Preheat the oven to 450 degrees. Coat 8 cupcake tins with cooking spray.

2 In a medium bowl, toss together the shredded potatoes, ¼ teaspoon of salt, and the melted butter until the potatoes are evenly coated. Press the mixture onto the bottom and sides of the prepared cupcake tins. Bake the nests at 450 degrees for 15 to 20 minutes until golden.

3 Heat the oil in a medium saucepan over medium-high heat; sauté the onions and mushrooms until they're lightly browned. Stir in the milk, cream cheese, parsley flakes, ¼ teaspoon of salt, pepper, and pimento. Stir the mixture until the cheese melts. Stir in the shrimp and wine, simmering just until the ingredients are warmed. Serve in the potato nests.

Per serving: Calories: 314; Total fat: 17g; Saturated fat: 10g; Cholesterol: 269mg; Sodium: 213mg; Carbohydrates: 22g; Fiber: 1g; Sugar: 2g; Protein: 16g.

Midday Munchables, Gluten-Free Style

A human being can only consume so many peanut butter and jelly sandwiches before the body screams for something new for lunch. The primary issue for celiacs is that the bread needed to make sandwiches is often — ahem — less than adequate in the taste department. (That was as tactful as I could be, considering many gluten-free breads resemble crumbly cardboard.) Lucky for you, this book contains recipes for excellent breads (see Chapter 9).

Gluten-free lunches seem to be a challenge for many people. Rest assured that your choices are vast.

Variety is the key. Switch foods and alter combinations to make lunch an event of anticipation. One day add deviled or hard-boiled eggs; the next day add salsa and gluten-free tortilla chips. Include veggies as often as possible, whether it's carrot sticks with dip or celery stuffed with peanut butter. If time is a factor, add no-fuss items like applesauce, gelatin cups, or flavored yogurt; or pack a few gluten-free crackers to have with cheese slices or to spread with hummus. For a treat, take a sandwich made from gluten-free sweet bread slices spread with cream cheese.

Meals on the move

If you work, you probably have little time in the morning to dawdle in the kitchen preparing a homemade bag lunch. For kids on a gluten-free diet, the problem is compounded because many children are picky eaters. But with a little preplanning and unlimited ingenuity, you can create many viable alternatives, even if you're on the run.

Miracles of the microwave

What *did* we do without microwaves? Fortunately, most workplaces and even schools have microwaves that employees or teachers can use. These appliances can be a lifesaver when you've made something at home and need to warm it up for your midday meal.

One idea is to make your own "lunchables" from dinner leftovers. Nearly every grocery store carries divided, plastic, lidded containers that are ideal for making these handy lunches. To prevent spoilage, freeze your meal in the container so you take a frozen package with you in the morning; by lunchtime, it will be thawed and ready to heat.

Other gluten-free foods conducive to being warmed in a microwave include pizza, lasagna, eggplant parmigiana, crustless quiche, and twice-baked potatoes.

If you're making mashed potatoes for dinner, bake the potatoes (instead of boiling them); remove most of the insides (also referred to as "guts") to make the mashed potatoes, and leave the skins intact. Then make your own potato skins topped with cheddar cheese, sliced green onions, and crumbled bacon (Chapter 15 has a potato skins recipe if you need a little more direction). Potato skins make a fun lunch for kids and adults.

Another fun microwavable lunch is a hot dog topped with American cheese and wrapped in a corn tortilla (wrap it all in waxed paper to heat in the microwave). Tamales, quesadillas, and Chinese stir-fry add variety to your lunch and warm easily in the microwave, too.

Think about a thermos

If you think a thermos is just for coffee, think again. Ah, so you think you're quite the adventurer because you've been brave enough to spoon chili or stew into a thermos? Now think even further outside the box — be daring!

Pack a gluten-free bun and spoon sloppy joe mix into the insulated container. By the way, many sloppy joe mixes available at the grocery store — even generics — are gluten-free.

You can also fill a thermos with boiling water and add corn on the cob, or one or two hot dogs. A thermos is great for taco meat (spoon it on top of a salad at lunchtime), pork and beans, hot dog slices and beans, or sausage in barbecue sauce. Rice dishes and gluten-free pasta entrees — everything from Spanish rice and beans, to gluten-free pasta marinara, to fettuccini Alfredo, to macaroni and cheese — hold well in a thermos.

Quickie cold lunches

If you're cool with cold, there's no end to your lunch selections. For entrees, here are just a few suggestions. Remember, creativity is key:

- Baked or fried chicken or chicken wings
- Cold poached salmon, plain or spread with mayonnaise
- Shrimp with cocktail sauce
- Cold sliced steak, chicken, or sushi
- Tomato stuffed with tuna fish
- Cottage cheese with fruit

Satisfying salads

Salads are gaining popularity as a lunch entrée, whether it's a (gluten-free, of course) pasta salad, shrimp or crab salad, chicken Caesar salad, or chicken pineapple salad. You can also enjoy the traditional potato salad made with mayonnaise and a hint of mustard, or a Greek potato salad made with green pepper, onion, olive oil, and cider vinegar. A chef salad is an excellent way to use up leftovers in the refrigerator. And let's not forget healthy bean salad. (Chapter 16 features salad recipes.)

If the salad is your main dish, treat yourself to an antipasto of marinated cubes of pepperoni, shredded chicken, cheese, olives, tomato wedges, artichoke hearts, and pepperoncini.

Craving croutons on your salad? Try tortilla chips instead. You can also check out several varieties of gluten-free salad toppings in the veggie section of your grocery store.

Hot or cold sandwiches

Oh, sure, so the days of throwing together a sandwich with cheap and easy-to-find bread may be a thing of the past — but prepare to be amazed because you have plenty of sandwich options, even in the gluten-free world.

It's time to try new innovations with old favorites. The common favorites — chicken breast sandwich, toasted cheese sandwich, tuna sandwich, and sloppy joes — have been modified, altered, enhanced, disguised, and transformed into totally new creations of savory sustenance.

If you want something small to have with your sandwich, try coleslaw or marinated vegetables.

If you enjoy sandwiches made on gluten-free bread, break the routine of deli lunchmeats with meatloaf, egg salad, or Reuben sandwiches.

Okay, I'm the first to admit that gluten-free bread is — ahem — a matter of taste. Either ya do or ya don't do gluten-free breads. So if you don't want the bread, don't worry. You can improvise and make a sandwich out of just about anything else. Try wrapping lunchmeat around a piece of string cheese — or, if you're more daring, add a piece or two of marinated asparagus before wrapping. Make toothpick kabobs of cubes of lunchmeat, cheese, pickles, and olives.

Italian Grilled Cheese Sandwich

You've had grilled cheese . . . and grilled cheese with tomato slices . . . and perhaps even grilled cheese with bacon. But you've never had a grilled cheese sandwich like this. We're talking real flavor here — new window dressing for an old-time American standby.

Preparation time: *5 minutes*

Cooking time: *4 minutes*

Yield: *4 servings*

2 tablespoons olive oil

8 thin slices gluten-free olive oil bread

¼ cup prepared pesto

4 slices mozzarella cheese

2 tablespoons minced onion

2 red peppers, roasted and cut in half (or use canned, prepared red roasted peppers)

4 slices provolone cheese

4 slices deli ham

2 teaspoons brown mustard

1 Brush ¼ tablespoon of the oil on one side of each of the 2 slices of bread. Place them, oiled side down, in a large skillet.

2 Spread 1 tablespoon of the pesto on top of each of the two slices of bread in the skillet. Top each with a slice of mozzarella cheese, and then sprinkle 1 tablespoon of minced onion over the two slices, dividing evenly.

3 Lay a pepper half on top of the onion. Top each sandwich with a slice of provolone cheese. Lay a slice of ham on top of the provolone.

4 Spread ½ teaspoon of mustard on two slices of bread and place, mustard-side down, on top of the sandwich.

5 Brush ¼ tablespoon of oil on top of the 2 assembled sandwiches.

6 Grill the sandwiches over medium-high heat, 2 minutes per side, or until each side is golden. Press lightly with a spatula during cooking so the cheese melts completely. Repeat Steps 1 through 6 to make remaining two sandwiches. Use a griddle if you want to make all 4 sandwiches at the same time.

Per serving: Calories: 823; Total fat: 39g; Saturated fat: 13g; Cholesterol: 60mg; Sodium: 1,729mg; Carbohydrates: 91g; Fiber: 5g; Sugar: 17g; Protein: 26g.

Tuna Fish Sandwich Like No Other

Tuna isn't just for mayo anymore! After you try this recipe, whether you put the filling on bread, in a gluten-free pita or tortilla, or even spoon it atop shredded lettuce, you won't want to go back to the old tuna-and-mayo rendition.

Preparation time: *8 minutes*

Cooking time: *3 minutes*

Yield: *4 servings*

4 slices gluten-free olive oil bread

¼ green pepper, cut into thin julienne strips

⅛ red onion, sliced thin

½ cup baby spinach leaves

2 small plum tomatoes, sliced thin

⅛ teaspoon pepper

¼ teaspoon Italian seasoning

6.5-ounce can water-pack chunk tuna, drained

2 teaspoons Italian dressing

8 artichoke hearts

4 slices pepper cheese

1 Preheat the broiler. Place the bread slices in a 9-x-13-inch baking dish.

2 On each slice of bread, layer the green pepper, onion, spinach leaves, and tomato slices, dividing evenly.

3 In a small bowl, blend the pepper, Italian seasoning, tuna, and Italian dressing. Spoon the mixture on top of the tomato slices.

4 Cut the artichoke hearts in half. Lay 4 halves on each sandwich.

5 Lay 1 slice of pepper cheese on top of each sandwich.

6 Broil the sandwiches about 3 minutes or just until the cheese is melted.

Per serving: *Calories: 429; Total fat: 15; Saturated fat: 9g; Cholesterol: 40mg; Sodium: 632mg; Carbohydrates: 50g; Fiber: 3g; Sugar: 9g; Protein: 24g.*

Best-Ever Sloppy Joes

Double, triple, or quadruple this recipe when you host a birthday party for your children's friends or whenever you have your friends over to watch a game. Spoon several heaping spoonfuls of hamburger mix on top of a toasted gluten-free bun. Now close your eyes and savor the spicy harmony of flavors.

Preparation time: *15 minutes*

Cooking time: *10 minutes*

Yield: *4 servings*

1 tablespoon olive oil	*1 teaspoon yellow mustard*
1 pound lean ground beef	*½ teaspoon garlic powder*
1 medium onion, diced	*¼ teaspoon salt*
¼ green pepper, diced	*¼ teaspoon pepper*
1 teaspoon chili powder	*1 tablespoon brown sugar*
¼ teaspoon cayenne pepper	*2 teaspoons cider vinegar*
1 teaspoon paprika	*2 tablespoons gluten-free Worcestershire sauce*
½ teaspoon cumin	*8-ounce can tomato sauce*

1 In a medium skillet over medium-high heat, brown the ground beef, onion, and green pepper in oil, breaking the meat up with a fork.

2 Stir in the chili powder, cayenne pepper, paprika, cumin, mustard, garlic powder, salt, pepper, brown sugar, vinegar, Worcestershire sauce, and tomato sauce and simmer for 10 minutes, stirring often.

Per serving: *Calories: 257; Total fat: 10g; Saturated fat: 3g; Cholesterol: 68mg; Sodium: 829mg; Carbohydrates: 16g; Fiber: 3g; Sugar: 9g; Protein: 3g.*

Caesar Sandwich

Hail to the Caesar Sandwich! You can make this with deli chicken, but it's even better when it's made with leftover roasted or grilled chicken.

Preparation time: *4 minutes*

Cooking time: *None*

Yield: *1 serving*

2 slices gluten-free olive oil bread, toasted	2 teaspoons Caesar salad dressing
2 slices deli roasted chicken breast	1 hard-boiled egg, sliced
1 large romaine lettuce leaf	Dash pepper

1 Lay the chicken slices on top of 1 slice of toast, and then fold the lettuce leaf on top. Drizzle the dressing on top of the lettuce.

2 Lay the egg slices on top of the dressing and then sprinkle them with pepper. Top with the second piece of toast.

Tip: If you don't have Caesar salad dressing, use Italian dressing and add 1 teaspoon of grated Parmesan cheese.

Per serving: Calories: 717; Total fat: 29g; Saturated fat: 7g; Cholesterol: 254mg; Sodium: 1,168mg; Carbohydrates: 88g; Fiber: 4g; Sugar: 17g; Protein: 25g.

Wraps and Other Sandwich Containers

Do you like wraps? If you can't find a premade loaf of gluten-free bread to your liking and you haven't had time to bake your own bread, don't despair. There are other viable sandwich "containers."

If you haven't tried a peanut butter and jelly sandwich made on gluten-free waffles, you have a taste-treat awaiting you. Purchase corn tortillas made from either yellow or white corn. Corn taco shells, precooked of course, are a crisp, fun holder for a multitude of fillings. Pancakes and crepes make wonderful wraps. And lettuce leaves are the ideal holders for lunchmeat and cheese. (If you feel daring, use Belgian endive leaves; they're shaped like boats and make a neat container for tuna and chicken salads.)

Eata pita

Okay, you won't find them in every grocery store, but there *are* gluten-free pitas available. If you can't find them, don't worry — you can make a good homemade version. Because the alternative flours are heavier, you may not always be able to cut open the pocket of the pita without destroying the integrity of the bread (which means it very well may crumble and fall apart). The good news is that you can make a marvelous pita flatbread, sans pocket, that is thin enough so you can place the filling on the bread, and then fold the bread in half to form a sandwich (the Mediterranean equivalent of a taco). Flip to Chapter 9 for a good flatbread recipe.

If you'd like, avoid the wrap altogether and pack a sandwich filling (like tuna or egg salad) in a container and take along a gluten-free muffin. Gluten-free crackers are also an alternative, and they're now available in many different flavors and textures. You can probably find them at your neighborhood grocery store.

Corn tortillas are available just about anywhere. Even the new gluten-free "flour" tortillas are excellent, and you can find them in most health food stores, usually in the frozen-foods section or online. After you bring them home, keep them refrigerated if you plan to use them within the week, or freeze them. To soften the tortillas so they don't crack when you wrap them, place them between two sheets of dampened paper towels and microwave them for a few seconds.

Antipasto Lettuce Wraps

Belgian endive leaves were created to hold stuff. They're naturally boat-shaped and beg for a filling. You can eat these wraps right away, but they're even better if you cover and refrigerate the filling for a few hours to allow the flavors to blend.

Preparation time: 6 minutes

Cooking time: None

Yield: 4 servings

2 tablespoons olive oil

2 tablespoons cider vinegar

¼ teaspoon garlic powder

⅛ teaspoon pepper

¾ teaspoon dried oregano

1 small onion, minced

¼ green pepper, chopped

3 red peppers, roasted and sliced thin (or use canned, prepared red roasted peppers)

6.5-ounce can tuna fish, drained

2 ounces pizza pepperoni, slices halved

6-ounce jar marinated artichokes, drained and cut in half

8 Belgian endive leaves

1 In a medium bowl, whisk together the oil, vinegar, garlic powder, pepper, and oregano.

2 Add the onion, green pepper, red peppers, tuna fish, pepperoni, and artichokes and stir to blend.

3 Spoon the mixture into 8 endive leaves to form boat sandwiches.

Per serving: Calories: 232; Total fat: 17g; Saturated fat: 3g; Cholesterol: 28mg; Sodium: 720mg; Carbohydrates: 6g; Fiber: 1g; Sugar: 1g; Protein: 15g.

Reuben Quesadillas

These quesadillas are great eaten fresh off the griddle, but you can also make them ahead and pack them in a bag for lunchtime. Ideally, you fill the tortilla, and then fold it in half, but the gluten-free tortillas don't always cooperate. To avoid having the tortilla break apart, just cut it in half from the start.

Preparation time: *5 minutes*

Cooking time: *5 minutes*

Yield: *6 servings*

Three 10-inch gluten-free tortillas, cut in half	*8-ounce can sauerkraut, drained and rinsed*
1½ teaspoons hot mustard	*6 slices low-fat Swiss cheese*
8 ounces deli corned beef, sliced thin	

1 Spread 3 of the tortilla halves with ½ teaspoon of mustard.

2 Divide the corned beef in thirds; lay 1 portion on each of 3 halves of the tortilla.

3 Divide the sauerkraut in thirds; lay 1 portion on top of the corned beef on each tortilla.

4 Lay 2 slices of Swiss cheese on top of the sauerkraut on each quesadilla.

5 Cover each quesadilla with the remaining 3 tortilla halves.

6 Cut each tortilla semicircle in half to make a total of 6 halves.

7 Place the quesadillas in a large skillet that has been prewarmed over medium-high heat, and toast the quesadillas on each side until the tortillas are lightly browned and the cheese is melted.

Vary It! *You can substitute different ingredients for the contents of the quesadilla, using pastrami in place of the corned beef and/or provolone cheese in place of Swiss.*

Per serving: *Calories: 232; Total fat: 10g; Saturated fat: 3g; Cholesterol: 47mg; Sodium: 7143mg; Carbohydrates: 16g; Fiber: 1g; Sugar: 1g; Protein: 24g.*

☜ *Broiled Veggie Tortillas*

Serving these wedges makes a great lunch, but they also make the perfect appetizer. And you can easily adapt this recipe for a wrap. Instead of cutting the tortilla into wedges, spoon the vegetables onto two whole tortillas and then roll each one up. (See the tip in the introduction to this section for softening tortillas so you can roll them.) After baking, cut each tortilla wrap in half.

Preparation time: *15 minutes*

Cooking time: *7 minutes*

Yield: *4 servings*

1 tablespoon olive oil

¼ teaspoon minced garlic

¼ green pepper, cut into thin strips

½ small zucchini, sliced

¼ medium onion, sliced thin

½ small Portabella mushroom, cut in half and sliced thin

½ teaspoon dried parsley flakes

¼ teaspoon dried oregano

¼ teaspoon Italian seasoning

dash of salt

⅛ teaspoon pepper

10-inch rice flour tortilla, cut into 4 wedges

¼ cup crumbled feta cheese

1 Preheat the broiler.

2 In a large skillet, sauté the vegetables in olive oil on high heat until they're tender crisp, about 3 minutes. Stir in the parsley flakes, oregano, Italian seasoning, salt, and pepper.

3 Reassemble the tortilla wedges together to form a circle on a baking sheet.

4 Spoon the veggies evenly over the tortilla wedges and then sprinkle with feta cheese.

5 Broil for 7 minutes or until the tortillas are crisp.

Per serving: *Calories: 100; Total fat: 7g; Saturated fat: 2g; Cholesterol: 8mg; Sodium: 192mg; Carbohydrates: 8g; Fiber: 1g; Sugar: 2g; Protein: 3g.*

Turkey Roll-Ups

The beauty of these roll-ups is that each time you make them, you can vary the ingredients. One time substitute roast beef, American cheese, and watercress, or corned beef and Swiss cheese with mustard. Use thin tomato slices or banana pepper rings in place of the roasted peppers, or sliced pepperoncini in place of the banana peppers. Rice paper wraps are a nice exchange for the tortillas. Oh, so many choices!

Preparation time: *10 minutes*

Refrigeration time: *2 to 6 hours*

Cooking time: *None*

Yield: *4 servings*

10-inch gluten-free tortilla

1 tablespoon mayonnaise

2 ounces deli turkey breast, sliced thin

2 ounces provolone cheese, sliced thin

2 red peppers, roasted and sliced (or use canned, prepared red roasted peppers)

1 small cucumber, sliced very thin

½ cup baby spinach leaves

1 Spread the mayonnaise on one side of the tortilla.

2 Along one edge, layer the turkey and cheese on top of the mayonnaise.

3 Along that same edge, lay out the peppers and cucumber.

4 Sprinkle the spinach leaves over all.

5 Tightly roll up the tortilla. Wrap it in a damp paper towel, then in wax paper, and refrigerate for several hours.

6 When you're ready to serve the roll-up, remove the paper towel and wax paper, and slice the tortilla into 8 slices.

Per serving: *Calories: 135; Total fat: 6g; Saturated fat: 3g; Cholesterol: 26mg; Sodium: 291mg; Carbohydrates: 10g; Fiber: 1g; Sugar: 2g; Protein: 11g.*

Pizza (No Foolin')

When you first thought of cooking gluten-free, visions of bread and spaghetti floating away filled your mind. Chances are, the next looming image was pizza. Dispel those negative thoughts because you can have all three! You can make gluten-free pizza to your liking with thick or thin crust, but you'll need to add extra flavoring, usually in the form of Italian seasoning.

Thin crust? Thick crust? You decide. The recipe below is for a thicker crust. If you prefer a thinner crust pizza, use a larger pan and roll the dough thinner. The challenge with gluten-free pizza dough is in the spreading. To get a light textured crust, the dough must be sticky to work with. You can add extra flour if you want to roll out the dough, but the baked crust won't be as light as one that isn't rolled. When spreading the crust in the pan, dip your fingers in warm water to keep the dough from sticking to your hands.

⏷ Three-Cheese Pizza

This pizza is *so* far beyond the traditional concept. There's no sauce, but it doesn't need any because the cheeses melt and meld and mingle together to form a covering that surpasses sublime. It's more than a cheese bread, so the only appropriate name has to be "cheese pizza."

Tools: *Electric mixer*

Preparation time: *15 minutes*

Cooking time: *25 minutes*

Yield: *6 servings*

2 teaspoons sugar	¼ teaspoon garlic powder
1 packet (2½ teaspoons) quick rising yeast	1 teaspoon plus 2 tablespoons grated Romano cheese
⅔ cup warm water (115 degrees)	1 tablespoon plus ½ teaspoon olive oil
1⅓ cup gluten-free flour mixture	1 teaspoon cider vinegar
¾ cup nonfat dry milk powder	1 teaspoon honey
½ teaspoon salt	1 tablespoon cornmeal
½ teaspoon baking powder	4 ounces feta cheese, crumbled
1 teaspoon unflavored gelatin	1 cup shredded mozzarella cheese
1 teaspoon Italian seasoning	

1 Preheat the oven to 425 degrees.

2 In a small bowl, dissolve the sugar and yeast in warm water. Set aside for 5 minutes.

3 In a medium mixing bowl, whisk together the flour mixture, milk powder, salt, baking powder, gelatin, Italian seasoning, garlic powder, and 1 teaspoon of the Romano cheese.

4 In another small bowl, whisk together 1 tablespoon of olive oil, the vinegar, and honey.

5 Add the oil mixture to the flour mixture and stir until well blended.

6 Add the yeast water to the flour mixture, and use the electric mixer to beat the mixture on high speed for 3 minutes. The dough should be very soft and moist.

7 Grease the bottom of a 12-inch pizza pan with ½ teaspoon of olive oil and then sprinkle it with cornmeal.

8 With dampened hands, press the dough into the bottom of the pan, building up the sides a bit to hold in the toppings.

9 Bake the dough at 425 degrees for 10 minutes and then remove it from the oven and put on the toppings.

10 First sprinkle the feta cheese, then the mozzarella, then the remaining 2 tablespoons of the Romano cheese on top of the crust.

11 Return the pizza to the oven and bake it at 425 degrees for an additional 15 minutes, or until the top is nicely browned.

Tip: *For a pizza with a thinner crust, use a baking sheet; for a deep-dish pizza, use an 11-x-7-inch pan.*

Vary It! *This pizza base may be used to make the traditional pizza with tomato sauce, mozzarella, or provolone cheese, and your favorite toppings. Or you can make your own calzones by dividing the dough into 4 pieces; pat each piece out on a sheet of wax paper, place your favorite filling on one half, then fold the other half of the dough over and seal well (forming a half-moon shape), then bake your calzone at 425 degrees for 20 minutes or until lightly browned.*

Per serving: *Calories: 306; Total fat: 10g; Saturated fat: 6g; Cholesterol: 30mg; Sodium: 517mg; Carbohydrates: 39g; Fiber: 2g; Sugar: 8g; Protein: 14g.*

Quick Midday Casseroles

As much as Americans enjoy their sandwiches at lunchtime, sometimes you're ready for something different. When the hungries hit at noontime, the casserole recipes in this section can lend variety to your nourishment fare and leave your tummy feeling full and content.

Casseroles became popular in America during World War I when certain food items were scarce. Leftovers were chopped up and mixed with whatever else was available, and then put in a glass or metal pan and baked. The virtues of these easy-to-prepare meals are many.

You can prepare the ingredients ahead of time and then slide the pan in the oven just before you're ready to eat. Casseroles are flexible because they can encompass leftovers and often use inexpensive meats. And these one-pan dishes can be anything from a vegetable conglomeration (for example, the much-overused but still-popular green bean casserole) to main dishes and even desserts.

Here are some casserole hints that will make your life easier:

✔ When making a casserole, make two. It's just as easy to double the ingredients and then freeze half so you have a spare on those days when you don't have time to cook. Preferably you'll have time to let the frozen casserole thaw in the refrigerator overnight before baking. If you're baking the casserole from a frozen state, you may need to almost double the baking time. And be very careful about freezing casseroles in glass dishes. If a glass casserole dish is cold and is set on a hot oven rack, the dish can crack.

✔ If you're cooking for a small brood and don't want to buy a whole head of cauliflower, broccoli, or whatever because you'll have too much left over, pick up just the amount you need from the salad bar available at most grocery stores.

✔ Fresh herbs tend to lose their flavor during prolonged baking at high heat. If your casserole will bake for more than 20 minutes, it may be better to use dried herbs instead.

✔ To convert almost any casserole to *au gratin,* just stir in some shredded cheese and then mix together some grated cheese, gluten-free bread crumbs, and a little melted butter to sprinkle on top before baking.

Don't you hate it when a recipes calls for a 3-quart dish? You know what a 9-x-9-inch pan looks like, but which of your casserole dishes holds 3 quarts? The easiest way to find out is to fill a measuring cup with water and pour it into the most likely pan until you know its capacity.

Pepperoni Squares

Kids love these "nibbles." A pizza spin-off, these squares can be prepared the night before, covered, and refrigerated. Just before lunch, pop them in the oven. Or bake them ahead and then wrap them in foil to reheat in the oven. If you cut the pieces smaller (24 pieces per pan), you can serve the squares as an appetizer.

Tools: *Electric mixer*

Preparation time: *15 minutes*

Cooking time: *40 minutes*

Yield: *6 servings*

Nonstick cooking spray	*⅛ teaspoon red pepper flakes*
1 tablespoon olive oil	*½ cup shredded mozzarella cheese*
½ cup chopped onion	*⅛ teaspoon salt*
⅓ cup chopped green pepper	*Dash pepper*
2 eggs	*½ teaspoon Italian seasoning*
¾ cup whole milk	*2 ounces pizza pepperoni, slices quartered*
¾ cup gluten-free flour mixture	*1 cup spaghetti sauce*
1½ tablespoons dried parsley flakes	

1 Preheat the oven to 400 degrees. Spray a 9-x-9-inch baking dish with cooking spray.

2 In a small skillet, sauté the onions and green pepper in oil over medium heat, stirring often, until the vegetables are soft.

3 In a medium mixing bowl, use the mixer to whip together the eggs and milk. Add the flour and beat the mixture until it's smooth and thickened. Stir in the reserved onion and green pepper, parsley flakes, red pepper flakes, mozzarella cheese, salt, pepper, Italian seasoning, and pepperoni.

4 Transfer the mixture to the prepared baking pan and bake it at 400 degrees for 40 minutes. Cut into 6 pieces.

5 In a microwave-safe bowl, warm the spaghetti sauce to serve as a dipping sauce for the Pepperoni Squares.

Per serving: Calories: 229; Total fat: 11g; Saturated fat: 3g; Cholesterol: 84mg; Sodium: 510mg; Carbohydrates: 25g; Fiber: 4g; Sugar: 7g; Protein: 8g.

◌ *Enchilada Casserole*

Keep these enchiladas covered in the refrigerator to pop in the oven, toaster oven, or microwave when your tummy warns you that it's lunchtime. When dipping the tortillas in the tomato sauce, do it quickly or the tortillas will get so soft they may fall apart. For extra decadence, top with sour cream before serving.

Preparation time: *15 minutes*

Cooking time: *20 minutes*

Yield: *6 servings*

Nonstick cooking spray	*⅛ teaspoon pepper*
8-ounce can tomato sauce	*2½ teaspoons chili powder*
⅓ cup water	*½ teaspoon dried oregano*
5 drops hot pepper sauce	*½ teaspoon cumin*
½ medium onion, diced	*1 cup shredded Monterey Jack cheese*
1 clove garlic, minced	*½ cup plus 2 tablespoons shredded sharp cheddar cheese*
½ cup diced green pepper	
2 teaspoons olive oil	*Six 9-inch corn tortillas*
3 tablespoons fresh chopped parsley	*6 tablespoons refried beans*
⅛ teaspoon salt	

1 Preheat the oven to 350 degrees. Spray a 7-x-11-inch baking pan with cooking spray.

2 In a large skillet over medium-high heat, stir together the tomato sauce, water, and hot pepper sauce. Bring it to a boil, then lower the heat and let it simmer for 3 minutes. Remove the skillet from the heat and let the sauce cool slightly.

3 In a small skillet, sauté the onions, garlic, and green pepper in the oil over medium heat until the vegetables are softened but not browned. Stir frequently. Remove the skillet from the heat and let the veggies cool.

4 In a medium bowl, stir together the onion mixture, parsley, salt, pepper, chili powder, oregano, cumin, Monterey Jack cheese, and ½ cup of cheddar cheese.

5 Dip each tortilla quickly into the tomato sauce to coat both sides. Lay the tortilla on a flat surface and spread with 1 tablespoon of the refried beans.

6 Spoon the cheese mixture on top of the beans, dividing evenly among the 6 tortillas.

7 Roll the tortillas and arrange them in the prepared baking dish. Pour the remaining tomato sauce over the tortillas, and then sprinkle them with the remaining 2 table-spoons of cheddar cheese.

8 Cover the pan with foil and bake the enchiladas at 350 degrees for 20 minutes.

Per serving: Calories: 239; Total fat: 13g; Saturated fat: 7g; Cholesterol: 29mg; Sodium: 619mg; Carbohydrates: 21g; Fiber: 5g; Sugar: 3g; Protein: 12g.

Macaroni and Sausage Casserole

Several recent studies have shown that macaroni and cheese is the top budget-stretching main dish served in America. So it's already been determined that you probably like it (like that's any huge surprise!). Now, are you ready for a new twist to this ever-favorite dish?

Preparation time: 20 minutes

Cooking time: 30 minutes

Yield: 8 servings

Nonstick cooking spray

1 pound sausage (regular or spicy)

1 medium onion, diced

3 cups gluten-free pasta shells

8-ounce jar processed cheese

18-ounce can gluten-free ready-to-serve cream of mushroom soup

¼ teaspoon pepper

¾ cup gluten-free bread crumbs

2 tablespoons melted butter

1 Preheat the oven to 325 degrees. Spray a 9-x-13-inch baking dish with cooking spray.

2 In a large skillet, brown the sausage and onion over medium-high heat, breaking up the meat with a fork. Remove the skillet from the heat and drain off the fat.

3 Boil the pasta in water in a large saucepan until it's barely tender and then drain. Return the pasta to the saucepan and immediately stir in the cheese so it melts.

4 Stir in the sausage, soup, and pepper.

5 Spoon the mixture into the prepared baking dish.

6 In a small bowl, stir together the bread crumbs and melted butter. Sprinkle this over the macaroni and sausage.

7 Bake the casserole at 325 degrees for 30 minutes until hot and bubbly and the bread crumbs start to brown a little.

Per serving: Calories: 333; Total fat: 17g; Saturated fat: 9g; Cholesterol: 51mg; Sodium: 1,233mg; Carbohydrates: 31g; Fiber: 1g; Sugar: 4g; Protein: 15g.

Chapter 11

Something's Fishy 'Round Here

In This Chapter

▶ Catching some tips for preparing fish

▶ Sticking to simple seasonings and sauces

▶ Serving creative seafood dishes

Some people think fish is fish. But oh, how wrong they are. Think of the options. Do you want to cook it with dry heat (baking, barbecuing, blackening, bronzing, broiling, microwaving), or use moist heat (steaming, poaching), or fry the fish (deep-frying, pan-frying)? When you've made up your mind about how to cook it, then you're confronted with further queries: Should it be marinated? Stuffed? Breaded? Basted? Glazed? Served with a sauce?

Before you become totally overwhelmed with choices, take a look at some of the recipes in this chapter and realize that fish can make a fabulous dish!

Reeling in Compliments with Fish and Seafood Dishes

Unlike meat, fish is naturally tender and requires short cooking times at a high temperature. All fish and seafood are naturally gluten-free. Below are some general guidelines for cooking fish:

- ✔ Measure fish at its thickest part.

- ✔ Allow 10 minutes of cooking time per inch of thickness for fresh fish.

- ✔ Allow 20 minutes of cooking time per inch of thickness for frozen fish.

- ✔ Fish is ready when it's opaque but still juicy. Sometimes if you cook a filet until it flakes easily with a fork, it will be overdone and dried out.

  Raw fish is *translucent,* kind of like frosted glass. You certainly can't look through it, but it's not solid either. Cooked fish is *opaque* and solid, meaning you can't see through it at all.

- ✔ Baking fish in an aluminum pan can create a chemical reaction that leaves the fish tasting acidic. It's best to bake fish in a glass or stainless steel pan.

- ✔ *Do not overcook* or the fish will become tough.

Broiled, Baked, and Poached

Fish is a highly nutritious food commodity. It provides protein, far fewer calories than meat, and is rich in Omega-3 fatty acids. (Isn't it odd that we're always being told to stay away from fatty foods, yet certain fatty acids are good for us?)

Omega-3 has many health benefits including lowering triglycerides and helping to prevent heart disease and blood clots, improving brain function, as well as helping with high blood pressure, diabetes, strokes, depression, arthritis, allergies, circulation problems, ADHD, Alzheimer's disease, skin disorders, gout, and lowering the risk of osteoporosis in post-menopausal women. The primary source for this fatty acid is fatty fish such as salmon, mackerel, sardines, and herring. Opt to buy fish that comes from the deep sea (as opposed to farm-raised) so it will be as pollutant-free as possible.

**Cranberry Cornmeal Muffins, Breakfast
Biscuit Bread, Pumpkin Waffles**

Three Cheese Pizza, Reuben Quesadillas,
Parmesan Chicken with Fresh Tomato Salsa

**Cheesy Corn Chowder,
Taco Salad in Tortilla Shells**

Speedy Taco Wings, Cajun Stuffed
Mushrooms, Roulade Canapé

Spinach Mandarin Salad, French Baguettes,
Glazed Filet Mignon with Bleu Cheese

Spinach Pie, Cranberries and Yams

Honey Cinnamon Grahams, Trail Mix Bars

Pumpkin Cheesecake, Whoopee Pies,
Strawberry Almond Torte

Grilled Cajun Orange Roughy

This fish dish will definitely awaken your taste buds! The mild flavor of the orange roughy doesn't compete with the spicy paste, and the whole combination teases the tongue just a bit. If you like your foods super-hot, add more cayenne. Do not overcook the filets, or the fish may become tough.

Preparation time: *5 minutes*

Cooking time: *8 minutes*

Yield: *4 servings*

Nonstick cooking spray	*⅛ teaspoon salt*
Four 5-ounce orange roughy filets	*¼ teaspoon pepper*
2 tablespoons butter, melted	*¼ teaspoon cayenne pepper*
¼ teaspoon garlic powder	*¼ teaspoon thyme*
2 teaspoons paprika	*½ teaspoon oregano*
½ teaspoon cumin	*⅛ teaspoon sugar*

1 Preheat the broiler.

2 Using the cooking spray, grease an 8-x-10-inch baking dish. Rinse the filets, pat them dry, and lay them in a single layer in the baking dish.

3 In a small bowl, stir the butter, garlic powder, paprika, cumin, salt, pepper, cayenne pepper, thyme, oregano, and sugar into a paste.

4 Spoon ¼ of the mixture on top of each filet; spread the topping evenly over each piece of fish.

5 Broil the filets for 7 to 8 minutes or until the fish is baked through.

Per serving: *Calories: 164; Total fat: 7g; Saturated fat: 4g; Cholesterol: 100mg; Sodium: 216mg; Carbohydrates: 1g; Fiber: 1g; Sugar: 0g; Protein: 24g.*

Sesame Pretzel Fish

The fish may be prepared ahead, covered with plastic wrap, and refrigerated until you're ready to bake it. If bass is not available, you can substitute orange roughy. Orange roughy is not as thick as bass, so you may have to reduce the baking time. You can add additional sesame seeds to the crumb mixture if you like.

Preparation time: *10 minutes*

Cooking time: *20 minutes*

Yield: *4 servings*

Nonstick cooking spray	¼ teaspoon garlic powder
Two 2.65-ounce bags gluten-free sesame pretzel rings	½ cup fresh lemon juice (about 3 whole lemons)
½ teaspoon salt	1½ tablespoons brown mustard
¼ teaspoon pepper	Four 5-ounce filets of bass
¾ teaspoon dried dill	

1 Preheat the oven to 400 degrees. Spray a 9-x-13-inch baking dish with cooking spray.

2 Puree 1 bag of pretzels at a time in a blender; empty the crumbs into a gallon-size self-seal plastic bag.

3 Add the salt, pepper, dill, and garlic powder to the plastic bag; seal the bag and shake well to mix the ingredients.

4 In a shallow bowl, whisk together the lemon juice and brown mustard.

5 Rinse the filets and pat them dry. Place the filets in the lemon-mustard mixture and let them marinate for 3 minutes.

6 Remove the bass and place them in the bag with the crumbs. Seal the bag and shake it to coat the filets evenly.

7 Place each piece of fish in a single layer in the prepared baking dish and bake the filets at 400 degrees for 20 minutes.

Tip: *Ground pretzels, especially ones with sesame seeds, make an excellent coating for oven-baked chicken, too!*

Per serving: *Calories: 403; Total fat: 16g; Saturated fat: 5g; Cholesterol: 129mg; Sodium: 963mg; Carbohydrates: 24g; Fiber: 2g; Sugar: 2g; Protein: 39g.*

Salmon with Mustard Dill Sauce

Oh, my gosh! This recipe *so* surpasses "good!" If possible, use wild salmon. It's deeper in color and has a much richer taste than farm-raised salmon. Before preparing this dish, remove the skin from the salmon by using a very sharp, thin knife.

Preparation time: *5 minutes*

Cooking time: *15 minutes*

Yield: *4 servings*

1 teaspoon plus 3 tablespoons olive oil

Four 5-ounce wild salmon filets with the skin removed

½ teaspoon dried dill

¼ teaspoon crushed red pepper flakes

¼ teaspoon dried oregano

¼ teaspoon salt

¼ teaspoon minced garlic

3 tablespoons slivered almonds

2 green onions, chopped

2 tablespoons fresh lemon juice (about 1 whole lemon)

1 teaspoon brown mustard

¼ teaspoon pepper

1 Preheat the oven to 350 degrees.

2 Lightly oil an 8-x-11-inch baking dish with 1 teaspoon of olive oil. Rinse and pat the filets dry, and place the fish in a single layer in the dish.

3 Combine the dill, red pepper flakes, oregano, salt, garlic, almonds, onion, lemon juice, brown mustard, pepper, and 3 tablespoons of olive oil in a blender. Puree the ingredients for 10 seconds, scrape down the blender's sides with a spatula, and then puree for 10 more seconds.

4 Spread the sauce over the fish, dividing evenly.

5 Bake the filets at 350 degrees for about 15 minutes or until a fork inserted in the thickest part of the salmon turns easily.

Per serving: *Calories: 392; Total fat: 25g; Saturated fat: 4g; Cholesterol: 101mg; Sodium: 243mg; Carbohydrates: 3g; Fiber: 1g; Sugar: 1g; Protein: 38g.*

Poached Salmon Piccata

For all of you who are trying to squeeze into a bikini, this dish is low calories and lower in fat. Plus, it's simple to prepare and tastes delicious. The benefit of eating salmon is its high Omega-3 content. You may opt to serve this over a bed of gluten-free noodles or on a bed of cooked spinach.

Preparation time: *5 minutes*

Cooking time: *10 minutes*

Yield: *2 servings*

¾ cup water

¼ cup sherry

2 teaspoons fresh lemon juice

½ teaspoon gluten-free chicken bouillon granules

1 tablespoon capers, rinsed and drained

⅛ teaspoon salt

⅛ teaspoon pepper

1 teaspoon dried parsley flakes

¼ teaspoon dried dill

¼ teaspoon dried mint flakes

1 tablespoon butter

Two 5-ounce pieces wild salmon filets, thawed and skin removed

1 Place the water, sherry, lemon juice, bouillon granules, capers, salt, pepper, parsley flakes, dill, mint, and butter in a medium skillet over high heat. Bring the mixture to a boil.

2 Reduce the heat to medium and add the salmon. Cover the skillet and simmer the filets for 7 to 8 minutes (cook 10 minutes per inch of thickness at the thickest part) or until the fish flakes easily with a fork. (You won't need to turn the fish over during cooking.)

3 Remove the fish from the skillet with a wide spatula to prevent the salmon from breaking apart. Discard the remaining liquid in the pan.

Per serving: Calories: 282; Total fat: 15g; Saturated fat: 5g; Cholesterol: 92mg; Sodium: 701mg; Carbohydrates: 3g; Fiber: 0g; Sugar: 1g; Protein: 28g.

Seafood Crepes and Casseroles

The recipes in this section provide more-creative ways to get fish in your meals. And more fish is a good thing. Fish and seafood are lower in saturated fat, total fat, and calories than comparable portions of meat or poultry.

Oysters are the least-consumed seafood even though they are loaded with zinc, which has been proven to be an aphrodisiac. Rumor has it that Casanova, the infamous 18th-century lover, ate 50 oysters for breakfast every day!

Seafood Sole

Talk about "sole" food! If you prepare this dish for company, you may opt to stuff each piece of fish with the seafood mixture, and then roll it up, secure it with a toothpick, and pour the sauce over the top before baking. It makes a beautiful presentation . . . especially if you remember to remove the toothpicks before serving it! Be sure to use lump crabmeat because imitation crabmeat usually isn't gluten-free.

Preparation time: *15 minutes*

Cooking time: *30 minutes*

Yield: *4 servings*

Nonstick cooking spray	¼ teaspoon pepper
1 tablespoon butter	¼ teaspoon paprika
½ cup onion, chopped	18-ounce can ready-to-serve gluten-free cream of mushroom soup
7-ounce can sliced mushrooms, drained	
½ pound fresh, cooked medium shrimp, cut in half	¼ teaspoon gluten-free chicken bouillon granules
6-ounce can lump crabmeat, drained	2 teaspoons cornstarch
Four 6-ounce sole or flounder filets	¼ cup shredded sharp white cheddar cheese
¼ teaspoon salt	1 tablespoon dried parsley flakes

1 Preheat the oven to 400 degrees. Lightly grease a 9-x-9-inch baking dish with cooking spray.

2 Melt the butter in a large saucepan; add the onions and mushrooms and sauté them over medium heat until they're soft. Stir in the shrimp and crabmeat and heat the mixture.

3 Rinse the filets and pat them dry. Sprinkle the filets with salt, pepper, and paprika and lay them in the prepared baking dish. Spoon the shrimp mixture over the filets.

4 In a medium bowl, stir together the soup, bouillon granules, and cornstarch until the ingredients are blended. Stir in the cheese and parsley flakes. Pour the mixture over the casserole.

5 Bake the casserole at 400 degrees for 30 minutes.

Per serving: *Calories: 418; Total fat: 16g; Saturated fat: 7g; Cholesterol: 178mg; Sodium: 1,414mg; Carbohydrates: 13g; Fiber: 1g; Sugar: 2g; Protein: 54g.*

Salmon Crepes

Stuffed "anything" always makes an impressive presentation, but when you stuff crepes, you've achieved the peak of profound resplendence (or simply put, crepes look great plated). Chicken crepes are the usual offering, but these salmon crepes are a true taste triumph.

Preparation time: *15 minutes*

Cooking time: *10 to 15 minutes*

Yield: *4 servings*

Nonstick cooking spray	*¾ cup half-and-half*
1½ tablespoons butter	*1 egg*
1 green onion, sliced thin	*2 teaspoons sherry*
1 tablespoon cornstarch	*6-ounce can salmon, drained*
½ teaspoon salt	*4-ounce can mushroom stems and pieces, drained*
⅛ teaspoon pepper	
⅛ teaspoon dried thyme	*8 crepes (see the recipe in Chapter 9)*
⅛ teaspoon dried dill	*1 tablespoon grated Romano cheese*

1 Preheat the oven to 400 degrees. Using the cooking spray, grease a 9-x-9-inch baking dish.

2 In a medium saucepan, sauté the onion in butter over medium heat until the onion is soft but not browned.

3 Remove the pan from the heat.

4 In a small bowl, stir together the cornstarch, salt, pepper, thyme, dill, and half-and-half until well blended, and then add it to the butter and onions in the pan. Stir until blended.

5 Return the pan to the heat and cook the contents over medium heat, stirring constantly, until the mixture has thickened. Remove the pan from the heat.

6 In a medium bowl, whip the egg with a whisk. Very slowly, drizzle the half-and-half mixture into the egg, whisking constantly, until ¾ of the *roux* (the half-and-half mixture) has been incorporated. Stir the egg mixture into the remaining roux in the pan. Cook 1 minute over medium heat, stirring constantly, and then remove the pan from the heat.

7 Pour ¾ of the sauce into a medium bowl. Stir the sherry into the remaining sauce in the pan and set it aside.

8 Stir the salmon and mushrooms into the bowl with the reserved sauce.

9 Place a heaping tablespoon of the salmon mixture down the center of each crepe. Roll up the crepes, jelly-roll style, and place them in a single layer in the prepared baking dish. Pour the remaining sauce over the tops of the crepes, and then sprinkle with cheese.

10 Bake the crepes at 400 degrees for 10 to 15 minutes, or until they're heated through.

Per serving of 2 crepes: *Calories: 217; Total fat: 15g; Saturated fat: 9g; Cholesterol: 122mg; Sodium: 473mg; Carbohydrates: 9g; Fiber: 1g; Sugar: 2g; Protein: 13g.*

Seafood au Gratin

This absolutely delicious combination is perfect for a buffet table. Serve it with rice or gluten-free noodles to compete the entrée. Don't substitute milk for the half-and-half, or the sauce won't be as thick and rich. Use real crabmeat; the imitation crabmeat may not be gluten-free.

Preparation time: *15 minutes*

Cooking time: *30 minutes*

Yield: *6 servings*

Nonstick cooking spray	¼ cup sherry
3 tablespoons butter	14-ounce can quartered artichoke hearts
2 tablespoons cornstarch	Juice from artichokes
¼ cup plus 1¾ cups half-and-half	¾ pound crabmeat pieces
¼ teaspoon salt	½ pound raw shrimp, peeled and deveined
1 teaspoon dried parsley flakes	½ pound sea scallops, sliced into medallions
⅛ teaspoon dried red pepper flakes	⅓ cup slivered almonds
1 teaspoon minced dried onion	¼ cup grated Parmesan cheese
¾ cup shredded cheddar cheese	Paprika

1 Preheat the oven to 325 degrees. Grease a 9-x-13-inch glass baking dish with cooking spray.

2 In a medium saucepan, melt the butter.

3 In a small bowl, stir the cornstarch together with ¼ cup of the half-and-half until the mixture is smooth. Stir this into the butter in the pan.

4 Add the remaining half-and-half, salt, parsley, red pepper flakes, and dried onion to the cornstarch mixture. Over medium heat, cook the mixture, stirring constantly with a whisk, until the mixture has thickened.

5 Stir in the cheddar cheese until it melts. Remove from heat.

6 Drain the artichoke hearts, reserving the liquid. Stir the sherry and the artichoke juice into the sauce in the saucepan.

7 Place the artichoke hearts, crabmeat, shrimp, and scallops in the prepared baking dish.

8 Pour the cream sauce over the seafood. Sprinkle the top with almonds, Parmesan cheese, and very lightly with paprika.

9 Bake the seafood at 325 degrees for 30 minutes.

Per serving: *Calories: 461; Total fat: 27g; Saturated fat: 15g; Cholesterol: 183mg; Sodium: 667mg; Carbohydrates: 16g; Fiber: 4g; Sugar: 1g; Protein: 37g.*

Tuna Broccoli Casserole

Even people who don't like broccoli love this casserole. You can assemble this dish ahead of time, cover and refrigerate it, then bake it at dinnertime. Casseroles don't get much easier than this one. Don't omit the thyme — that's what gives this dish its special flavor. For this recipe, I used Progresso Creamy Mushroom Soup (which is already diluted). Because companies change their recipes and ingredients regularly, check the label ingredients to make sure the soup is gluten-free before you purchase it.

Preparation time: *15 minutes*

Cooking time: *25 minutes*

Yield: *6 servings*

Nonstick cooking spray

2 cups rice seashell pasta

2 tablespoons cornstarch

1 teaspoon gluten-free chicken bouillon granules

1 teaspoon dried minced onion flakes

¼ teaspoon dried thyme

1 tablespoon dried parsley flakes

¼ teaspoon pepper

⅛ teaspoon salt

12-ounce can tuna packed in water, drained

4-ounce jar chopped pimiento, drained

18-ounce can gluten-free cream of mushroom soup

3 tablespoons whole milk

10-ounce box frozen chopped broccoli, thawed

½ cup plus ¾ cup shredded Monterey Jack cheese

¼ cup seasoned gluten-free bread crumbs

¼ teaspoon paprika

1 Preheat the oven to 400 degrees. Using the cooking spray, grease a 9-x-9-inch baking dish.

2 In a medium saucepan, cook the pasta according to package directions, and then rinse and drain it.

3 In a large bowl, stir together the cornstarch, bouillon granules, onion flakes, thyme, parsley flakes, pepper, and salt. Add the pasta, tuna, pimiento, soup, milk, broccoli, and ½ cup of the cheese to the bowl. Stir to mix well.

4 Spoon the mixture into the prepared baking dish.

5 In a small bowl, stir together the remaining ¾ cup of cheese, bread crumbs, and paprika. Sprinkle this mixture on top of the casserole.

6 Bake the casserole at 400 degrees for 25 minutes.

Per serving: Calories: 385; Total fat: 13g; Saturated fat: 7g; Cholesterol: 40mg; Sodium: 406mg; Carbohydrates: 41g; Fiber: 3g; Sugar: 3g; Protein: 26g.

Chapter 12

Tastes Like Chicken: Poultry Dishes

In This Chapter

▶ Picking out popular chicken entrées

▶ Clucking over poultry casseroles

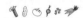
A barbecued chicken leg is hot off the grill, dripping with sauce, and sitting on your plate. You're starving, and the aroma is activating all of your sensory glands. Are you *really* going to use your fork and knife? Or are you going to dive down with both hands and pick it up? According to Emily Post, "Birds are not eaten with the fingers in company!" Fortunately, Miss Manners counters with the advice that hands can definitely be used in the enjoyment and consumption of said bird. (Like any of us really cares what either of them has to say!)

Few foods are as versatile as chicken. First, you need to decide what kind of chicken to buy — free-range or farm-raised, light meat or dark meat, whole chickens or separate parts, diced or shredded or strips, fresh or frozen, pre-marinated or plain, bone-in or boned. After you've made these decisions, then you have to figure out how you're going to prepare the bird. It can be grilled, stewed, baked, roasted, stuffed, broiled, boiled, oven-fried, deep-fried, pan-fried, microwaved, or cooked in a slow cooker. With all these choices, it can be difficult to pick just one.

The recipes in this chapter will come to your rescue. We have taken America's favorite food and dressed it up in new ways. Now the only decision you have to make is which of these recipes you're going to make first!

Flocking to Baked, Broiled, and Pan-Fried Dishes

Short of the chop-everything-into-one-baking-dish-and-cover-with-gluten-free-cream-of-mushroom-soup casseroles, the most common ways to prepare chicken are baked, broiled, and pan-fried. Below are some new ways to re-create the chicken dinner.

Honey Broiled Chicken

It doesn't seem possible that an entrée as simple to prepare as this one can taste so great. Your family will think you slaved for hours over a hot stove. (Go ahead, let them think that.) Use bone-in chicken pieces so the meat stays moist during broiling. If you opt to put the chicken on the grill, baste frequently with pan juices.

Preparation time: *8 minutes*

Cooking time: *35 minutes*

Yield: *4 servings*

Nonstick cooking spray	¼ teaspoon pepper
Four 6-ounce bone-in chicken thighs	½ teaspoon garlic powder
Juice from 1 lemon	5 teaspoons sugar
4 tablespoons butter	2 tablespoons brown mustard
½ teaspoon salt	4 teaspoons honey

1 Preheat the broiler. Spray a 9-x-9-inch baking dish with nonstick spray.

2 Place the chicken, skin side up, in the baking dish. Squeeze the lemon juice over the chicken.

3 Melt the butter in a small saucepan. Remove the saucepan from the heat and stir in the salt, pepper, and garlic powder. Spoon the butter sauce over the chicken thighs.

4 Broil the chicken for 20 minutes, turning once.

5 In a small bowl, stir together the sugar, mustard, and honey. Brush half of the mixture over the chicken pieces and return to the broiler for 10 minutes. Turn the chicken pieces over, brush with the remaining sauce, and broil for 5 minutes more.

Per serving: Calories: 201; Total fat: 13g; Saturated fat: 8g; Cholesterol: 65mg; Sodium: 638mg; Carbohydrates: 11g; Fiber: 0g; Sugar: 11g; Protein: 8g.

Corn Chip Chicken

Kids of all ages will love this. The coating stays crisp, and it's every bit as good as fried chicken. The breading will stick regardless of whether you keep the skin on the pieces. For convenience, you can bread the chicken ahead, cover it, and refrigerate it until baking time. This recipe uses chicken legs, but you can use the pieces your family likes best. Serve this once, and your family will beg you to make it again!

Tools: *Blender*

Preparation time: *10 minutes*

Cooking time: *45 minutes*

Yield: *5 servings*

9.75-ounce bag corn chips

¼ teaspoon pepper

½ teaspoon Cajun seasoning

¼ teaspoon garlic powder

1 teaspoon paprika

4 tablespoons melted butter

5 whole chicken legs (leg and thigh)

1 Preheat the oven to 375 degrees.

2 Pour half of the corn chips into a blender and purée; pour the fine crumbs into a self-seal plastic bag. Repeat with the second half of corn chips.

3 Add the pepper, Cajun seasoning, garlic powder, and paprika to the corn chips and mix well to distribute the spices evenly.

4 Dip one chicken piece into the melted butter, and then place it in the bag. Seal the bag and shake it to coat the chicken with crumbs. Repeat with the remaining chicken pieces.

5 Place the chicken in an 8-x-11-inch baking dish.

6 Bake the chicken at 375 degrees for 40 to 45 minutes, or until the chicken is just cooked through. (You don't need to turn the chicken pieces during cooking.)

Per serving (breaded without skin): Calories: 630; Total fat: 35g; Saturated fat: 37g; Cholesterol: 170mg; Sodium: 540mg; Carbohydrates: 32g; Fiber: 4g; Sugar: 0g; Protein: 41g.

Parmesan Chicken with Fresh Tomato Salsa

You may find it a little tricky to get the cheese coating to stick to the chicken. What works best is to pound the cheese in with the flat side of a meat mallet. Add no salt to the chicken — the cheese provides all the salt needed.

Tools: *Meat mallet*

Preparation time: *15 minutes*

Cooking time: *15 minutes*

Yield: *4 servings*

Four 4-ounce boneless skinless chicken breasts

8 teaspoons sherry

¼ teaspoon plus ¼ teaspoon pepper

2 cups coarsely shredded Parmesan cheese (do not use canned grated cheese)

⅓ cup gluten-free bread crumbs

1 tablespoon plus 3 tablespoons olive oil

½ medium onion, chopped

½ small green pepper, chopped

½ teaspoon minced garlic

2 teaspoons Italian seasoning

¼ teaspoon salt

4 plum Roma tomatoes, chopped

2 tablespoons minced fresh parsley

1 On a cutting board and using the meat mallet, pound the thicker portion of each chicken breast to make the thickness of the pieces uniform.

2 Pour the sherry into a shallow bowl.

3 Mix ¼ teaspoon of pepper, the cheese, and bread crumbs together on a sheet of wax paper.

4 Dip each chicken breast in the sherry, moistening both sides, and then press the breasts firmly into the cheese mixture, covering both sides of each breast. Use a meat mallet to help the cheese adhere to the meat.

5 In a medium skillet over medium heat, sauté the onion, green pepper, and garlic in 1 tablespoon of olive oil, stirring frequently, until the vegetables are tender. Stir in the Italian seasoning, salt, ¼ teaspoon of pepper, tomatoes, and parsley. Continue cooking until the mixture is heated through.

6 Preheat a large nonstick skillet over medium-high heat. Add 3 tablespoons of oil. Set the breasts in the skillet and cook 5 to 6 minutes per side, until the cheese is light golden and the chicken is cooked through.

7 Remove the breasts from the skillet and set them on paper toweling to drain the excess oil.

8 To serve, place the chicken breasts on a serving platter and spoon the tomato salsa over the chicken breasts.

Per serving: Calories: 449; Total fat: 26g; Saturated fat: 10g; Cholesterol: 83mg; Sodium: 1,034mg; Carbohydrates: 61g; Fiber: 1g; Sugar: 2g; Protein: 38g.

Creole Chicken

As the Caribbean song so aptly says, "Hot! Hot! Hot!" I've tamed this version of Creole Chicken somewhat to accommodate most tastes, but if you like *really* spicy hot food, add more cayenne pepper.

Preparation time: *10 minutes*

Cooking time: *50 minutes*

Yield: *4 servings*

1 tablespoon olive oil	8-ounce can tomato sauce
2 cloves garlic, minced	1 cup water
1 medium onion, thinly sliced	2 bay leaves
2 ribs celery, thinly sliced	½ teaspoon salt
½ green pepper, finely diced	⅛ rounded teaspoon cayenne pepper
1 tablespoon dried parsley flakes	Four 5-ounce bone-in skinless chicken breasts

1 Preheat the oven to 350 degrees.

2 In a medium skillet over medium heat, sauté the garlic, onion, celery, and green pepper in oil, stirring frequently, until tender (about 4 minutes).

3 Stir in the parsley flakes, tomato sauce, water, bay leaves, salt, and cayenne pepper. Simmer 2 more minutes.

4 Place the chicken in a 9-x-9-inch baking dish. Pour the sauce over the chicken.

5 Bake the chicken at 350 degrees for 35 minutes and then cover with foil and bake another 15 minutes until the chicken is very tender.

Per serving: Calories: 194; Total fat: 5g; Saturated fat: 0g; Cholesterol: 68mg; Sodium: 707mg; Carbohydrates: 8g; Fiber: 2g; Sugar: 5g; Protein: 29g.

Stuffed Rock Cornish Game Hens

Ask the butcher to cut each hen in half. Hens come defeathered, but they tend to have a few straggling hairs, so clean the hens well before prepping. (How impressive would it be to set this fancy presentation in front of guests . . . and then they spot hairs protruding from the carcass? There goes the ambiance!) Soak the rice early in the day.

Preparation time: *25 minutes*

Cooking time: *1½ hours*

Yield: *4 servings*

1 cup rice	3 tablespoons slivered almonds
2 Rock Cornish game hens, halved	1 large red pepper, roasted and chopped
2 tablespoons olive oil	¼ teaspoon dried dill
¼ teaspoon plus ¼ teaspoon salt	¼ teaspoon dried mint
¼ teaspoon plus ¼ teaspoon pepper	2 teaspoons dried parsley flakes
½ teaspoon paprika	½ cup half-and-half
1 tablespoon plus 2 tablespoons butter	2 tablespoons cornstarch
5 cups gluten-free chicken broth, divided	2 teaspoons brown mustard
½ cup sherry	2 ounces (about ½ cup) shredded Swiss cheese
2 green onions, sliced thin	

1 Early in the day, put the rice in a small bowl and cover it with water. Let it soak for several hours, and then rinse the rice in a strainer under cold water until the water runs clear. Drain.

2 Preheat the oven to 500 degrees.

3 Rub the oil over the hens, inside and out. Place the hens in a 9-x-13-inch baking dish, cut side down. Sprinkle them with ¼ teaspoon of salt and ¼ teaspoon of pepper, and the paprika. Cut 1 tablespoon of the butter into small pieces and place it on top of the hens. Pour 2 cups of the chicken broth and the sherry into the pan around the hens.

4 Bake the hens at 500 degrees for 5 minutes, and then lower the heat to 350 degrees and continue baking for 15 minutes. Cover the hens with foil and bake for 25 minutes more, or until the leg twists easily.

5 In a medium saucepan, sauté the onion and almonds in 2 tablespoons of butter over medium heat, stirring frequently, until the onion has softened. Add the roasted red pepper, 1 cup of chicken broth, ¼ teaspoon each of salt and pepper, dill, mint, and parsley. Bring to a boil.

6 Lower the heat and stir in the rinsed, drained rice. Cover the pan and cook approximately 15 minutes, or until the moisture has been absorbed. Remove from the heat.

7 In a small saucepan, stir together 2 cups of chicken broth, the half-and-half, cornstarch, and mustard. Using a whisk, stir until the mixture is smooth. Stir in the cheese and cook, stirring constantly, over medium heat until the sauce thickens.

8 To serve, place a compressed mound of rice on each dish. Place a hen half on top, and then spoon the sauce over the top.

Per serving: Calories: 871; Total fat: 52g; Saturated fat: 19g; Cholesterol: 217mg; Sodium: 1,853mg; Carbohydrates: 49g; Fiber: 3g; Sugar: 2g; Protein: 39g.

Poultry Casseroles That Will Fly Off the Plate

Think of casseroles as energy conservation. You bake everything in one pot, so you usually only have to clean one pot after dinner. You don't have to dish out a vegetable, a starch, and an entrée — with one large spoon, you can serve up an entire meal.

Casseroles also fall into the category of food conservation and utilization. Do you have two carrots at the bottom of your vegetable bin that are starting to dry out and one last green onion that's starting to outlive its prime? Chop them up, sauté them in a little oil until they're soft, and then add them to any casserole. It's a much wiser alternative than waiting two more days and then throwing them out. Other ingredients that are prime candidates for adding to casseroles include that partially used bag of peas in the back of your freezer, the last cube of gluten-free chicken bouillon that's been sitting in your cupboard since 1998, and bits of fresh spinach that are left in the bag from that spinach salad you made four days ago.

If you're looking for something besides gluten-free breadcrumbs to top your casseroles, try crushed Funyuns, crushed corn chips or potato chips, crushed gluten-free cereals, crumbled bacon, shredded cheese (add this toward the end of the baking time), gluten-free cracker crumbs, or chopped nuts.

Easy Company Chicken

Who really wants to spend all of their time in the kitchen preparing foods the day before company arrives? Casseroles don't get much easier than this one. And when your friends ring your doorbell, do you want to be stuck in the kitchen preparing last-minute foods, or would you rather be sitting down and enjoying their company? This casserole fills the bill because you can make it ahead and then bake it while you bond with your guests. This recipe was made with Progresso Creamy Mushroom Soup. At time of purchase, read the label to determine whether the soup is still gluten-free. The crackers used for this recipe were Blue Diamond Nut Thins Country Ranch, though most any gluten-free cracker works. Again, read the label before purchasing.

Preparation time: *10 minutes*

Cooking time: *50 minutes*

Yield: *6 servings*

6 large chicken thighs

18-ounce can gluten-free cream of mushroom soup (not condensed)

1½ cups plus ½ cup shredded sharp cheddar cheese

1.25-ounce package gluten-free taco seasoning mix

½ cup milk

2 cups crushed gluten-free crackers

1 Preheat the oven to 375 degrees.

2 Place the chicken thighs in an 8-x-11-inch baking dish.

3 In a medium bowl, stir together the soup, 1½ cups of cheese, taco seasoning mix, and milk. Spoon the mixture over the chicken.

4 Sprinkle with crushed crackers.

5 Cover the pan with foil and bake the casserole at 375 degrees for 40 minutes.

6 Remove the foil and sprinkle the casserole with the remaining ½ cup of cheese. Return the dish to the oven to bake for 10 minutes more, or until the cheese has melted.

Per serving: *Calories: 298; Total fat: 20g; Saturated fat: 11g; Cholesterol: 49mg; Sodium: 661mg; Carbohydrates: 15g; Fiber: 1g; Sugar: 4g; Protein: 14g.*

Grecian Chicken with Pasta

You have choices: Are you going to use rice pasta? Corn pasta? Lentil pasta? Each of these pastas requires a slightly different length of cooking time, so follow the package directions for cooking. That being said, for this recipe, don't cook the spaghetti as long as the package directs because the pasta is also baked after it's boiled. The gluten-free pastas tend to get mushy when overcooked.

Preparation time: *15 minutes*

Cooking time: *1 hour, 15 minutes*

Yield: *5 servings*

3 tablespoons butter

3½-pound chicken, cut into serving pieces

1 onion, chopped

Two 8-ounce cans tomato sauce

2 cups gluten-free chicken broth

¼ cup white wine

2 teaspoons cinnamon

½ teaspoon salt

¼ teaspoon pepper

1 pound gluten-free spaghetti (or other pasta)

3 tablespoons grated Parmesan cheese

1 Preheat the oven to 350 degrees.

2 Sauté the chicken pieces and onions in the butter in a large skillet over medium-high heat until the chicken is browned on both sides. Transfer the chicken and onions to a roasting pan.

3 Stir in the tomato sauce, chicken broth, white wine, cinnamon, salt, and pepper. Bake the chicken at 350 degrees for 1 hour, or until the chicken is very tender. (If the chicken gets too brown before it's cooked through, cover the pan with foil for the remainder of the baking time.)

4 Boil the spaghetti in a large saucepan of boiling water until the pasta is just barely tender, and then drain.

5 When the chicken is tender, stir the spaghetti into the chicken and sauce and return the pan to the oven for 15 minutes, stirring the spaghetti every 5 minutes. (You may need to add a little water to the sauce.)

6 Remove the casserole from the oven and sprinkle the top with cheese.

Per serving: *Calories: 904; Total fat: 41g; Saturated fat: 14g; Cholesterol: 171mg; Sodium: 1,112mg; Carbohydrates: 84g; Fiber: 4g; Sugar: 5g; Protein: 43g.*

Chicken Pot Pie

This dish is as Americana as it gets. Almost anything in the vegetable bin in your refrigerator that may be showing signs of age can be chopped up and added to this — asparagus, mushrooms, zucchini, broccoli, cauliflower, green beans, tossed salad (*Aha!* Just kidding about the tossed salad!). You can add the rest of that half-used jar of chopped pimento or roasted red peppers, too.

Tools: *Rolling pin*

Preparation time: *40 minutes*

Cooking time: *40 minutes*

Yield: *6 servings*

Pot Pie Pie Crust (see the following recipe)	*3 cups cooked, cubed chicken*
Nonstick cooking spray	*¼ teaspoon salt*
½ cup diced carrots	*¼ teaspoon pepper*
½ cup diced celery	*¼ cup cornstarch*
4 small red potatoes, chopped	*1 cup plus 1 cup gluten-free chicken broth*
1 small onion, chopped	*1 egg yolk*
½ cup frozen peas, thawed	*2 tablespoons water*

1 Preheat the oven to 400 degrees.

2 Make the Pot Pie Pie Crust.

3 Roll out half of the dough and place it in a 9-inch pie plate that has been sprayed with cooking spray.

4 Boil the carrots, celery, potatoes, and onions in water in a medium saucepan until they're tender. Drain.

5 In a large bowl, stir together the boiled vegetables, peas, chicken, salt, and pepper.

6 Place the cornstarch in a medium saucepan and add 1 cup of broth; whisk until the mixture is smooth. Put the pan on the stove over medium heat.

7 Stir in the remaining chicken broth and cook, stirring constantly, until the mixture has thickened. Remove from the heat.

8 Pour the gravy over the chicken and vegetables in the bowl and mix until the gravy is evenly distributed.

9 Spoon the mixture into the pastry-lined pie plate.

10 Roll out the remaining dough and place it on top of the pie. Seal the edges and *flute* (see the Tip paragraph at the end of the recipe for the how-to).

11 In a small bowl, whisk the egg yolk with 2 tablespoons of water. Brush on the pie crust.

12 Bake the pot pie at 400 degrees for 40 minutes, or until the crust is baked through.

Tip: To flute the pie crust, tuck the edges of the top crust under the edges of the bottom crust to assure a firm seal so the filling won't escape during baking.

Pot Pie Pie Crust

1¾ cups gluten-free flour mixture

¾ cup cornstarch

2½ teaspoons baking powder

¼ teaspoon dried thyme

¾ teaspoon salt

1 tablespoon sugar

¾ cup shortening

1 egg, slightly beaten

1 tablespoon vinegar

1 In a medium bowl, whisk together the flour mixture, cornstarch, baking powder, thyme, salt, and sugar.

2 With a pastry blender or two knives, cut in the shortening until the mixture resembles fine crumbs.

3 Stir the egg and vinegar into the flour mixture. Add ice water, 1 tablespoon at a time, and blend in just until the dough sticks together and forms a ball.

4 Divide the dough in half and roll each half into a ball.

5 Working on a flat surface, place each ball between two sheets of plastic wrap.

6 With a rolling pin, roll each dough ball into a 10-inch circle. Use as directed in the Chicken Pot Pie recipe.

Per serving: Calories: 703; Total fat: 30g; Saturated fat: 8g; Cholesterol: 126mg; Sodium: 949mg; Carbohydrates: 66g; Fiber: 5g; Sugar: 5g; Protein: 26g.

Slow Cooker Chicken with Spinach and Mushrooms

If you work outside the home, or if you opt to take the kids swimming all day instead of staying at home to cook in a hot kitchen, then this is the meal for you. In the morning, dump everything into a slow cooker, put on the lid, and then go enjoy your day. This meal is excellent served over rice or gluten-free noodles.

Tools: *Slow cooker*

Preparation time: *5 minutes*

Cooking time: *8 hours*

Yield: *4 servings*

Two 10-ounce boxes frozen, chopped spinach, thawed

8-ounce can sliced mushrooms, with liquid

18-ounce can gluten-free ready-to-serve cream of mushroom soup

¼ cup sherry

1 packet gluten-free dry onion soup mix

½ teaspoon pepper

¼ teaspoon dried thyme

Four 5-ounce skinless chicken thighs

1 Stir together all the ingredients, except the chicken, in the slow cooker.

2 Add the chicken thighs and stir them in so they're covered with the sauce.

3 Cover and cook on low for 8 hours.

Per serving: *Calories: 401; Total fat: 9g; Saturated fat: 2g; Cholesterol: 63mg; Sodium: 1,520mg; Carbohydrates: 19g; Fiber: 6g; Sugar: 4g; Protein: 21g.*

Chapter 13

Meat Matters

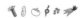
*I*f you're a vegetarian or cooking for one, you can skip this chapter and head to Chapter 14. But for those meat-and-potatoes people, or even those who love a healthy, veggie-filled lifestyle but enjoy the protein-packed punch of a tasty lean meat, read on.

The recipes in this chapter delve into the delights of beef, pork, and lamb. Sorry, but there are no recipes for buffalo, venison, antelope, wild turkey, or alligator, but being the fan I am of interesting foods, I'd suggest finding a recipe for your favorite off-beat meat and modifying it to be gluten-free if you're up for the challenge. If you need help modifying recipes, take a look at Chapter 7 for some pointers. And if you're looking for seafood and chicken recipes, see Chapters 11 and 12, respectively.

Gluten-Free . . . If You're Game

Yes, meat is gluten-free . . . initially. If you buy roasts, chops, or any other whole piece of meat, there's nothing to be concerned about from a gluten standpoint. If, however, you pick up a package of marinated beef kabobs or preseasoned pork tenderloin, you'll need to check what ingredients have been used in the marinade and seasonings.

When you buy meat from the deli department, be careful. Most of the premium meats sold there are solid meat, but some of the less expensive brands may use extenders. *Extenders* are inexpensive fillers and binders that can include wheat; they can enhance the flavor of processed meats, but they're primarily added to expand and extend the product. These fillers must be listed on the label, and manufacturers must list wheat on the label — so if you're reading carefully, you'll find it.

And then there's the enigma surrounding ground meats. If you pick up a package that says "ground beef," wouldn't you assume it was just beef that was ground up? Well, that may not necessarily be so. Some (granted, not many) meat processors add fillers that contain wheat products to their ground meats. Again, the ingredients in the fillers must be listed on the package ingredient label, but you still have to read the label to make sure it's safe for you to eat.

The Main Attractions: Beef, Pork, and Lamb

Three grades of beef are sold in grocery stores: prime, choice, and select.

- **Prime** is juicier and more tender than the other two grades because it has the most *marbling* (a fancy word for "fat specks").

- **Choice** beef is moderately marbled and generally slightly more "mature" than prime beef. It's the most popular grade purchased because it isn't as expensive as prime and it's more tender than select.

- **Select** is the leanest, so ultimately it's the healthiest, but because it has the least amount of marbling, it's usually tougher, less juicy, and less flavorful.

Let's see now . . . On one hand you have tender, juicy, flavorful; on the other hand you have healthier. And then you have the beef that's in the middle of the road. It's really a matter of preference.

Pork today is 35 percent to 50 percent leaner than it was just 30 years ago. Unfortunately, pork dries out when it's overcooked, primarily because of the lower fat content. You can avoid overcooking pork by paying close attention to the internal temperature with an accurate instant-read thermometer. Pork is cooked through when the thermometer registers 160 degrees. Always let the meat *rest* (that's a fancy word for letting it sit for a few minutes after it's cooked) before serving or carving so the juices can be reabsorbed into the center.

If you aren't partial to the taste of lamb, chances are you tasted mutton. Meat from older sheep is called *mutton,* and most people think it tastes disgusting, whereas the taste of spring lamb is succulent, delicious, and moist. When buying leg of lamb, you may find it challenging to figure out how much you need because of the bone. You're safe if you buy 1 pound for every two people to be served.

Glazed Filet Mignon with Blue Cheese

If you can take a second mortgage out on your home to afford the fillets, this definitely is the entrée to select when you want to totally impress someone. It takes almost no time to prepare, looks gorgeous, and tastes divine. To complete the ambiance and plate presentation, serve the steak on a bed of fresh or sautéed watercress. This recipe calls for blue cheese. Some blue cheese, like Gorgonzola, is made from mold grown on wheat bread, but many brands of blue cheese are now made synthetically and contain no wheat mold. Shropshire, Frigo, and Kraft are just three of the gluten-free blue cheeses on the market, but still check the ingredient label every time you purchase the cheese to be sure the product is still gluten-free.

Preparation time: *7 minutes*

Cooking time: *10 minutes*

Yield: *4 servings*

¼ teaspoon salt	Four 4-ounce filet mignons
¼ teaspoon pepper	2 tablespoons gluten-free soy sauce
⅛ teaspoon paprika	2 teaspoons balsamic vinegar
⅛ teaspoon cumin	2 teaspoons dry red wine
⅛ teaspoon garlic powder	2 tablespoons butter
⅛ teaspoon cayenne pepper	4 tablespoons gluten-free blue cheese

1 In a small bowl, stir together the salt, pepper, paprika, cumin, garlic powder, and cayenne pepper.

2 Rub the spices onto both sides of the steaks.

3 In the same small bowl, combine the soy sauce, vinegar, and wine. Set the mixture aside.

4 Heat a nonstick skillet over medium-high heat.

5 Melt the butter in the skillet, and then add the steaks. Cook for 1 minute on each side to brown.

6 Reduce the heat to medium and cook for 3 minutes.

7 Turn the steaks. Pour the soy mixture over the meat and continue to cook for 3 to 4 more minutes (depending on the thickness of the steaks and the desired doneness).

8 Spoon 1 tablespoon of the blue cheese on top of each steak. Cover the pan with a lid to seal in the steam until the cheese begins to melt.

Per serving: *Calories: 336; Total fat: 21g; Saturated fat: 10g; Cholesterol: 117mg; Sodium: 880mg; Carbohydrates: 2g; Fiber: 0g; Sugar: 1g; Protein: 33g.*

Asian Chop Suey

Chop suey is a dish that traditionally consists primarily of vegetables, but may also include meat, poultry, or seafood. Here, it's served with sticky rice, which is actually a type of rice, not necessarily the method of cooking. Sticky rice is short-grain rice that is glutinous and sticky when cooked. (*Glutinous* doesn't refer to the gluten found in wheat, rye, or barley and, when derived from rice, is permissible on a gluten-free diet.)

Preparation time: *30 minutes, plus 2 hours (or overnight) to marinate meat*

Cooking time: *30 minutes*

Yield: *6 servings*

4 tablespoons plus 1 teaspoon sesame oil, divided	2½ cups water
1 teaspoon sugar	4 green onions, sliced on the diagonal
½ teaspoon ginger	¼ pound sliced mushrooms
¼ teaspoon plus ¼ teaspoon salt	2 stalks celery, sliced
¼ teaspoon pepper	2 cups fresh broccoli florets, sliced
3 tablespoons gluten-free soy sauce	1 large carrot, sliced thin on the diagonal
2 tablespoons sherry	8-ounce can baby corn, drained
1 pound flank steak, sliced thin across grain	¾ cup bamboo shoots, rinsed
1½ cups short-grain (sticky) rice	18 snow pea pods
⅓ cup pine nuts	2 tablespoons cornstarch
	1 cup gluten-free chicken broth

1 Place 2 tablespoons of the sesame oil, the sugar, ginger, ¼ teaspoon of the salt, the pepper, soy sauce, and sherry in a gallon-size self-seal bag; seal the bag and shake it to combine the contents evenly.

2 Add the meat, reseal the bag, and marinate the meat for 2 hours or overnight in the refrigerator.

3 Before mealtime, soak the rice for 5 minutes in enough warm water to cover it; drain the rice and rinse it with cold water.

4 In a medium saucepan, sauté the pine nuts in 1 teaspoon of the sesame oil over medium-high heat, stirring frequently, until the nuts are lightly browned. Add the 2½ cups water; turn the heat to high, and bring to a boil.

5 Stir in the drained rice, and then cover the pan, lower the heat, and simmer the rice and nuts for 20 minutes, or until the liquid has been absorbed. Remove the pan from the heat and let it stand for 10 minutes.

6 In a wok or a large skillet, heat 1 tablespoon of the sesame oil. Remove the meat from the marinade and stir-fry it over high heat until it's browned on the outside. (Cook for about 1 minute for medium rare. Don't overcook the meat or it will become tough.) Remove the meat to a plate.

7 Heat the remaining 1 tablespoon of oil in the same skillet or wok. Add the onions, mushrooms, celery, broccoli, and carrots. Stir-fry over high heat for 1 minute.

8 Add the corn, bamboo shoots, snow peas, and the remaining ¼ teaspoon of salt. Continue to stir-fry for 1 minute more. Add the reserved marinade and cook for 2 minutes.

9 Stir in the meat and heat 30 seconds or until the meat is warmed.

10 Place the cornstarch in a small bowl. Slowly whisk in the chicken broth until the mixture is smooth.

11 Pour the cornstarch mixture over the meat and vegetables and stir constantly over medium heat until the sauce thickens and the ingredients are evenly coated (about 12 seconds).

Per serving: Calories: 508; Total fat: 18g; Saturated fat: 3g; Cholesterol: 262mg; Sodium: 802mg; Carbohydrates: 9g; Fiber: 4g; Sugar: 33g; Protein: 34g.

The pros of eating plenty of protein

Do you ever wonder what all the hype is about protein? Well for one thing, cells are made up mostly of protein. For another, protein helps the body resist disease. And we know that every adult needs a minimum of 1 gram of protein for every 10 pounds of body weight to keep from slowly breaking down our tissues. And then there's the fact that protein helps maintain our energy levels throughout the day. Okay, so maybe protein *is* good for us.

Beef, pork, chicken, fish, beans, and other high-protein foods can help you feel full for a longer period of time, and the body uses up more energy to digest these proteins (that's good). But just because protein is good for us, doesn't mean you should eat unlimited amounts. Too much protein can weaken our bones and can sometimes be tough on the kidneys (that's bad).

Beef Pot Roast a la Mushrooms

The directions for this recipe tell you to cut the meat into cubes. If you prefer to leave the roast whole, add a half hour to the roasting time. Let the whole roast cool, and then cut it into thin slices. (This makes the best cold sandwich!) The beef is excellent served over gluten-free noodles.

Preparation time: *10 minutes*

Cooking time: *3 hours*

Yield: *4 servings*

2 pounds lean chuck steak, cut into 1-inch cubes

⅛ teaspoon plus ⅛ teaspoon salt

¼ teaspoon plus ⅛ teaspoon pepper

3 tablespoons chopped parsley

2 green onions, sliced

2 tablespoons gluten-free soy sauce

1 cup water

14.5-ounce can gluten-free beef broth

2 tablespoons Italian salad dressing

1 clove garlic, minced

2 tablespoons butter

16 ounces fresh mushroom slices

1 tablespoon minced parsley

1 Preheat the oven to 350 degrees.

2 Place the steak cubes in a 9-x-9-inch baking pan. Add ⅛ teaspoon of salt, ¼ teaspoon of pepper, the chopped parsley, onions, soy sauce, water, beef broth, Italian salad dressing, and garlic. Cover the pan securely with heavy-duty foil.

3 Roast the steak at 350 degrees for 3 hours.

4 Melt the butter in a large skillet. Add the mushrooms, ⅛ teaspoon of salt, ⅛ teaspoon of pepper, and the minced parsley and sauté on high heat, stirring often, until the mushrooms are browned and glazed.

5 To serve, spoon the beef onto a plate, and then spoon the mushrooms on top.

Tip: You can also prepare this meat in a slow cooker — just be sure to reduce the water to ¼ cup.

Per serving: *Calories: 421; Total fat: 23g; Saturated fat: 10g; Cholesterol: 163mg; Sodium: 1,382mg; Carbohydrates: 4g; Fiber: 1g; Sugar: 2g; Protein: 47g.*

Glazed Corned Beef

Never have you eaten corned beef like this. The mustard and dark corn syrup combine to create a phenomenal taste that infiltrates every pore of the meat. You'll definitely want to make extra so you'll have leftovers for corned beef sandwiches the next day.

Preparation time: *10 minutes*

Cooking time: *2 hours, 50 minutes*

Yield: *4 servings*

2½-pound lean corned beef brisket	1 clove garlic, quartered
2 onions, peeled and quartered	3 whole cloves
2 bay leaves	½ cup dark corn syrup
¼ teaspoon pepper	1 tablespoon brown mustard

1 Put the corned beef brisket in a large saucepan or Dutch oven. Add enough water to cover.

2 Add the onion, bay leaves, pepper, garlic, and cloves.

3 Bring to a boil; reduce the heat, cover, and simmer for 2 hours and 45 minutes, or until the meat is very tender.

4 In a small saucepan, stir together the corn syrup and mustard. Bring to a boil; reduce the heat and simmer for 5 minutes, stirring occasionally. Let the glaze cool.

5 Preheat the broiler.

6 Remove the brisket from the water and discard the water and vegetables.

7 Trim the excess fat from the beef place it in a broiler pan.

8 Spoon the glaze over the top of the meat.

9 Broil the brisket for 3 to 4 minutes, or until the meat is heated through. Watch the meat closely and remove it from the broiler as soon as it's glazed.

Tip: If you want to save time at dinnertime, you can simmer the corned beef ahead of time, and then slice it and set it in a broiler pan that is lined with foil. Shape the foil closely around the meat slices to keep the slices as close as possible and shaped in a loaf. Just before serving, spoon the glaze over the meat and broil until the meat has warmed and is glazed.

Per serving: *Calories: 704; Total fat: 42g; Saturated fat: 13g; Cholesterol: 153mg; Sodium: 3,313mg; Carbohydrates: 38g; Fiber: 1g; Sugar: 13g; Protein: 42g.*

Pork Chops with Caramelized Onions

It's amazing what adding a speck of brown sugar to sliced onions in a skillet will do to transform these vegetable slivers into delicacies. The caramelized onions give pork chops an entirely new depth of taste. You definitely want to watch the cooking time closely with these pork chops so they remain moist and tender.

Preparation time: 20 minutes, plus 2 hours to marinate meat

Cooking time: 10 minutes

Yield: 4 servings

Four ¾-inch thick pork chops	1 large white onion, sliced thin
½ cup marsala wine	7-ounce can sliced mushrooms, drained
Nonstick cooking spray	1 teaspoon brown sugar
¼ teaspoon salt	⅓ cup hot water
⅛ teaspoon pepper	1 gluten-free chicken bouillon cube
8 slices bacon	

1 Place the pork chops and wine in a gallon-size self-seal bag and marinate the meat for 2 hours in the refrigerator.

2 Preheat the broiler. Spray a 8-x-11-inch baking dish with cooking spray.

3 Remove the chops from the marinade and sprinkle them with salt and pepper. Set them in the prepared baking dish.

4 In a large skillet, cook the bacon, drain it on paper toweling, and then crumble it. Reserve 2 tablespoons of the bacon drippings.

5 Add the onions and mushrooms to the drippings in the skillet and cook over medium heat, stirring occasionally, until the onions begin to soften.

6 Stir the brown sugar into the skillet and cook for 5 minutes longer, or until the onions are completely browned.

7 In a small bowl, stir together the water and bouillon until the cube has dissolved. Add this to the onions and boil until the liquid is reduced by half, scraping up any browned bits from the bottom of the skillet.

8 Stir in the bacon.

9 Broil the pork chops for about 5 minutes per side, or just until the meat is cooked through and the internal temperature reaches 160 degrees.

10 Spoon the onion-mushroom mixture over the pork chops to serve.

Per serving: Calories: 529; Total fat: 38g; Saturated fat: 14g; Cholesterol: 128mg; Sodium: 1,320mg; Carbohydrates: 5g; Fiber: 1g; Sugar: 2g; Protein: 37g.

Baked Pork Chops

At the beginning of this section I state that if you overcook pork chops, they become tough. This dish is the exception. The longer you bake this dish, the more tender the meat becomes, until it gets so tender that it falls off the bone.

Preparation time: 10 minutes

Cooking time: 2 hours

Yield: 4 servings

Four ¾-inch thick bone-in pork chops	½ cup chopped celery
½ teaspoon salt	½ cup chopped onion
¼ teaspoon pepper	1 tablespoon brown sugar
2 tablespoons olive oil	1 teaspoon yellow mustard
8-ounce can tomato sauce	¼ teaspoon cinnamon
1 cup water	

1 Preheat the oven to 350 degrees.

2 Sprinkle both sides of the pork chops with salt and pepper. In a large skillet, brown the chops in oil over medium-high heat.

3 After the chops are browned, place them in a shallow baking dish.

4 In a small bowl, stir together the tomato sauce, water, celery, onion, brown sugar, and mustard; pour the mixture over the chops.

5 Cover the pan with foil and bake the chops at 350 degrees for 45 minutes. Then uncover them and continue baking for 45 minutes more, or until the chops are so tender that they almost fall apart.

Tip: *When you serve the pork chops, you should have some sauce in the pan to spoon over the chops. If, during cooking, you see that the sauce is drying out and being absorbed too much, you may need to add a little water. Don't add more than 1 cup of water at a time. If you are baking in a glass dish, make sure the water being added is very hot because adding cold water can cause the dish to break.*

Per serving: *Calories: 544; Total fat: 27g; Saturated fat: 8g; Cholesterol: 172mg; Sodium: 761mg; Carbohydrates: 9g; Fiber: 2g; Sugar: 7g; Protein: 62g.*

Best Spare Ribs You'll Ever Eat!

The "best spare ribs you'll ever eat" isn't a guess or a boast — it's a fact! These are finger-licking, can't-get-enough, memory-making spare ribs.

Tools: *Dutch oven*

Preparation time: *1 hour*

Cooking time: *40 minutes*

Yield: *4 servings*

1 tablespoon brown sugar

¼ cup cider vinegar

5 cups water

1 tablespoon gluten-free beef bouillon granules

2 tablespoons molasses

¼ cup ketchup

2 teaspoons dry mustard

1 teaspoon gluten-free Worcestershire sauce

⅛ teaspoon cloves

½ teaspoon chili powder

¼ teaspoon cayenne pepper

3 pounds baby back ribs (2 slabs)

1 Early in the day (or the day before), put the sugar and vinegar in a large Dutch oven. Reduce over medium heat about 8 minutes until the vinegar and sugar form a syrup. (Watch carefully because the syrup will suddenly darken in color.)

2 Immediately add the water and bouillon granules. Stir in the molasses, ketchup, dry mustard, Worcestershire sauce, cloves, chili powder, and cayenne pepper. Bring it to a boil.

3 Cut each slab of ribs into smaller sections. Add them to the saucepan and simmer for 20 minutes.

4 Remove the pan from the heat. Remove the ribs and place them in a dish. Cover and refrigerate.

5 Cook the liquid over medium heat until it becomes thick and syrupy (about 25 minutes), stirring constantly during the last 5 minutes.

6 Remove the pan from the heat and pour the sauce into a bowl. (Yield will be about 1 cup of basting sauce.) Cool the sauce, then cover and refrigerate it.

7 Before dinner, preheat the oven to 350 degrees.

8 Place the ribs on a nonstick baking dish, with the underside facing up.

9 Baste well with the sauce and bake at 350 degrees for 20 minutes. Turn the ribs over and baste generously. Continue to bake for 20 to 25 minutes.

Per serving: *Calories: 607; Total fat: 28g; Saturated fat: 10g; Cholesterol: 218mg; Sodium: 673mg; Carbohydrates: 16g; Fiber: 0g; Sugar: 13g; Protein: 67g.*

Lamb Chops with Tiered Topping

Get out of the mind-set that lamb chops have to be broiled. If you have always broiled lamb chops before, you're in for a real treat with this baked version. This relatively easy-to-assemble entrée is impressive because people never tire of tiered.

Preparation time: *15 minutes*

Cooking time: *42 minutes*

Yield: *6 servings*

1 tablespoon minced garlic	*Six 4-ounce loin lamb chops*
3 tablespoons minced fresh mint (leaves only)	*6 thick lemon slices, seeds removed*
¼ cup minced fresh parsley	*6 large, firm white mushroom caps*
2 tablespoons gluten-free soy sauce	*⅛ teaspoon salt*
2 tablespoons plus 2 tablespoons butter, softened	*¼ teaspoon pepper*
	6 tablespoons shredded mozzarella cheese

1 Preheat the oven to 350 degrees. Line an 8-x-11-inch baking dish with foil, leaving enough overhang to cover the pan after it's filled.

2 In a small bowl, use a fork to mash together the garlic, mint, parsley, soy sauce, and 2 tablespoons of the butter.

3 Place the lamb chops in the lined baking dish.

4 Cover the tops of the chops with the herb mixture, dividing the mixture evenly. If any herb sauce remains in the bowl, drizzle it over the chops.

5 Lay 1 lemon slice on top of each chop.

6 Melt the remaining 2 tablespoons of butter; roll the mushroom caps in butter to coat. Set one cap on top of each lamb chop.

7 Sprinkle the chops with salt and pepper.

8 Seal the foil. Bake the chops at 350 degrees for 40 minutes.

9 Remove the chops from the oven and turn on the broiler. Fold back the foil. Sprinkle the cheese on top of the chops. Broil for 2 minutes, or until the cheese has melted.

Per serving: Calories: 308; Total fat: 28g; Saturated fat: 13g; Cholesterol: 75mg; Sodium: 530mg; Carbohydrates: 5g; Fiber: 1g; Sugar: 2g; Protein: 15g.

Barbecue Lamb Shanks

You've done the barbecue chicken and ribs bit; now it's time to expand your horizons to barbecue lamb. Cooking time may vary a bit depending on the size of the shanks. This succulent meat falls off the bone. Lamb shanks frequently have to be ordered from the meat department at your grocery store ahead of time.

Preparation time: *15 minutes*

Cooking time: *2 hours*

Yield: *4 servings*

4 lamb shanks, about ½ pound each	*½ cup water*
¼ teaspoon paprika	*1 tablespoon brown sugar*
¼ teaspoon garlic powder	*1 large onion, chopped*
¾ teaspoon salt	*1 tablespoon cider vinegar*
¼ teaspoon pepper	*½ teaspoon dry mustard*
2 tablespoons olive oil	*¼ teaspoon gluten-free Worcestershire sauce*
½ cup ketchup	

1 Preheat the oven to 325 degrees.

2 Sprinkle the lamb shanks with paprika, garlic powder, salt, and pepper.

3 In a large skillet or Dutch oven over medium-high heat, brown the shanks on all sides in the oil. Transfer the meat to an 8-x-11-inch baking dish.

4 Stir the ketchup, water, brown sugar, onion, vinegar, mustard, and Worcestershire sauce into the skillet, scraping any browned bits from the bottom of the pan. Spoon this mixture on top of the lamb shanks and cover the baking dish with foil.

5 Bake at 325 degrees for 2 hours, or until the meat is very tender.

Per serving: *Calories: 627; Total fat: 44g; Saturated fat: 20g; Cholesterol: 161mg; Sodium: 878mg; Carbohydrates: 15g; Fiber: 1g; Sugar: 12g; Protein: 42g.*

Mixing Up Meals with Ground Meats

Bad news and good news . . . Ground meats have issues that aren't associated with whole cuts of meats. In whole cuts, the interior of the meat is essentially sterile; bacteria are isolated to the surface. When meat is ground, bacterial contamination from the surface can be distributed throughout the meat.

Now the good news: Ground meat is now *irradiated* (zapped with rays), which kills the bacteria. And if you cook the meat properly as described in the following recipes, you won't have anything to worry about.

When buying ground meats, ask the butcher if the meat has had fillers added. Some stores add wheat-based fillers to ground hamburger. Sausage is always questionable, so read the label ingredients carefully.

Meatballs in Wine Sauce

Put away all of your other meatballs-in-some-kind-of-sauce recipes because you won't need them anymore. Whether these are served with toothpicks for a cocktail party or served over rice for dinner, the taste of these meatballs is remarkable. Use the most porous gluten-free bread you can find for toasting. This is one recipe where you can't take a shortcut by substituting garlic powder for the cloves of garlic.

Preparation time: *15 minutes*

Cooking time: *40 minutes*

Yield: *4 servings*

2 slices porous gluten-free bread, toasted	*2 tablespoons butter*
1 pound lean ground beef	*3 ounces (½ of a 6-ounce can) tomato paste*
1 egg	*½ teaspoon sugar*
¼ teaspoon salt	*½ cup red wine*
¼ teaspoon pepper	*1½ cups water*
2 cloves garlic, minced	

1 Crumble the toast into a medium bowl. Add the ground beef, egg, salt, pepper, and garlic. Mix thoroughly.

2 Form the meat mixture into small balls, and then roll into football-shaped ovals. You should have about 24 meatballs.

3 In a large skillet over medium heat, brown the meatballs in butter, turning frequently.

4 Add the tomato paste, sugar, red wine, and water, cover, and simmer for 30 minutes, adding more water only if needed.

Per serving: Calories: 310; Total fat: 14g; Saturated fat: 7g; Cholesterol: 137mg; Sodium: 478mg; Carbohydrates: 12g; Fiber: 2g; Sugar: 4g; Protein: 26g.

BBQ Meatloaf

The easiest way to crush the crackers for this recipe is to put them in a plastic bag and use a rolling pin. (This method makes less noise than using a hammer!) A blender is also effective in crushing the crackers, but then you have a big blender to wash (whereas the rolling pin stays clean). And if you have any leftover meatloaf, meatloaf sandwiches are always a big hit!

Preparation time: 15 minutes

Cooking time: 55 minutes

Yield: 4 servings

Nonstick cooking spray	1 teaspoon gluten-free Worcestershire sauce
2 tablespoons olive oil	1 teaspoon gluten-free soy sauce
½ cup onion, minced	1 pound lean ground beef
½ cup green pepper, minced	¼ teaspoon salt
1 clove garlic, minced	¼ teaspoon pepper
½ cup fresh parsley, chopped	½ cup shredded cheddar cheese
½ teaspoon gluten-free beef bouillon granules	⅓ cup gluten-free crushed crackers
2 tablespoons water	3 tablespoons gluten-free barbecue sauce
1 egg	

1 Preheat the oven to 350 degrees. Spray a 9-x-9-inch baking dish with cooking spray.

2 Over medium heat, sauté the onions, green pepper, and garlic in oil in a large skillet, stirring frequently, until the vegetables are tender and very lightly browned.

3 Stir in the parsley, bouillon granules, and water. Simmer, stirring, until the liquid has been absorbed. Remove the skillet from the heat and let it cool slightly.

4 In a medium bowl, whisk together the egg, Worcestershire sauce, and soy sauce. Add the ground beef, salt, pepper, and sautéed vegetables. Combine until well mixed.

5 Mix in the cheese and crushed crackers.

6 Transfer the meat mixture to the baking dish. Shape the meat into a loaf about 3 inches thick; smooth the top.

7 Brush the top of the loaf with the barbecue sauce.

8 Bake at 350 degrees for 55 minutes, or until the center of the loaf is no longer pink. Let the loaf stand for 5 minutes before slicing.

Tip: *You can portion the meat mixture into four muffin tins for individual meat pies. The muffin-sized loaves only take about 40 minutes to bake at 350 degrees.*

Per serving: Calories: 398; Total fat: 23g; Saturated fat: 8g; Cholesterol: 137mg; Sodium: 738mg; Carbohydrates: 18g; Fiber: 1g; Sugar: 7g; Protein: 29g.

Italian Hamburger Pasta Casserole

Who doesn't love pasta? Make up a large pan of this for the gang, add a tossed salad, and dinner is ready. Leftovers fit nicely into a thermos for lunch — don't forget to pack a fork!

Preparation time: *15 minutes*

Cooking time: *60 minutes*

Yield: *10 servings*

1 pound gluten-free pasta shells or elbow macaroni	*¾ teaspoon dried basil*
2 tablespoons olive oil	*½ teaspoon salt*
2½ pounds lean ground beef	*¼ teaspoon pepper*
2 medium onions, diced	*14.5-ounce can diced tomatoes with juice*
3 cloves garlic, minced	*Two 15-ounce cans tomato sauce*
3 tablespoons minced fresh parsley	*1 cup water*
¾ teaspoon cinnamon	*½ cup grated Parmesan cheese*

1 Preheat the oven to 350 degrees.

2 In a large saucepan, boil the pasta, stirring occasionally, until the pasta is barely tender (about 6 minutes). Rinse it under cold running water, and then drain in a colander.

3 Add the olive oil to the same saucepan, and brown the beef, onions, and garlic over medium-high heat, breaking up the meat with a fork.

4 Stir the parsley, cinnamon, basil, salt, pepper, diced tomatoes and juice, tomato sauce, and 1 cup of water into the meat mixture and simmer, stirring often, for 3 minutes. Stir in the pasta and mix to blend.

5 Spoon the mixture into a 9-x-13-inch pan. Sprinkle the top with cheese.

6 Bake the dish at 350 degrees for 1 hour.

Per serving: Calories: 404; Total fat: 21g; Saturated fat: 4g; Cholesterol: 73mg; Sodium: 766mg; Carbohydrates: 47g; Fiber: 3g; Sugar: 5g; Protein: 27g.

Meatballs in Lemon Sauce

How many times in your life have you boiled meatballs? If the answer is zero, you're in for a taste treat. The flavor emitted from the meatballs as they cook converts the water in the pan into a wonderful broth.

Tools: *Dutch oven, electric mixer*

Preparation time: *15 minutes*

Cooking time: *35 minutes*

Yield: *4 servings*

1 pound lean ground beef	*¼ cup uncooked rice*
1 small onion, minced	*3 tablespoons cornstarch*
¼ teaspoon salt	*1 tablespoon olive oil*
¼ teaspoon pepper	*2 eggs*
2 tablespoons chopped fresh parsley	*Juice of 1 lemon*
½ teaspoon dried mint	*Salt to taste*

1 In a medium bowl, mix together the ground beef, onion, salt, pepper, parsley, mint, and rice.

2 Shape the mixture into balls a little smaller in size than a ping-pong ball. You'll have about 24 meatballs.

3 Dust the meatballs lightly in cornstarch.

4 Place the meatballs in a Dutch oven and add enough water to cover them. Add the oil. Bring the water to a boil, and then lower the heat to medium-low and let the meatballs simmer for 30 minutes.

5 In a medium mixing bowl, use the mixer to whip the eggs for 2 minutes. Add the lemon juice.

6 Remove the pan with the meatballs from the stove.

7 Add ⅔ of the meatball broth, in a slow steady stream, to the eggs, whipping constantly. Taste the sauce; add salt to taste.

8 Pour the lemon sauce over the meatballs and the remaining sauce in the in the Dutch oven and cook for 2 minutes over very low heat. (Don't permit the mixture to boil or the eggs will curdle.) Serve immediately.

Vary It! *If you're mentally prepared to break all previous culinary boundaries, you can substitute ground lamb for the ground beef.*

Per serving: *Calories: 337; Total fat: 13g; Saturated fat: 5g; Cholesterol: 188mg; Sodium: 248mg; Carbohydrates: 18g; Fiber: 1g; Sugar: 1g; Protein: 35g.*

Marinated Kielbasa

Of course, you should always read the ingredients of any package you buy, but this holds especially true when buying sausage. Many fillers used in making sausage contain wheat and wheat byproducts. Fortunately, many brands of gluten-free sausage are available. You can make this recipe with gluten-free kielbasa, bratwurst, or any of the plain, hot, or flavored sausages. And just when you thought you didn't have to make any more choices . . .

Preparation time: *5 minutes, plus 1 hour to marinate*

Cooking time: *10 minutes*

Yield: *4 servings*

1½ tablespoons dark corn syrup

2 teaspoons olive oil

¼ teaspoon powdered ginger

1 teaspoon brown mustard

1 teaspoon gluten-free Worcestershire sauce

1 teaspoon gluten-free soy sauce

1 pound kielbasa links

1 Place the corn syrup, oil, ginger, mustard, Worcestershire sauce, and soy sauce in a gallon-size self-seal bag. Swish it around to blend the ingredients.

2 Add the kielbasa to the bag. Seal the bag and push the sausage around so it's evenly covered with marinade.

3 Refrigerate the sausage for at least 1 hour.

4 Preheat the broiler.

5 Remove the kielbasa from the bag and place it on a broiler pan. Drizzle the marinade over the top of the meat.

6 Broil the meat for approximately 10 minutes, turning several times, until the kielbasa is barely charred on the outside and cooked through.

Per serving: Calories: 298; Total fat: 22g; Saturated fat: 7g; Cholesterol: 79mg; Sodium: 137mg; Carbohydrates: 11g; Fiber: 0g; Sugar: 2g; Protein: 15g.

Greek Hamburger Vegetable Casserole

This casserole takes a little extra time to prepare, but every moment is worth it. This goes *so* beyond eggplant parmigiana! Although this casserole is more than substantial as an entrée, it doubles as an excellent side dish on a buffet. If you don't tell the kids that there's eggplant in it, they'll love it, too.

Preparation time: *35 minutes*

Cooking time: *45 minutes*

Yield: *6 servings*

Nonstick cooking spray	½ teaspoon cinnamon
2 tablespoons olive oil	1 large zucchini, sliced ¼ inch thick
½ pound lean ground beef	1 large yellow squash, sliced ¼ inch thick
2 cloves garlic, minced	1 medium eggplant, peeled, sliced ¼ inch thick
1 medium onion, diced	1½ tablespoons cornstarch
¼ cup water	1 cup milk
¼ cup white wine	1 tablespoon butter
2 tablespoons tomato paste	1 egg
2 tablespoons minced fresh parsley	⅛ teaspoon nutmeg
½ teaspoon salt	½ cup small curd cottage cheese
½ teaspoon pepper	½ cup gluten-free bread crumbs, divided
1 teaspoon dried oregano	⅓ cup grated Romano cheese, divided

1 Preheat broiler. Spray a baking sheet and a 9-x-9-inch baking dish with cooking spray.

2 Add the olive oil to a medium skillet and brown the beef, garlic, and onion, breaking the meat up with a fork.

3 Add the water, wine, tomato paste, parsley, salt, pepper, oregano, and cinnamon. Simmer it on low heat, stirring frequently, until all the liquid has been absorbed. Remove from the heat.

4 Place zucchini, squash, and eggplant on the baking sheet. Spray the tops of the vegetables with the cooking spray. Broil the vegetables, turning once. Remove the zucchini and squash when both sides are golden. The eggplant may not brown as much as the squash, but it's done baking when it's tender.

5 In a small saucepan, stir together the milk and cornstarch. Turn on the heat to medium and warm the milk, stirring constantly with a whisk, until the mixture has thickened. Stir in the butter until it melts. Remove from the heat and cool slightly.

6 Whisk the egg in a small bowl until it's frothy. Stir in the nutmeg and cottage cheese. Stir this into the milk mixture.

7 Preheat the oven to 350 degrees. Sprinkle 2 tablespoons of the bread crumbs on the bottom of the baking dish.

8 Layer half of the broiled vegetables in the prepared dish. Spoon half of the meat mixture over the top vegetables. Sprinkle with half of the remaining bread crumbs and half of the Romano cheese. Repeat the layers. Smooth the cottage cheese mixture over the top. Sprinkle the remaining bread crumbs over the top.

9 Bake the dish at 350 degrees for 45 minutes, or until the topping is golden. Cool slightly before cutting.

Tip: *Make this dish on the weekend and freeze it before baking if you want to serve it on a busy weeknight. Just remember to thaw it before baking.*

Per serving: Calories: 310; Total fat: 16g; Saturated fat: 7g; Cholesterol: 86mg; Sodium: 723mg; Carbohydrates: 21g; Fiber: 5g; Sugar: 8g; Protein: 21g.

Chapter 14

Making Memories with Meatless Dishes

Meatless dishes are perceived to be a challenge on a gluten-free diet because so many vegetarian or vegan dishes use pasta. The good news is that *lots* of really great gluten-free pastas are available; the other good news is that veggies are gluten-free! All of them!

So let's talk veggies, starting with the incredible side dishes you can make with very little effort.

Veggin' Out with Side Dishes

Side dishes with veggies add flavor, nutrition, and color to a dinner plate. For a festive presentation, sprinkle the dish with minced parsley before putting the vegetables on the plate. If you want to get really wild and crazy, add some edible flowers, like nasturtiums.

Cooking vegetables is somewhat of an art, and we have some helpful hints to help you make the best of your veggies. Here are a few suggestions to keep in mind:

✔ All vegetables that grow above ground can start cooking in boiling water.

✔ For those that grow beneath the ground (beets, turnips, and so on), start in cold water.

✔ Many vegetables can be grilled (leeks, onions, asparagus, eggplant, and so on). Just slather them with a little olive oil and some seasonings before grilling.

✔ Salted eggplant absorbs less fat than unsalted eggplant when it's fried or sautéed. Sprinkle the slices with salt and place them in a colander in the sink. Let them set for 30 minutes, and then rinse the slices in cool water and pat them dry with paper towels.

✔ Peeled sweet potatoes can be substituted for white potatoes in many recipes.

✔ Whether you steam, grill, roast, stir-fry, or pan-fry your veggies, try to include them in as many meals as possible.

By adding a tossed salad, some of the selections in this section can double as a meatless entrée.

Broccoli Cauliflower Combo

The topping on this casserole is "fun" — crumbled Funyuns are used. As of the writing of this book, Funyuns (sold in the chips aisle) are gluten-free. Should the ingredients on the package change, you can use crushed potato chips instead.

Preparation time: *8 minutes*

Cooking time: *30 minutes*

Yield: *6 servings*

Nonstick cooking spray	*1½ cups processed cheese*
10-ounce box frozen cauliflower	*18-ounce can gluten-free ready-to-serve*
Two 10-ounce boxes frozen broccoli	*cream of mushroom soup*
2 tablespoons slivered almonds	*1 cup plus 1 cup crushed Funyuns*

1 Preheat the oven to 350 degrees. Spray a 9-x-9-inch baking dish with cooking spray.

2 Place the cauliflower and broccoli in a medium saucepan and cover the vegetables with water.

3 Bring the water to a boil, and then simmer the vegetables for 2 minutes.

4 Drain the vegetables in a colander, and then transfer them to the prepared baking dish.

5 Sprinkle the almonds over the vegetables.

6 In a small mixing bowl, stir together the cheese, soup, and 1 cup of crushed Funyuns; pour the mixture over the broccoli and cauliflower.

7 Sprinkle the remaining 1 cup of crushed Funyuns on top of the casserole.

8 Bake the vegetables at 350 degrees for 30 minutes.

Per serving: *Calories: 288; Total fat: 17g; Saturated fat: 7g; Cholesterol: 23mg; Sodium: 948mg; Carbohydrates: 25g; Fiber: 6g; Sugar: 6g; Protein: 12g.*

Glazed Carrots with Walnuts

Carrots add so much color to a plated dish, and making an impressive side dish simply doesn't get any easier than this. You can use pecans in place of the walnuts and pure maple syrup in place of the brown sugar.

Preparation time: *5 minutes*

Cooking time: *8 minutes*

Yield: *4 servings*

3 cups baby carrots	*¼ teaspoon cinnamon*
2 tablespoons butter	*⅛ teaspoon salt*
3 tablespoons chopped walnuts	*⅛ teaspoon pepper*
1½ tablespoons brown sugar	

1 Put the carrots in a medium saucepan and cover them with water. Boil until they're tender but not mushy. Drain.

2 While the carrots are draining, melt the butter in the same saucepan and add the walnuts.

3 Sauté the nuts for 1 minute, and then add the sugar, cinnamon, salt, and pepper. Stir to combine.

4 Stir in the carrots until they're evenly coated with the glaze.

Per serving: *Calories: 140; Total fat: 9g; Saturated fat: 4g; Cholesterol: 15mg; Sodium: 112mg; Carbohydrates: 141g; Fiber: 2g; Sugar: 11g; Protein: 1g.*

Spinach Pie

If you cut the slices of this pie a bit larger, this dish doubles as a meatless entrée. You can prepare it ahead, cover and refrigerate it, and then bake it just before dinner. After removing the dish from the oven, let it set for 10 minutes before cutting.

Preparation time: *15 minutes*

Cooking time: *45 minutes*

Yield: *12 servings*

Nonstick cooking spray

3 tablespoons butter

1 medium onion, chopped

3 large eggs

16-ounce container small curd cottage cheese

1 cup grated mozzarella cheese

1 cup grated Parmesan cheese

¼ teaspoon salt

½ teaspoon pepper

1 teaspoon dried dill

10-ounce box frozen chopped spinach, thawed and squeezed dry

1 Preheat the oven to 350 degrees. Spray a 9-inch pie plate with cooking spray.

2 Melt the butter in a large skillet over medium heat. Add the onion and sauté until tender, about 8 minutes.

3 In a large bowl, whisk the eggs lightly.

4 Stir in the cottage cheese, mozzarella, Parmesan cheese, salt, pepper, and dill.

5 Stir in the onions and spinach until everything is well blended

6 Spoon the mixture into the prepared pie plate.

7 Bake the pie at 350 degrees for 45 minutes, or until a knife inserted near the center comes out clean. If the pie begins to brown too much on top before being cooked through, cover it with a piece of foil.

8 Let the pie rest for 10 minutes before cutting it into 12 wedges.

Per serving: *Calories: 177; Total fat: 11g; Saturated fat: 7g; Cholesterol: 81mg; Sodium: 484mg; Carbohydrates: 4g; Fiber: 1g; Sugar: 1g; Protein: 16g.*

Stuffed Acorn Squash

The first ingredient in this recipe, 1 large acorn squash, has a qualifier after it — "halved and seeded." Sure, that's easy to write down, but have you ever tried to cut an acorn squash in half? The shell is harder than titanium! The easiest way to accomplish this feat is to take a strong, pointed knife and first make jabs that cut through the skin around the center of the vegetable. Then take a butcher knife and press down along the "jabbed" line . . . and good luck! This dish makes a beautiful presentation.

Preparation time: *15 minutes*

Cooking time: *1 hour*

Yield: *2 servings*

1 large acorn squash, halved and seeded

1 cup water

2 tablespoons butter, melted

½ teaspoon bottled lemon juice

¼ teaspoon cinnamon

2 tablespoons brown sugar

1 medium red or golden delicious apple, peeled, cored, and chopped fine

2 tablespoons chopped pecans

1 Preheat the oven to 375 degrees.

2 Place the squash, cut side down, on a small baking dish.

3 Pour the water onto the bottom of the dish and bake the squash at 375 degrees for 35 minutes. Remove the squash from the oven and discard the water in the pan.

4 In a bowl, stir together the butter, lemon juice, cinnamon, brown sugar, apple, and pecans.

5 Mound the apple mixture on top of the squash halves, dividing evenly.

6 Place the squash back in the baking dish, cut side up, and continue baking it at 375 degrees for another 30 to 35 minutes or until the flesh is tender when poked with a fork. If the top browns too much, cover it with foil during the last 15 minutes of baking.

Per serving: *Calories: 294; Total fat: 14g; Saturated fat: 8g; Cholesterol: 30mg; Sodium: 94mg; Carbohydrates: 45g; Fiber: 5g; Sugar: 20g; Protein: 3g.*

Cranberries and Yams

Did you know that yams and sweet potatoes are not related botanically? Yams are the starchier, but softer, of the two. In the United States, we just *think* we are buying yams. They are labeled "yams," and they may look darker than sweet potatoes, but they are merely a different variety of sweet potato, one with a softer center than those labeled "sweet potatoes."

Preparation time: *15 minutes*

Cooking time: *20 minutes*

Yield: *4 servings*

Nonstick cooking spray

2 large yams, peeled

¼ teaspoon cinnamon

¼ teaspoon plus ⅛ teaspoon salt

¼ teaspoon cumin

⅛ teaspoon pepper

¼ teaspoon garlic powder

2 tablespoons dried cranberries

2 teaspoons butter

1 large pear, peeled, cored, and cut into ½-inch cubes

¼ cup coarsely chopped pecans

¼ teaspoon ginger

1 teaspoon brown sugar

½ teaspoon balsamic vinegar

1 Preheat the oven to 450 degrees. Spray a baking sheet with cooking spray.

2 Cut each yam in half crosswise, and then into wedges.

3 In a plastic, self-seal bag, combine the cinnamon, ¼ teaspoon of salt, cumin, pepper, and garlic powder.

4 Add the yams. Seal the bag and shake it until the yams are evenly coated.

5 Lay the yam wedges in a single layer on the prepared baking sheet.

6 Bake the yams at 450 degrees for 30 to 35 minutes, or until the wedges are very tender, turning the yams once during baking.

7 While the yams bake, place the cranberries in a bowl of hot water to soak and soften for 5 minutes. Drain.

8 Melt the butter in a large nonstick skillet.

9 Add the pears and pecans and sauté them over medium heat until the pears are tender and golden, about 4 minutes, stirring frequently.

10 Stir in the cranberries, ginger, brown sugar, vinegar and remaining ⅛ teaspoon of salt, and heat until the sauce is warmed.

11 To serve, spoon the cranberry sauce over the yams.

Per serving: *Calories: 186; Total fat: 7g; Saturated fat: 2g; Cholesterol: 5mg; Sodium: 279mg; Carbohydrates: 31g; Fiber: 5g; Sugar: 13g; Protein: 2g.*

Carrot and Zucchini Latkes

The only thing that these latkes are missing is a dollop of sour cream on top. Enjoy them as a side dish, or serve several as a main entrée. The gluten-free bread crumbs in the recipe are readily available at most health food stores. The bread crumbs will stay fresher longer if you keep the unused portion in the freezer.

Preparation time: *15 minutes*

Cooking time: *10 minutes*

Yield: *6 latkes*

½ pound carrots

1 medium zucchini

1 small onion

1 egg

1 tablespoon plus 1 teaspoon cornstarch

¼ teaspoon salt

¼ teaspoon pepper

¼ teaspoon dried dill

1 tablespoon grated Romano cheese

¼ cup gluten-free Italian seasoned bread crumbs

2 tablespoons olive oil

1 Grate the carrots, zucchini, and onion using the large holes of a box grater.

2 Place the vegetables in the center of several thicknesses of paper toweling. Bring up the ends of the toweling and twist them together to form a pouch. Holding the pouch over the sink, squeeze out the excess moisture from the vegetables.

3 Place the vegetables in a medium bowl. Add the egg, cornstarch, salt, pepper, dill, Romano cheese, and bread crumbs, and mix well.

4 Heat the oil in a large skillet over medium heat.

5 For each latke, spoon 1 large spoonful of the mixture carefully into the pan. Immediately use the side and back of the spoon to form the mixture into a flat round. Cook about 4 minutes per side, or until browned.

6 Remove the latke from the skillet; drain on a paper towel. Repeat with the remaining mixture.

Per serving: *Calories: 204; Total fat: 11g; Saturated fat: 2g; Cholesterol: 72mg; Sodium: 345mg; Carbohydrates: 23g; Fiber: 3g; Sugar: 5g; Protein: 5g.*

Roasted Asparagus with Mustard Dressing

These asparagus are absolutely delicious, so you probably won't have any leftovers. But if you do, cover and refrigerate them because they're also amazing when served cold.

Preparation time: *6 minutes*

Cooking time: *15 minutes*

Yield: *4 servings*

1 bunch thin asparagus (approximately 28 stalks)

1 tablespoon plus 3 tablespoons olive oil

2 tablespoons brown mustard

¼ teaspoon salt

⅛ teaspoon pepper

1 tablespoon balsamic vinegar

1 teaspoon sugar

1 Preheat the oven to 400 degrees.

2 Wash the asparagus, and break off and discard the tough ends. Place the stalks in a baking dish.

3 Drizzle the stalks with 1 tablespoon of oil and toss to coat evenly. Spread the asparagus in a single layer.

4 Bake the asparagus at 400 degrees for 10 minutes, or until they're almost tender-crisp.

5 In a small bowl, whisk together the remaining 3 tablespoons of oil, mustard, salt, pepper, vinegar, and sugar.

6 Pour the mustard glaze over the asparagus and return it to the oven for 5 minutes.

Per serving: *Calories: 160; Total fat: 14g; Saturated fat: 2g; Cholesterol: 0mg; Sodium: 237mg; Carbohydrates: 7g; Fiber: 1g; Sugar: 4g; Protein: 3g.*

Packing Some Punch with Pastas and Starches

While veggies may be good for us, let's face it — nothing beats a great bowl of pasta or a side of potatoes. We're talking good, stick-to-your-ribs foods here.

The gluten-free pastas taste every bit as good as traditional wheat pasta if you take a little care with the preparation. When boiling gluten-free pasta, add a little oil to the pot of water. Oil helps prevent the pasta from sticking together. Also add some salt. Salt raises the temperature of the boiling water, enabling the pasta to cook more quickly without falling apart.

The alternative flour pastas and macaronis become gooey and mushy if you overcook them. As soon as they're *al dente* (a fancy word for "just about tender"), remove the pan from the stove, drain off the water, and then rinse the pasta under cold running water (unless a recipe directs otherwise).

To serve the pasta with a sauce, add some sauce to the pot you used to cook the pasta and bring it to a boil. Add the rinsed and drained pasta, and then heat, stirring occasionally, just until the strands are hot, and serve immediately. If you're going to use the pasta in a casserole that will be baked, you don't need to reheat the pasta after you drain it.

The variety of alternative pastas available is increasing almost daily. Corn and rice are still the mainstays. Corn pasta is a bit coarser and grainier, takes a little longer to cook, and has a more distinctive taste. It also holds together better. Rice pasta has no distinctive taste, so it absorbs the sauce's flavor. It cooks more quickly than the corn-based products, so you need to pay close attention when it nears al dente. If it's overcooked, it can fall apart — but cooked al dente, it's fabulous.

Although rice and corn are the most common alternative pastas on the grocery shelves, you can also buy gluten-free pasta that's made from the following flours:

- White sweet potato
- Milo
- Water chestnut
- Arrowroot
- Yam
- Lotus
- Cassava
- Quinoa
- Amaranth
- Buckwheat
- Lentil

After corn and rice pasta, lentil definitely weighs in as the next most popular. It's darker in color, but the taste is very good and it resists the mushy factor. Quinoa pasta is pretty widely available these days, too, and is *loaded* with nutrition! (See Chapter 3 for the lowdown on most of these flours.)

Buckwheat pasta often has wheat flour added to it. Don't assume the buckwheat pasta is pure buckwheat. Be sure to read the label!

The Ultimate Macaroni and Cheese

This macaroni and cheese is the most delicious version you'll ever have the pleasure of consuming. The culinary gratification borders on the euphoric. You can assemble this dish ahead and freeze it (thaw it before baking), or you can cover and refrigerate it until shortly before dinner. Served with a side salad, it can double as an entrée.

Preparation time: *30 minutes*

Cooking time: *30 minutes*

Yield: *9 servings*

Nonstick cooking spray	*4 tablespoons butter*
8-ounce box rice penne pasta	*1 teaspoon salt*
2 cups milk	*¾ cup shredded Romano cheese, divided*
½ cup whipping cream	

1 Preheat the oven to 350 degrees. Spray a 9-x-9-inch baking dish with cooking spray.

2 In a medium saucepan, cook the pasta as the package directs, boiling only for 6 minutes. Rinse and drain the pasta.

3 In the same saucepan, stir together the milk and whipping cream. Remove a ½ cup of the milk mixture and set it aside.

4 Bring the remaining milk mixture to a simmer and add the drained pasta.

5 Cook the milk and pasta over medium heat, stirring frequently, about 10 minutes, or until the mixture thickens and most of the milk is absorbed.

6 Add the butter and salt and stir until the butter melts.

7 In the prepared baking dish, layer half the macaroni, and then half of the cheese. Repeat the layers.

8 Pour the reserved milk over the top of the pasta.

9 Bake the pasta at 350 degrees for 30 minutes, or until the top begins to brown around the edges. Let the dish cool for 10 minutes before slicing.

Per serving: *Calories: 227; Total fat: 12g; Saturated fat: 7g; Cholesterol: 36mg; Sodium: 326mg; Carbohydrates: 23g; Fiber: 0g; Sugar: 3g; Protein: 7g.*

Spaghetti Marinara

No two people in the world make their marinara sauce quite the same way. This sauce is thick and will stick to the pasta. Many tomato-based dishes taste better the next day, and this marinara sauce is no exception. If you have the time, make the sauce the day before, and cover and refrigerate the pan to allow the flavors to blend before reheating and spooning it onto your pasta.

Preparation time: *10 minutes*

Cooking time: *25 minutes*

Yield: *4 servings*

1½ tablespoons virgin olive oil	½ teaspoon dried basil
2 medium onions, chopped	½ teaspoon dried oregano
¼ cup grated carrots	¼ teaspoon cinnamon
3 cloves garlic, finely minced	¼ teaspoon salt
28-ounce can crushed tomatoes	¼ teaspoon pepper
8-ounce can tomato sauce	2 teaspoons sugar
2 tablespoons chopped fresh parsley	12-ounce box rice spaghetti

1 Heat the oil in a large saucepan over medium heat. Sauté the onions, carrots, and garlic until tender, stirring frequently (about 5 minutes).

2 Stir in the tomatoes, tomato sauce, parsley, basil, oregano, cinnamon, salt, pepper, and sugar. Heat the sauce to boiling, and then reduce the heat to low. Cover and simmer the sauce for 20 minutes.

3 Prepare the spaghetti as the package directs. Spoon the marinara sauce over the cooked pasta.

Per serving: *Calories: 414; Total fat: 6g; Saturated fat: 1g; Cholesterol: 0mg; Sodium: 606mg; Carbohydrates: 82g; Fiber: 6g; Sugar: 9g; Protein: 5g.*

Parmesan Potatoes

Think super-simple. This side dish is pretty and tasty enough to serve to company, yet simple enough to accompany any family meal.

Preparation time: 5 minutes

Cooking time: 40 minutes

Yield: 4 servings

3 tablespoons olive oil	⅛ teaspoon pepper
¼ teaspoon garlic powder	¼ teaspoon Italian seasoning
2 tablespoons grated Romano cheese	4 medium to large unpeeled red-skinned potatoes, cut in quarters lengthwise
⅛ teaspoon salt	

1 Preheat the oven to 375 degrees.

2 Place the potatoes in an 8-x-11-inch baking dish.

3 Pour the oil over the potatoes. Sprinkle the garlic powder, Romano cheese, salt, pepper, and Italian seasonings over the potatoes.

4 Bake the potatoes at 375 degrees uncovered for 40 minutes, or until tender.

Vary It! You can substitute dried dill for the Italian seasoning, melted butter for the oil, and Romano cheese for the Parmesan.

Per serving: *Calories: 202; Total fat: 11g; Saturated fat: 2g; Cholesterol: 1mg; Sodium: 366mg; Carbohydrates: 25g; Fiber: 2g; Sugar: 2g; Protein: 0g.*

Twice-Baked Sweet Potatoes

Is it really worth all the effort to bake, then scoop, then mash, then stuff, then top, then rebake sweet potatoes? Yes, yes, and yes again! Deep inside of you, you know this is the perfect side dish for autumn, but you'll have the urge to make it all year long.

Tools: Electric mixer

Preparation time: 15 minutes

Cooking time: 90 minutes

Yield: 4 servings

2 large sweet potatoes or yams, cut in half lengthwise

Nonstick cooking spray

3 tablespoons milk

3 tablespoons maple syrup

½ teaspoon vanilla

¼ teaspoon salt

1 egg

3 tablespoons gluten-free flour mixture (see Chapter 8 for the recipe)

3 tablespoons brown sugar

3 tablespoons butter, melted

3 tablespoons finely chopped pecans

1 Preheat the oven to 375 degrees.

2 Put the halves of the potatoes together to form a whole potato, and wrap each potato in foil.

3 Bake the potatoes at 375 degrees for about 1 hour until they're tender but not mushy.

4 Cool the potatoes slightly, and then scoop out the centers, leaving enough potato to hold the shape of the skin. Place the scooped-out centers in a large mixing bowl.

5 Lower the oven temperature to 325 degrees. Spray an 8-x-11-inch baking dish with cooking spray.

6 Using a mixer, whip the potato pulp until it's smooth. Add the milk, maple syrup, vanilla, salt, and egg, and continue to whip until the pulp is light and fluffy.

7 Spoon the filling into the potato shells, dividing evenly.

8 Place the shells in the prepared baking dish.

9 In a small bowl, use a fork to blend together the flour mixture and brown sugar. Add the butter and continue to blend with the fork until the dry ingredients are evenly moistened.

10 Stir in the pecans.

11 Crumble sugar mixture over the potatoes. Bake the potatoes at 325 degrees for 30 minutes.

Tip: *Sweet potatoes have a relatively low glycemic index (see Chapter 4 for more on that), making them far healthier for you than white potatoes.*

Per serving: Calories: 384; Total fat: 21g; Saturated fat: 7g; Cholesterol: 77mg; Sodium: 238mg; Carbohydrates: 46g; Fiber: 3g; Sugar: 22g; Protein: 5g.

Mashed Potatoes with Caramelized Onions

The caramelized onions and cheese give this creation a unique flavor that dictates you have a second helping (and sometimes a third)!

Tools: *Ricer or electric mixer*

Preparation time: *25 minutes*

Cooking time: *20 minutes*

Yield: *4 servings*

2 tablespoons olive oil	1 teaspoon salt
1 cup sliced onions	¼ teaspoon pepper
½ teaspoon brown sugar	¾ cup milk
4 large Idaho potatoes	⅔ cup shredded white sharp cheddar cheese
¼ cup butter, softened	

1 In a large skillet, heat the oil. Stir in the onions and brown sugar, and cook over medium heat for about 10 minutes, or until the onions are browned and glazed, stirring frequently.

2 Peel the potatoes. Cut each potato in half crosswise, and then cut each half into quarters.

3 Place the potatoes in a large saucepan and cover them with water. Bring the water to a boil and boil for 20 minutes, or until the potatoes are tender. Drain.

4 Place small batches of potatoes in a ricer and rice the potatoes into a mixing bowl. If you don't have a ricer, place the potatoes in the mixing bowl and whip the potatoes smooth with the mixer. Add the butter, salt, and pepper, and blend well.

5 Add the milk to the potatoes and whip until they're light and fluffy.

6 Whip in the onions and cheese just until they're evenly distributed and blended.

7 Either serve the potatoes immediately or transfer the mixture to a casserole dish that has been sprayed with nonstick cooking spray, cover, and refrigerate. To reheat the potatoes, bake the covered casserole at 400 degrees for 20 minutes.

Vary It! *If you want even richer potatoes, use half-and-half in place of the milk.*

Per serving: *Calories: 536; Total fat: 26g; Saturated fat: 13g; Cholesterol: 55mg; Sodium: 814mg; Carbohydrates: 66g; Fiber: 6g; Sugar: 6g; Protein: 12g.*

Serving Vegetable Dishes as the Main Attraction

Anyone who is vegan or vegetarian has already discovered some of the fascinating and delectable things that can be done with vegetables. A meat-and-potatoes person may need a little more convincing that it's possible to fill an empty stomach *and* enjoy the meal with no meat present. This section includes a few entrees that will convince anyone that meat isn't needed to satisfy the tummy at mealtime.

If you're innovative, select a vegetable large enough to stuff. Hollow it out, chop up the center, and sauté with onions and green pepper. Add "something" (rice, pasta, and/or veggies) to the onions and peppers, restuff the vegetable, and top it off with gluten-free bread crumbs, shredded cheese, or a sauce, and then bake. Each time you opt to do this, select a different veggie for the shell, a different filling, and a different topping.

Gluten-free lasagna noodles are another source for creativity. *Parboil* (partially cook by boiling) the noodles *slightly,* and then drain. (If the noodles are fully cooked, they'll fall apart when you assemble the casserole.) Don't rinse the noodles because they need to keep the starch intact for a cohesive finished product. If you use enough sauce in the casserole, you don't even need to parboil. Simply lay the noodles in a pan, top with a filling of your choice, repeat the layers, spread with a sauce, and bake.

> ### Quinoa-Stuffed Tomatoes

If you're wondering what in the heck *quinoa* (pronounced *keen*-wah) is, it's a gluten-free grain that's jam-packed with nutrients. The small, beaded form is used in this recipe; it's also an excellent substitute for couscous and for use in *tabbouleh* (a Middle Eastern salad). For this recipe, the tomatoes, once baked, need to be firm enough to hold their shape, yet soft enough to cut easily with a fork. Select large, ripe (but not too soft) tomatoes. You don't use the tomato pulp in this recipe, so place the pulp in a self-seal bag to use in a stew or pasta sauce another day.

Preparation time: *30 minutes*

Cooking time: *20 minutes*

Yield: *4 servings*

4 large tomatoes	¼ teaspoon dried thyme
1 cup water	¼ teaspoon dried mint
2 teaspoons butter	2 teaspoons dried parsley flakes
2 teaspoons olive oil	14-ounce can gluten-free chicken broth
½ teaspoon minced garlic	½ cup uncooked quinoa
2 green onions, minced	2 tablespoons fresh lemon juice
½ teaspoon salt	10-ounce box frozen chopped spinach, thawed and drained well
¼ teaspoon pepper	
½ teaspoon dried dill	3 tablespoons crumbled feta cheese

1 Preheat the oven to 350 degrees.

2 Cut ½ inch off the stem side of each tomato and discard the lid. Hollow out the insides.

3 Place the tomato shells in a 9-x-9-inch baking dish, cut side down.

4 Pour the water around the tomatoes, cover the dish with foil, and bake the tomatoes at 350 degrees for 15 to 20 minutes until the skins are slightly softened but firm enough to hold their shape. Remove the tomatoes from the oven and drain off the hot water.

5 In a large nonstick saucepan, sauté the garlic and onions in the butter and oil over medium-high heat until the onion is tender, stirring frequently.

6 Stir in the salt, pepper, dill, thyme, mint, and parsley.

7 Add the chicken broth and bring it to a boil.

8 Lower the heat to medium-low, stir in the quinoa, cover the pan, and simmer the broth slowly for 20 minutes, or until the broth has been absorbed and the quinoa is tender.

9 With a fork, stir in the lemon juice and spinach until everything is well combined. Stir in the feta cheese.

10 Stuff the tomatoes with the quinoa mixture. Cover the pan with foil.

11 Bake the stuffed tomatoes at 350 degrees for 20 minutes.

Per serving: *Calories: 222; Total fat: 10g; Saturated fat: 4g; Cholesterol: 17mg; Sodium: 815mg; Carbohydrates: 28g; Fiber: 6g; Sugar: 7g; Protein: 11g.*

Spinach Lasagna

Very little in life provides the satisfaction of consuming an Italian dinner, and this one ranks high on the list in the satisfaction department. This entrée is guaranteed to provide you with genuine gastronomical gratification. Serve it with a tossed salad, and your dinner is complete. Take care not to overcook the noodles when parboiling them.

Preparation time: *35 minutes*

Cooking time: *45 minutes*

Yield: *6 servings*

½ cup hot water

1 gluten-free chicken bouillon cube

8-ounce box gluten-free lasagna noodles

1 medium onion, chopped

2 teaspoons minced garlic

1 tablespoon olive oil

2½ cups spaghetti sauce

¾ teaspoon Italian seasoning

¼ teaspoon pepper

1½ cups gluten-free small curd cottage cheese

½ cup plain yogurt

¼ cup grated Romano cheese

10-ounce box frozen chopped spinach, thawed and squeezed dry

1½ cups shredded mozzarella cheese

1 Preheat the oven to 350 degrees.

2 In a small bowl, stir together the hot water and bouillon cube until the cube dissolves.

3 In a medium saucepan over medium heat, sauté the onion and garlic in oil until tender, stirring frequently.

4 Stir in the broth (bouillon cube and water), spaghetti sauce, Italian seasoning, and pepper; simmer slowly for 15 minutes.

5 In a medium bowl, stir together the cottage cheese, yogurt, Romano cheese, and spinach.

6 In a medium saucepan, boil the noodles according to the package directions, boiling only for 10 minutes. Drain the water and rinse the noodles very quickly with cold water so they're cool enough to handle (you want them to retain their starch).

7 Spread ¼ of the sauce in an 8-x-11-inch baking dish. Lay 1 layer of noodles on top of the sauce. Spread ½ of the spinach mixture over the noodles, and then ⅓ of the mozzarella. Repeat the layers, ending with the sauce and mozzarella.

8 Bake the lasagna uncovered at 350 degrees for 45 minutes. Let the lasagna set for 10 minutes before cutting.

Per serving: *Calories: 388; Total fat: 14g; Saturated fat: 6g; Cholesterol: 29mg; Sodium: 911mg; Carbohydrates: 45g; Fiber: 5g; Sugar: 8g; Protein: 22g.*

Cheese-Stuffed Zucchini

This dish blends the tastes from the Mediterranean to make an entrée that you can also serve as a side dish.

Preparation time: *20 minutes*

Cooking time: *45 minutes*

Yield: *4 servings*

Nonstick cooking spray

2 medium zucchini, each cut in half lengthwise

2 teaspoons olive oil

1 cup finely chopped onion

1 cup finely chopped green pepper

2 cloves garlic, minced

1 cup finely chopped plum tomatoes

¾ teaspoon dried oregano

¼ cup chopped fresh parsley

¼ teaspoon salt

¼ teaspoon pepper

¼ teaspoon dried dill

¼ teaspoon dried mint

¾ cup crumbled feta cheese

4 teaspoons gluten-free Italian seasoned bread crumbs

1 Preheat the oven to 350 degrees. Spray a 9-x-9-inch baking dish with cooking spray.

2 Carefully remove the pulp from each zucchini half, leaving a ¼-inch thick shell. Chop the pulp.

3 Heat the oil in a large nonstick skillet. Add the onion, green pepper, and garlic. Sauté over medium heat, stirring frequently, until the vegetables are soft (about 5 minutes).

4 Stir the tomatoes, zucchini pulp, oregano, parsley, salt, pepper, dill, and mint into the onion mixture. Reduce the heat and cook over medium-low heat for 5 minutes, stirring occasionally. Remove from the heat; cool for 5 minutes.

5 Stir in the cheese.

6 Stuff each zucchini shell with about ½ cup of the onion mixture. Sprinkle the tops with bread crumbs.

7 Set the zucchini "boats" in the prepared baking dish.

8 Bake the zucchini at 350 degrees for 30 minutes, or until the bread crumbs are lightly browned and the shells are tender.

Vary It! *Here's a novel idea: If you grow your own zucchini, try stuffing the flowers from the plant before the vegetable begins to develop. Pick the flowers when they are large, wash them well, and then stuff and bake them.*

Per serving: *Calories: 165; Total fat: 9g; Saturated fat: 5g; Cholesterol: 25mg; Sodium: 610mg; Carbohydrates: 17g; Fiber: 4g; Sugar: 7g; Protein: 7g.*

Italian Stuffed Cabbage

If you've ever tried to peel the leaves off of a head of cabbage to make stuffed cabbage leaves, you know it's not quite that simple. But it's not that hard, either. You can retrieve the leaves from a head of cabbage in two ways. First, though, you have to peel off and toss out the coarse outer leaves because they'll be tough and too thick to be pliable enough for stuffing.

Method 1: Blanch the head of cabbage in boiling water, and then plunge it into cold water to stop the cooking. After the head is cool, separate it into leaves. **Method 2:** Freeze the head of cabbage. After it thaws, the leaves should peel off nicely.

Long-grain rice works best in these rolls. Pack the cabbage loosely, allowing room for the rice to expand.

Preparation time: *55 minutes*

Cooking time: *1 hour*

Yield: *8 servings*

1 large cabbage	2 teaspoons salt
1 zucchini	1 teaspoon pepper
1 carrot	½ teaspoon cumin
2½ cups uncooked rice	½ teaspoon cinnamon
2 medium onions, minced	2 drops hot pepper sauce
½ bunch fresh parsley, minced	¾ cup water
½ teaspoon garlic powder	¼ cup olive oil
1 teaspoon Italian seasoning	Two 26-ounce jars spaghetti sauce

1 Cut the core out of the cabbage.

2 Place the cabbage, core down, in a large saucepan. Add about 3 cups of water and steam the cabbage, covered, until the outer leaves turn bright green. Remove the softened leaves, and then return the cabbage to the pot and repeat until all the cabbage leaves have been removed.

3 Preheat the oven to 350 degrees.

4 Shred the zucchini and carrot into a large bowl.

5 Add the remaining ingredients except the spaghetti sauce and cabbage leaves. Stir to mix well. Stir ½ cup of the spaghetti sauce into the rice mixture.

6 Stuff each cabbage leaf with 3 tablespoons of the rice mixture. (Use slightly more rice mixture for the larger cabbage leaves and slightly less mixture for the small, inside cabbage leaves.) Fold in one side of the leaf to cover the filling, and then roll the cabbage.

7 Spread 1 cup of the spaghetti sauce on the bottom of a 9-x-13-inch baking dish.

8 Lay the cabbage rolls in the pan, seam side down.

9 Pour 2½ cups of the spaghetti sauce over the top of the rolls.

10 Cover the pan with foil and bake the rolls at 350 degrees for 1 hour, adding a little water if needed.

11 Warm the remaining 2 cups of spaghetti sauce to pour over the rolls just before serving.

Per serving: Calories: 431; Total fat: 10g; Saturated fat: 1g; Cholesterol: 581mg; Sodium: 909mg; Carbohydrates: 78g; Fiber: 8g; Sugar: 15g; Protein: 11g.

Artichoke Lasagna

Garlic, fresh mushrooms, artichokes, cheese, wine, and whipping cream — these ingredients combine to form a creation that will tantalize and satisfy any discerning palate. When you're making this dish, be very careful not to overboil the noodles; you want them firm enough to handle. You can assemble this dish ahead of time and either refrigerate it or freeze it until you're ready to bake it. (If you freeze it, thaw it before baking.) When removing the lasagna from the oven, let it set for 5 minutes before cutting.

Preparation time: 45 minutes

Cooking time: 30 minutes

Yield: 9 servings

Garlic Sauce (see the following recipe)

¼ teaspoon plus ¼ teaspoon salt

1 tablespoon olive oil

9 rice lasagna noodles

1 tablespoon butter

4 ounces fresh mushrooms, chopped

2 cloves garlic, minced

14-ounce can artichoke hearts, drained and minced

½ cup sherry

¼ teaspoon pepper

Nonstick cooking spray

2 tablespoons grated Parmesan cheese

(continued)

1 Preheat the oven to 350 degrees.

2 Fill a large saucepan with water and bring it to a boil. Add ¼ teaspoon of salt and the olive oil. Add the noodles and cook them about 8 minutes, until they're almost tender. Drain the water. Return the noodles to the pan and keep them submerged in cold water until they're needed.

3 Melt the butter in a large skillet over medium heat. Add the mushrooms and garlic and sauté them over medium heat for about 6 minutes, stirring frequently.

4 Add the artichokes and sherry and cook the vegetables until the liquid is absorbed.

5 Stir in the remaining ¼ teaspoon of salt and the pepper.

6 Spray an 8½-x-6½-inch baking dish with cooking spray.

7 Spoon a small amount of the Garlic Sauce on the bottom of the pan. Lay 3 noodles over the sauce (not overlapping). Spoon ⅓ of the sauce over the noodles. Repeat the layers two more times.

8 Sprinkle the Parmesan cheese over the top.

9 Bake the lasagna at 350 degrees for 30 minutes, or until the top is just browning. Cool for 5 minutes before cutting into squares.

Garlic Sauce

3 cloves garlic, unpeeled	*⅛ teaspoon salt*
1 tablespoon olive oil	*¼ teaspoon pepper*
1 tablespoon sherry	*¼ cup finely grated Parmesan cheese*
1 cup whipping cream	*Dash nutmeg*

1 Place the garlic in a small piece of foil; drizzle the olive oil over the cloves. Seal the packet and bake about 30 minutes, or until the garlic is soft. Remove the garlic from the oven.

2 When the garlic is cool, squeeze it into a small bowl (discarding the skins) and mash it with a fork.

3 Place the mashed garlic in a small saucepan. Add the sherry, whipping cream, salt, and pepper. Simmer the sauce slowly, stirring constantly, until the mixture has been reduced and thickened.

4 Remove the sauce from the heat. Stir in the Parmesan cheese and nutmeg.

Per serving: *Calories: 250; Total fat: 14g; Saturated fat: 7g; Cholesterol: 36mg; Sodium: 363mg; Carbohydrates: 24g; Fiber: 1g; Sugar: 1g; Protein: 5g.*

Part III

Dishes to Enjoy Before, After, or Any Time

In this part . . .

We explore new and intriguing recipes outside of the usual three square meals a day: beyond toast for breakfast, beyond that sandwich at lunch, and certainly beyond the typical dinner. The pages are jammed with tempting appetizers, salads, soups, snacks, and desserts.

Chapter 15

Appetizing Appetizers

In This Chapter

▶ Knowing what to serve when

▶ Can't-resist dips and grab-and-go goodies

▶ Hot munchies straight from the oven

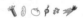
Appetizers, hors d'oeuvres, starters, antipasto, gustus, mezethes, tapas, maza, mezze, zakuski, dim sum, smorgasbord . . . an appetizer by any other name is still an appetizer.

It seems a little ironic that we *eat* to build an appetite, but that's the idea. Appetizers are small servings of foods served before a meal to whet the appetite, or they can be served alone to enable people to dawdle over small servings of different dishes. Serving appetizers stretches out a social gathering while guests circulate, talk, bond, and mingle.

Choosing the Right Appetizers for the Occasion

Conjure up in your mind all those appetizers you've been offered at parties over the years. Celery sticks with plain cream cheese. Crackers with spray cheese. Chips and dip made from sour cream and onion soup mix. Herring in dill sauce. Aren't you tired of these things? Wouldn't you rather serve something with more character and spice? Something a bit more memorable? Bland appetizers merely fill the belly, whereas appetizers with pizzazz actually assault the senses and get guests craving more.

Be creative in your food choice. Balance hot and cold dishes, rich and mild foods, and try to include at least one vegetarian offering. Assortment is the key. Pick foods that are party-friendly — people will most likely be walking around, so you don't want to serve foods that are too sticky, messy, or greasy. Better choices are items that people can pick up easily and eat with two fingers.

Here are a few ideas to get your creative juices flowing:

- ✔ Consider serving something where people can participate, like assembling their own mini-tacos on corn tortillas or in corn taco shells and adding their own toppings, fillings, or condiments.

- ✔ Rice papers (available at Asian markets), when soaked in water for 2 minutes, become very pliable and make the perfect wrapper for appetizers. You can use these wrappers to make mini-Reuben wraps with pastrami and Swiss cheese and a dab of gluten-free brown mustard (to be served hot or cold). Or spread the rice papers with cream cheese, and then top with gluten-free chunky salsa, shredded lettuce, crisp-cooked bacon, and some guacamole. Roll these up and you have one delicious appetizer.

- ✔ A great assemble-ahead appetizer is Eggplant Pizza. Brown slices of eggplant in your broiler, top with a small amount of gluten-free spaghetti sauce, sprinkle with Italian seasoning, and then top off with a slice of provolone cheese. Pop it in the microwave to melt the cheese, and it's ready to serve.

- ✔ In the summertime, make use of your grill. Early in the day, assemble mini-kabobs (shrimp, chicken, beef, veggies), or wrap mushrooms in bacon and brush them with gluten-free barbecue sauce. Let your friends grill their own appetizers.

To add some sanity to the day of the party, choose appetizers that you can make ahead and store in the refrigerator or freezer until it's time to serve them. If guests are coming for dinner, choose lighter appetizers so people don't fill up on them, but prepare enough so that your guests stay busy munching and meandering in the living room or family room (so they'll stay out of your kitchen and let you work at plating the dinner). Plan on about four appetizers per person. If you're offering two appetizers, that would average two of each selection per person. If you're only serving appetizers, then you'd better make a bit larger quantity of each. Figure on eight to nine pieces per guest.

If you're hosting a party, chances are that most of your guests aren't on a gluten-free diet. But hey, it's your party! Stop making "their appetizers" and "your appetizers." Make gluten-free appetizers that everyone can enjoy!

Taking a Dip with Cold Appetizers

If you're planning an event that will last an entire afternoon or evening, keep in mind that some foods shouldn't remain at room temperature for longer than two hours at the most. When serving foods that need refrigeration (dips, deviled eggs, meats or seafood, anything with mayonnaise), put out partial amounts and refill the platter from the refrigerated stash.

In the case of cold dips, an easy way to keep them cool longer is to set the dip bowl into a slightly larger bowl that has been filled with ice. Or think outside the bowl. Spoon the dip into a hollowed-out small head of cabbage, squash, or large green or red pepper, and then set this into the bowl with ice.

Although you can't gauge exactly how much chips and dip your friends will consume, a pretty good approximation is to have ¼ cup of chip dip per person when other snacks are also served.

Shrimp Deviled Eggs

Everyone seems to love deviled eggs, and this recipe is an exceptional treat. You probably have your own recipe for hard-boiled eggs, and if you want to use it, that's fine. But if you've never boiled eggs before, I include a process that works every time.

Preparation time: *10 minutes*

Cooking time: *11 minutes*

Yield: *6 servings*

3 eggs	*¼ teaspoon dried dill*
1 teaspoon plus dash of salt	*¼ teaspoon lemon juice*
8 large cocktail shrimp, cooked and deveined	*⅛ teaspoon pepper*
2 tablespoons plus 1 teaspoon mayonnaise	*Paprika*
¼ teaspoon mustard	*Dash Salt*

1 Place the eggs in a single layer in a medium saucepan with enough cold water to cover them. Add a teaspoon of salt to the pan to help prevent the eggshells from cracking. Bring the water to a boil over high heat. As soon as the water starts to boil, let the eggs cook for exactly 11 minutes, and then remove the pan from the heat. Set the pan in the sink and run cold water over the eggs to stop them from further cooking.

2 Dice the shrimp and set them aside.

3 Peel the eggs and cut them in half lengthwise. Carefully remove the yolks and place them in a medium bowl. Set the egg whites aside.

4 Mash the yolks with the back of a fork. Add the mayonnaise, mustard, dill, lemon juice, pepper, and a dash of salt and stir until the mixture is smooth.

5 Stir in the shrimp until it's evenly distributed.

6 With a small spoon, refill the egg white halves, mounding the yolk mixture on top.

7 Sprinkle the tops lightly with paprika, cover, and refrigerate until serving time.

Per serving: *Calories: 68; Total fat: 5g; Saturated fat: 1g; Cholesterol: 122mg; Sodium: 116mg; Carbohydrates: 2g; Fiber: 0g; Sugar: 1g; Protein: 5g.*

🍅 Feta Supreme Spread

Make this spread ahead so it has plenty of time for the flavors to blend. Slather it on gluten-free pita wedges or gluten-free crackers to make an easy appetizer. You can also use it as a sandwich spread or sprinkled over a Greek salad.

Preparation time: *5 minutes*

Refrigeration time: *2 hours*

Cooking time: *None*

Yield: *2 cups*

8 ounces feta cheese	*½ teaspoon dried oregano*
1½ tablespoons fresh lemon juice (1 lemon)	*¼ teaspoon garlic powder*
1 tablespoon red wine vinegar	*⅛ teaspoon cumin*
3 tablespoons olive oil	*¼ teaspoon pepper*

1 With a fork, crumble the feta in a medium bowl.

2 Add the lemon juice, red wine vinegar, olive oil, oregano, garlic powder, cumin, and pepper and continue to blend with a fork until everything is mixed.

3 Cover the bowl with plastic wrap and refrigerate the spread for several hours.

Per serving: *Calories: 121; Total fat: 11g; Saturated fat: 5g; Cholesterol: 25mg; Sodium: 316mg; Carbohydrates: 2g; Fiber: 0g; Sugar: 1g; Protein: 4g.*

Roulade Canapé

Although this concoction makes a great lunch, the directions below call for slicing the *roulades* (rolled slices of meat stuffed with filling) to convert them to *canapés* (another fancy word for appetizer). This may be one of the simplest recipes you'll ever make; it's also one of the most impressive to look at.

Preparation time: *5 minutes*

Refrigeration time: *2 hours*

Cooking time: *None*

Yield: *24 pieces*

3 ounces cream cheese, softened

1 cup baby spinach leaves, rinsed

2 whole roasted red peppers, each cut in half

4 slices deli ham

4 slices deli turkey

1 Cut the ham and turkey slices the same sizes (approximately the size of a slice of bread).

2 Spread cream cheese on each of the ham slices, dividing evenly.

3 Place 1 slice of turkey on top of each ham slice.

4 Spread the spinach leaves on top of the turkey slices, and then place a red pepper half at one end of each slice.

5 Starting at the narrow end of the meat, roll each into a roulade.

6 Wrap each individual roulade tightly in plastic wrap and refrigerate for 4 or more hours.

7 To serve, remove the plastic wrap and cut each roulade into 6 rounds with a serrated knife. Place the pieces, cut side up, on a platter.

Per serving: *Calories: 47; Total fat: 3g; Saturated fat: 2g; Cholesterol: 15mg; Sodium: 181mg; Carbohydrates: 1g; Fiber: 0g; Sugar: 1g; Protein: 4g.*

Crabmeat Dip

If you and your friends are going to munch, get out those gluten-free crackers and munch on something *good!* This crab dip is just a bit different than most, but it's oh so tasty.

Preparation time: *10 minutes*

Refrigeration time: *2 hours*

Cooking time: *None*

Yield: *2 cups*

4.5-ounce can crabmeat, drained and flaked	*¼ teaspoon dried dill*
1 hard-boiled egg, shelled and minced	*1 green onion, minced*
¼ cup mayonnaise	*¼ teaspoon gluten-free Worcestershire sauce*
¼ cup sour cream	*½ teaspoon dried parsley flakes*
1 teaspoon lemon juice	*¼ teaspoon salt*
½ teaspoon dry mustard	*⅛ teaspoon pepper*

1 In a medium bowl, stir together all the ingredients, mixing well to blend thoroughly.

2 Cover and chill the dip for at least 2 hours for flavors to blend.

Per serving: *Calories: 88; Total fat: 7g; Saturated fat: 2g; Cholesterol: 59mg; Sodium: 284mg; Carbohydrates: 3g; Fiber: 0g; Sugar: 1g; Protein: 4g.*

Tortilla Sticks

These sticks are perfect for snacking, but they're also the perfect accompaniment for soups or a pasta dinner. They're even great eaten hot from the oven. Beware . . . you can't eat just one! These are also tasty when sprinkled with sesame seeds before baking.

Preparation time: *5 minutes*

Cooking time: *8 minutes*

Yield: *20 pieces*

Nonstick cooking spray	*3 tablespoons grated Parmesan cheese*
Two 8-inch rice flour tortillas	*⅛ teaspoon garlic powder*
2 tablespoons butter, melted	*¼ teaspoon Italian seasoning*

1 Preheat the oven to 400 degrees. Spray a nonstick baking sheet with the nonstick cooking spray.

2 Brush one side of each tortilla with the melted butter, and then sprinkle it with the cheese, garlic powder, and Italian seasoning. Press the toppings into the tortillas so they stick.

3 With a clean pair of scissors, cut each tortilla into ten ¾-inch-wide strips. Place the strips on the baking sheet.

4 Bake at 400 degrees for 8 minutes, or until the strips are light golden and crisp.

Per serving: *Calories: 26; Total fat: 2 g; Saturated fat: 0.8 g; Cholesterol: 4 mg; Sodium: 35 mg; Carbohydrates: 2. Fiber: 0 g; Sugar: 0 g; Protein: 1 g*

Hors D'oeurves from the Oven

The hot appetizers in this section are perfect for any occasion. Whether you're having a formal cocktail party at home (does anyone still have those?) or friends over to watch a game on TV, or you're going to a picnic or tailgate party, these offerings will impress your friends. Appetizers bring cohesiveness to any gathering. People gather around the food, so make sure that the food is absolutely irresistible!

⏱ Hot Taco Bake

When you think of "taco bake," is soufflé the first thing that pops into your mind? If not, start making that connection. Whether you serve this with gluten-free crackers or tortilla chips or lots of assorted veggies, this creamy concoction is sure to be a hit with your friends. Spread any leftover dip on gluten-free corn tortillas and warm them in the microwave or oven for lunch or a quick snack.

Preparation time: *5 minutes*

Cooking time: *40 minutes*

Yield: *3 cups*

Nonstick cooking spray

½ onion, minced

¼ green pepper, minced

1 tablespoon olive oil

16 ounces cream cheese, softened

16 ounces sour cream

9-ounce can bean dip

1.25-ounce package gluten-free taco seasoning mix

1 cup shredded cheddar cheese

½ cup grated hot pepper cheese

1 Preheat the oven to 325 degrees. Using the nonstick cooking spray, grease a 9-inch-square baking dish.

2 In a small skillet, slowly sauté the onion and green pepper in oil over medium heat until they're soft. Remove from the heat.

3 Using a mixer, whip the cream cheese until it's light. Add the sour cream and continue to whip until the mixture is blended and smooth.

4 Whip in the bean dip and taco seasoning. Stir in the cheddar cheese, onions, and green pepper.

5 Spoon the mixture into the prepared baking dish.

6 Sprinkle the pepper cheese on top.

7 Bake the dip at 325 degrees for 25 minutes, or until it's lightly browned on top.

Per serving: *Calories: 286; Total fat: 27g; Saturated fat: 16g; Cholesterol: 72mg; Sodium: 524mg; Carbohydrates: 6g; Fiber: 0g; Sugar: 1g; Protein: 8g.*

Baked Potato Skins

You've had potato skins before, but not like these! Make plenty of extras because no one can stop after eating just one! When scooping out the potato center, don't go all the way to the skin. Leave an inner lining of potato so it can hold its shape. You won't need the pulp, so spoon the scooped-out centers into a self-seal bag to make potato pancakes at another time.

Preparation time: *15 minutes*

Cooking time: *60 minutes*

Yield: *12 servings*

6 medium russet potatoes

2 tablespoons butter

1 teaspoon minced garlic

⅛ teaspoon pepper

4 ounces crumbled gluten-free blue cheese

3 slices bacon, cooked crisp and crumbled

3 tablespoons gluten-free seasoned bread crumbs

2 tablespoons grated Parmesan cheese

1 Preheat the oven to 400 degrees.

2 Rinse each potato and then cut it in half. Put the two halves back together and wrap the potato in foil. Repeat with the remaining potatoes. Put them on the oven rack and bake for 45 minutes. Let the potatoes cool for 15 minutes. (***Note:*** Leave the oven on because you'll put the skins back in to reheat them and melt the cheese.)

3 Remove the foil. Using a small spoon, scoop out the centers of each potato half.

4 In a small skillet, melt the butter. Add the garlic and pepper and sauté them in the butter over medium heat. Using a pastry brush, brush the inside of each potato half with the butter mixture.

5 Sprinkle the blue cheese inside of each potato half and then top with the bacon crumbles.

6 In a small bowl, stir together the bread crumbs and Parmesan cheese; sprinkle the mixture on top of the bacon.

7 Place the potato skins on a baking sheet and bake at 400 degrees for 15 minutes, or until the skins are hot and crisp.

Per serving: Calories: 172; Total fat: 33g; Saturated fat: 5g; Cholesterol: 26mg; Sodium: 424mg; Carbohydrates: 15g; Fiber: 2g; Sugar: 1g; Protein: 8g.

🍅 Artichoke Squares

Aren't squares of any kind wonderful? They're so convenient to serve. You can assemble them ahead of time, they bake by themselves while you prepare for company, and you usually don't need forks to enjoy them. Although these squares are listed as an appetizer, if you cut the pieces a little larger, they can double as a vegetable dish at dinner. *Warning:* Don't buy marinated artichokes or this dish will be too bitter.

Preparation time: *10 minutes*

Cooking time: *35 minutes*

Yield: *16 pieces*

3 tablespoons olive oil

8 green onions, sliced thin

½ teaspoon minced garlic

4 eggs

½ teaspoon dried mint

1 teaspoon dried dill

1 teaspoon gluten-free Worcestershire sauce

15-ounce can artichoke quarters, drained and chopped

1 cup shredded Swiss cheese

3 tablespoons gluten-free seasoned bread crumbs

1 Preheat the oven to 325 degrees. Oil an 8-inch-square baking dish.

2 Add the olive oil to a small skillet and sauté the onion and garlic over medium heat until they're soft. Let the mixture cool slightly.

3 With a whisk, whip the eggs in a large bowl until they're frothy. Stir the mint, dill, and Worcestershire sauce into the eggs.

4 Stir in the artichokes, cheese, onions, and garlic.

5 Smooth the mixture into the prepared baking dish. Sprinkle the bread crumbs over the top.

6 Bake at 325 degrees for 35 minutes, or until the bread crumbs are lightly browned.

7 Let the dish cool slightly before cutting.

Per serving: *Calories: 76; Total fat: 6g; Saturated fat: 2g; Cholesterol: 59mg; Sodium: 64mg; Carbohydrates: 3g; Fiber: 1g; Sugar: 1g; Protein: 4g.*

Speedy Taco Wings

Get out lots of napkins because these wings are "finger-lickin' good!" Preparation is less than a half hour from the time you take the chicken out of the refrigerator to the time you sit down to relish these remarkable tidbits. For those who want to bump up the heat a degree or two, add a little extra cayenne and chili powder to the mix.

Preparation time: *5 minutes*

Cooking time: *20 minutes*

Yield: *20 pieces*

¼ cup olive oil

20 pieces disjointed chicken wings

1.25-ounce package gluten-free taco seasoning mix

¼ teaspoon cayenne pepper

¾ teaspoon Cajun seasoning

½ teaspoon chili powder

1 Preheat the oven to 400 degrees. Lightly oil an 8-x-11-inch baking dish.

2 Pour the oil into a self-seal bag. Add the chicken pieces, seal the bag, and push the pieces around until they're evenly coated with oil.

3 Add the taco seasoning mix, cayenne pepper, Cajun seasoning, and chili powder to another self-seal bag.

4 Remove the oil-coated chicken pieces from their bag and add them to the seasoning bag; push (or shake) the pieces around until they're evenly coated with the dry mix. Place the chicken in the prepared baking dish.

5 Bake the wings at 400 degrees for 20 minutes, or until the chicken pieces are cooked through and the tops are beginning to brown.

Per serving: Calories: 136; Total fat: 11g; Saturated fat: 2g; Cholesterol: 22mg; Sodium: 443mg; Carbohydrates: 3g; Fiber: 0g; Sugar: 0g; Protein: 5g.

Cajun Stuffed Mushrooms

These morsels are tangy and will tantalize the tip of your tongue. But if you thrive on five-alarm foods that virtually disintegrate your taste buds, then use gluten-free hot sausage and add more Cajun seasoning.

Preparation time: *15 minutes*

Cooking time: *35 minutes*

Yield: *24 mushroom caps*

Nonstick cooking spray	¾ teaspoon Cajun seasoning
24 large mushrooms	2 teaspoons dried parsley flakes
½ pound gluten-free spicy sausage	½ teaspoon cumin
1 cup chopped onion	1 cup mayonnaise
¼ cup minced green pepper	¾ cup grated Parmesan cheese
½ teaspoon garlic powder	

1 Preheat the oven to 350 degrees. Line an 9-x-13-inch baking dish with foil; spray the foil with nonstick cooking spray.

2 Clean the mushrooms, removing the stems. Set the caps aside. Chop the stems.

3 In a large skillet, brown the sausage, onion, green pepper, and mushroom stems over medium heat, breaking the meat up with a fork. Stir in the garlic powder, Cajun seasoning, parsley flakes, and cumin.

4 Pile the stuffing into the mushroom caps. Set the caps, stuffing side up, in the prepared baking dish.

5 In a small bowl, stir together the mayonnaise and Parmesan cheese. Spoon the mixture on top of each mushroom cap.

6 Bake the mushrooms at 350 degrees for 35 minutes, or until the cheese is golden.

Per mushroom: *Calories: 8; Total fat: 7 g; Saturated fat: 2 g; Cholesterol: 7 mg; Sodium: 143 mg; Carbohydrates: 1 g; Fiber: 0 g; Sugar: 1 g; Protein: 2 g*

Chapter 16

Salads with Pizzazz

In This Chapter

▶ Tossing the varietal veggies

▶ Fruit can be fun, too

▶ Slipping in some meat

Admittedly, this chapter *has* to be one of the easiest to write. After all, most salads are naturally gluten-free, aren't they? Seriously, when was the last time you shopped for salad-makin's and had to read a label — other than croutons and toppings, of course. "Ingredients: carrot." Hmmm, better look that one up to make sure it's on the approved list of gluten-free ingredients. *Not!*

Best of all, fruits and veggies — aka salad makin's — are a great source of nutrition. Loaded with antioxidants, vitamins, and minerals, they're also a great source of fiber and even water.

In this chapter, I show you lots of ways to jazz up a salad with fruits, veggies, and other ingredients you may not have thought to add to the mix. I also offer some ideas for making gluten-free salads that would otherwise be on the no-no list and show you how to incorporate meat into your salads for a little extra protein and flavor.

If you're making meatloaf, stuffed peppers, sweet breads, or muffins, shred some carrots and/or zucchini into them. They'll add flavor and moisture, and you'll be getting more vitamins without much extra effort. Or you can add chopped green pepper and onion to almost any meat, casserole, or vegetable dish.

Fruit and Vegetable Options

Before you even begin to create a salad, you have to make choices. What kind of lettuce will you select? Will it be iceberg (which has almost no nutritional value), leaf lettuce, spinach, spring field greens, or something more exotic like watercress or Bibb lettuce? A good rule of thumb to remember is that the darker the green, the better it is for you.

When making a fruit salad, begin by placing a handful of crisp greens on a dish, and then use your imagination. Experiment by adding the less common fruits like pomegranate seeds, sliced dates, black raspberries, grapefruit sections, sliced persimmons, or mango cubes.

For vegetable salads, you can jazz up a salad by

- Replacing the cucumber with zucchini
- Substituting sliced roasted red peppers for the tomatoes
- Using feta cheese crumbles instead of shredded cheddar or mozzarella cheese
- Tossing in kalamata olives in place of the ripe olives

Think of some of the alternative options offered at salad bars. Why not borrow some of these ideas to spruce up your own salads? You can include

- Marinated asparagus tips or artichoke hearts
- Peas or snow pea pods
- Diced beets
- Teeny cubes of ham or shredded tuna
- Marinated beans (green, kidney, black, navy)
- Corn kernels
- Nuts (walnuts, pecans, cashews, almonds)
- Raw cauliflower or broccoli
- Sprouts (alfalfa or bean)
- Seeds (poppy, sesame, sunflower)

Life is full of decisions. When you have your salad assembled, what are you going to use for dressing? For a fruit salad, whisk 1 tablespoon of jam into gluten-free Italian dressing and drizzle it over the salad. When tossing a veggie salad, you can choose from a wide variety of gluten-free salad dressings on the market.

No dressing in the cupboard or refrigerator? Not to worry. One of the best salad dressings is still a blend of olive oil and vinegar with seasonings.

Minestrone Salad

This is an antipasto in cut-up form. This tasty salad should be made ahead and then refrigerated to allow the flavors to blend. You can use elbow pasta in place of the shells. *Note:* Don't rinse the pasta if you want the dressing to stick to it.

Preparation time: 15 minutes

Cooking time: 8 minutes

Refrigeration time: 3 hours

Yield: 8 servings

½ cup rice pasta shells	¼ teaspoon pepper
3 tablespoons olive oil	½ teaspoon sugar
2 tablespoons cider vinegar	15.5-ounce can light red kidney beans, rinsed and drained
1 tablespoon balsamic vinegar	
1 tablespoon dried parsley flakes	1 carrot, sliced thin
¾ teaspoon dried oregano	1 medium zucchini, sliced thin
½ teaspoon dried basil	½ green pepper, chopped
½ teaspoon dried mint flakes	1 medium yellow onion, sliced thin
¼ teaspoon salt	⅛ pound pepperoni, slices halved

1 In a medium saucepan, boil the pasta according to the package directions; drain.

2 In a large bowl, whisk together the oil, vinegars, parsley, oregano, basil, mint, salt, pepper, and sugar. Add the pasta and the kidney beans, carrot, zucchini, green pepper, onion, and pepperoni. Toss well to coat the pasta and veggies evenly with the dressing.

3 Cover the salad and refrigerate it for several hours to allow the flavors to blend.

Per serving: Calories: 149; Total fat: 8g; Saturated fat: 2g; Cholesterol: 8mg; Sodium: 318mg; Carbohydrates: 15g; Fiber: 4g; Sugar: 2g; Protein: 4g.

↻ *Marinated Artichoke Salad*

Marinated salads need "bonding" time in the refrigerator to meld all the flavors together. This is the perfect picnic salad because it has no mayonnaise and no fresh greens to wilt.

Preparation time: *5 minutes*

Refrigeration time: *3 hours*

Cooking time: *None*

Yield: *6 servings*

7.5-ounce jar marinated artichokes, reserve juice	*¼ teaspoon pepper*
8-ounce jar marinated button mushrooms, reserve juice	*¼ teaspoon dried dill*
	¼ teaspoon dried oregano
1 large tomato, cut into chunks	*⅛ teaspoon dried mint*
3 cups broccoli florets	*3 tablespoons olive oil*
¼ teaspoon salt	

1 Combine the artichokes, mushrooms, tomato, and broccoli in a large bowl.

2 In a small bowl, whisk together the juices from the artichokes and mushrooms, the salt, pepper, dill, oregano, mint, and oil. Pour the dressing over the vegetables and toss to coat evenly.

3 Cover and refrigerate the salad for several hours to allow the flavors to blend.

Tip: *If you have salad left over, cut up the ingredients, lay them on a piece of gluten-free pita bread or pizza crust, and then melt a slice of mozzarella cheese on top. You have an instant lunch.*

Per serving: *Calories: 95; Total fat: 7g; Saturated fat: 1g; Cholesterol: 0mg; Sodium: 265mg; Carbohydrates: 7g; Fiber: 3g; Sugar: 2g; Protein: 3g.*

☙ *Frosted Fruit Salad*

Fruit never had it so good! This dressing is better than fabulous. Prepare this salad the same day you plan to serve it. Even though this makes a great dinner salad, it can easily double as a dessert.

Tools: *Electric mixer*

Preparation time: *20 minutes*

Cooking time: *None*

Yield: *8 servings*

⅓ cup sweetened condensed milk	*8-ounce can crushed pineapple*
3 ounces cream cheese, softened	*½ cup coarsely chopped walnuts*
2 tablespoons orange marmalade	*½ pint fresh strawberries, hulled and sliced*
½ teaspoon vanilla	*½ pint fresh blueberries*
15.25-ounce can sliced peaches, drained and cut in thirds	*3 ripe kiwis, peeled and sliced*

1 In a large mixing bowl, whip together the condensed milk, cream cheese, marmalade, and vanilla using the electric mixer, until the ingredients are fluffy and well blended.

2 Drain the peaches and pineapple well using a sieve or a colander.

3 Stir the peaches, pineapple, walnuts, strawberries, blueberries, and kiwi into the cream cheese mixture until the salad is blended.

Per serving: *Calories: 233; Total fat: 10g; Saturated fat: 3g; Cholesterol: 16mg; Sodium: 55mg; Carbohydrates: 33g; Fiber: 3g; Sugar: 27g; Protein: 4g.*

☕ *Spinach Mandarin Salad*

Everyone has been told to eat more fresh fruits and vegetables. This luscious salad combines both. When you toast the pine nuts, watch them carefully. After they start to brown, they can burn quickly.

Preparation time: *8 minutes*

Cooking time: *6 minutes*

Yield: *4 servings*

¼ cup pine nuts	2 teaspoons honey
2 tablespoons orange juice	½ teaspoon brown mustard
1½ tablespoons balsamic vinegar	4 cups fresh baby spinach leaves
2 tablespoons olive oil	¼ red onion, sliced thin
⅛ teaspoon salt	15-ounce can mandarin oranges, drained
⅛ teaspoon pepper	

1 Preheat the oven to 400 degrees.

2 Place pine nuts in a small skillet that has been sprayed with nonstick spray. On medium-high heat, toast the nuts, stirring frequently, until they are lightly browned. Remove the pan from the stove and cool.

3 In a small bowl, whisk together the orange juice, vinegar, oil, salt, pepper, honey, and mustard.

4 In a large bowl, toss together the spinach and dressing until evenly coated.

5 Add the onion, oranges, and pine nuts and toss till evenly distributed.

Per serving: *Calories: 199; Total fat: 13g; Saturated fat: 1g; Cholesterol: 0mg; Sodium: 114mg; Carbohydrates: 19g; Fiber: 2g; Sugar: 17g; Protein: 2g.*

☞ *Luscious Lentil Salad*

Before you say, "Yuk! Lentil Salad!" try this one. If you like marinated bean salads, you'll love this salad. It's ideal to pack in a small, covered container for brown-bag lunches with a muffin.

Preparation time: 10 minutes

Cooking time: 8 minutes

Refrigeration time: 2 hours

Yield: 4 servings

⅓ pound lentils	¼ teaspoon dried oregano
3 tablespoons olive oil	1 small onion, chopped
2 tablespoons balsamic vinegar	¼ green pepper, chopped
¼ teaspoon salt	1 rib celery, sliced thin
⅛ teaspoon pepper	½ carrot, sliced thin
¼ teaspoon dried dill	1 tablespoon chopped fresh parsley
⅛ teaspoon dried mint flakes	

1 Place the lentils in a small saucepan and cover with water. Bring the water to a rolling boil, and boil about 15 minutes, or until the lentils are tender but not mushy. Rinse the lentils under cold water, and then drain.

2 Place the lentils in a medium bowl. Add the oil, vinegar, salt, pepper, dill, mint, oregano, onion, green pepper, celery, carrot, and parsley to the bowl. Stir the lentils well to coat them evenly.

3 Cover the salad and refrigerate it for 2 hours to allow the flavors to blend.

Per serving: Calories: 168; Total fat: 10g; Saturated fat: 1g; Cholesterol: 0mg; Sodium: 163mg; Carbohydrates: 15g; Fiber: 5g; Sugar: 4g; Protein: 5g.

☙ Potato Salad Nicoise

The beauty of this salad is that you can make it ahead, cover it, and refrigerate it until serving time. It's hearty enough to serve as a main entrée. And because it doesn't contain any mayonnaise, it's the perfect choice for picnics.

Preparation time: *35 minutes*

Cooking time: *15 minutes*

Refrigeration time: *2 hours*

Yield: *4 servings*

16 small white gourmet potatoes or small red-skinned potatoes	¼ teaspoon garlic powder
	¼ teaspoon salt
4 eggs	¼ teaspoon pepper
2 cups frozen, cut green beans	2 teaspoons dried parsley flakes
2 green onions, sliced thin	½ teaspoon Italian seasoning
4 Roma tomatoes, sliced	2 tablespoons cider vinegar
12 pitted black olives	¼ cup olive oil
1 teaspoon brown mustard	croutons (see the following recipe)

1 Place potatoes in a medium saucepan. Cover with water and bring to a boil. Boil for 20 minutes or until potatoes are just fork tender. Rinse in cold water to cool them down. When cool, slide off the skins and discard skins.

2 Place eggs in a small saucepan. Cover with water and bring to a boil. Boil for 11 minutes and then remove eggs to a colander and rinse well with cold water. When cool enough to handle, peel eggs, discarding shells. Quarter eggs and set aside.

3 Place the beans in a medium saucepan and cover them with water. Bring the beans to a boil and cook them until they're fork tender; rinse the beans in cold water and then drain them. Place the beans in a large bowl.

4 Quarter the potatoes and add them to the beans. Add the green onions, tomatoes, and olives to the bowl.

5 In a small bowl, whisk together the mustard, garlic powder, salt, pepper, parsley flakes, Italian seasoning, vinegar, and oil; pour the dressing over the potato mixture and gently blend to distribute the dressing evenly. Cover the potato salad and refrigerate it for 2 hours.

6 Just before serving, toss in the croutons (see the following recipe) and garnish with the egg wedges.

Gluten-Free Croutons

⅛ teaspoon salt

⅛ teaspoon pepper

¼ teaspoon Italian seasoning

¼ teaspoon garlic powder

1 teaspoon grated Romano cheese

2 tablespoons olive oil

3 slices gluten-free bread

1 Preheat the oven to 300 degrees.

2 In a medium bowl, whisk together the salt, pepper, Italian seasoning, garlic powder, cheese, and oil.

3 Cut the bread into ½-inch cubes.

4 Add the bread cubes to the bowl and toss them until the oil mixture is evenly distributed.

5 Spoon the bread cubes onto a baking sheet and bake them at 300 degrees for 35 minutes, or until the bread is toasted, stirring occasionally. Watch closely so that the cubes don't burn.

Per serving: Calories: 570; Total fat: 28g; Saturated fat: 5g; Cholesterol: 212mg; Sodium: 657mg; Carbohydrates: 68g; Fiber: 10g; Sugar: 7g; Protein: 15g.

Combining Greens with Meats

Unadorned, lettuce is just a side dish that periodically appears near your plate at lunch or dinner. Even though additional ingredients can be added to the lettuce, some people still relegate salads to summer buffets and lunches for those on diets. It's time to reevaluate that thinking. By adding meat and some fiber (sunflower seeds, poppy seeds, sesame seeds, tomatoes, raw baby zucchini, or even flax seed), a salad suddenly becomes a hearty, healthy, great-tasting meal in a bowl.

Asian Pork Salad

Pork and soy sauce (gluten-free, of course) are natural go-togethers. Pork tenderloin is a very tender meat if it's not overcooked. Because the pieces are cut so small (*julienne* or matchstick pieces) in this recipe, they need very little cooking time.

Preparation time: *10 minutes*

Refrigeration time: *3 hours*

Cooking time: *8 minutes*

Yield: *2 servings*

Dressing (see the following recipe)

½ pound pork tenderloin, cut into thin slices, then julienned

1 tablespoon plus 2 teaspoons olive oil

2 teaspoons plus 2 teaspoons gluten-free soy sauce

1 clove garlic, minced

¼ teaspoon cayenne pepper

¼ teaspoon ginger

¼ teaspoon dried mint

3 tablespoons fresh lemon juice

8 snow peas

¼ green pepper, cut in half, then julienned

1 onion, sliced

4 sprigs fresh parsley, chopped

3 cups (1 bunch) watercress, trimmed

1 teaspoon sesame seeds

1 Place the pork, 1 tablespoon of olive oil, 2 teaspoons of soy sauce, garlic, cayenne pepper, ginger, mint, and lemon juice in bowl. Blend the ingredients well, and then cover and refrigerate for 3 hours to marinate the meat.

2 Heat 2 teaspoons of olive oil in a large skillet or wok over medium heat. Remove the pork from the marinade (discarding the marinade) and sauté the pork until no pink shows (about 2 minutes).

3 Add the snow peas, green pepper, onions, and parsley to the skillet and sauté for 1½ minutes on high heat. (The vegetables should be crisp.) Drizzle 2 teaspoons of soy sauce over the pork mixture and toss. Remove the skillet from the heat.

4 Place the watercress on two dinner plates, dividing evenly. Spoon the pork and vegetables on top.

5 Whisk the dressing to mix and then drizzle it on top of the salads. Sprinkle the salads with sesame seeds.

Dressing

½ teaspoon brown mustard

1½ teaspoons gluten-free soy sauce

1 tablespoon balsamic vinegar

2 tablespoons olive oil

⅛ teaspoon pepper

Dash cayenne pepper

In a small bowl, whisk together the mustard, soy sauce, vinegar, oil, pepper, and cayenne pepper. Cover the dressing and refrigerate it until needed.

Per serving: Calories: 496; Total fat: 33g; Saturated fat: 6g; Cholesterol: 106mg; Sodium: 1,050mg; Carbohydrates: 13g; Fiber: 2g; Sugar: 5g; Protein: 38g.

Baked Chicken Salad

Who doesn't like chicken? Thanks to the mayo, celery, and green pepper, this dish qualifies as a hot salad. And talk about convenience: You can used boiled, broiled, fried, grilled, or roasted chicken breast in this recipe — just whatever you have on hand or leftover from a previous meal.

Preparation time: *10 minutes*

Cooking time: *30 minutes*

Yield: *4 servings*

2 boneless, skinless chicken breasts, cooked	*1 teaspoon dried parsley flakes*
1 cup chopped celery	*¼ cup chopped onion*
¼ cup slivered almonds	*1¼ cups mayonnaise*
3 tablespoons chopped green pepper	*1 cup crushed potato chips*

1 Preheat the oven to 350 degrees. Grease a 9-inch-square baking dish.

2 Cut the cooked chicken breasts into ½-inch cubes, and place them in a large bowl.

3 Add the celery, almonds, green pepper, parsley, onion, and mayonnaise to the bowl. Using a rubber spatula, mix until the ingredients are well combined.

4 Spoon the mixture into the prepared pan. Sprinkle potato chips over the top.

5 Bake the chicken salad at 350 degrees for 30 minutes.

Vary It! *You can use buttered gluten-free bread crumbs in place of the potato chips.*

Per serving: Calories: 490; Total fat: 33g; Saturated fat: 5g; Cholesterol: 70mg; Sodium: 662mg; Carbohydrates: 26g; Fiber: 2g; Sugar: 6g; Protein: 24g.

Taco Salad in Tortilla Shells

Are you tired of sprinkling a few gluten-free tortilla chips on top of a salad so you can call it a taco salad? This recipe tweaks the taco! Get the larger, 10-inch gluten-free corn tortillas so you can create your own taco shells.

Preparation time: *1 hour*

Cooking time: *10 minutes*

Yield: *4 servings*

4 taco shells (see the following recipe)	*1 small head iceberg lettuce*
1 pound lean ground beef	*3 green onions, sliced thin*
1 tablespoon olive oil	*3 plum tomatoes, diced*
1.25-ounce envelope gluten-free taco seasoning mix	*1 cup shredded cheddar cheese*
1 cup water	*½ cup Italian dressing*
8-ounce can light red kidney beans, rinsed and drained	

1 Make the taco shells and set them aside.

2 In a large skillet, brown the beef in the oil over medium-high heat, breaking the meat up with a fork.

3 Stir in the taco seasoning and water. Add the kidney beans and simmer the mixture gently until the moisture has been absorbed, stirring occasionally. Remove the skillet from the heat.

4 Cut the lettuce crosswise into thin strips and place it in a large bowl.

5 Add the green onions, tomatoes, cheese, ground beef, and dressing; toss the ingredients to blend well.

6 Serve the salad in the tortilla shells.

Tortilla Shells

Four 8-inch corn tortillas   *Nonstick cooking spray*

1 Preheat the oven to 400 degrees.

2 Wrap the tortillas in a damp paper towel. Warm them in the microwave for 15 seconds to soften.

3 Spray the outside of a 6- or 7-inch round glass bowl or baking dish (large custard cups work great) with the cooking spray.

4 Mold 1 tortilla over the bottom of the inverted bowl or baking dish.

5 Bake the tortilla at 400 degrees for 15 minutes, or until the tortilla is very crisp and lightly browned.

6 Carefully remove the shell from the bowl and set it aside to cool. Repeat Steps 3, 4, and 5 with the remaining tortillas.

Tip: *If you have more than one bowl or baking dish that is 6 or 7 inches in diameter, you can bake several tortillas at a time, cutting down on the baking time.*

Per serving: *Calories: 52; Total fat: 1g; Saturated fat: 0g; Cholesterol: 0mg; Sodium: 11mg; Carbohydrates: 11g; Fiber: 2g; Sugar: 0g; Protein: 1g.*

Marinated Steak Salad

To get the most flavor from this salad, write a note to yourself to marinate the steak early in the morning or overnight so it will absorb all the essence of the seasonings. Although this recipe is even better when the steak is grilled over an open fire, using the broiler is a very good alternative. Gluten-free croutons have not been added to this salad, but they make an excellent addition.

Preparation time: *10 minutes*

Refrigeration time: *2 hours*

Cooking time: *15 minutes*

Yield: *8 servings*

3 tablespoons gluten-free soy sauce	*6 cups baby spinach leaves*
3 tablespoons balsamic vinegar	*½ cup thin, diagonally cut carrot slices*
¼ teaspoon ginger	*½ cup thinly sliced cucumber*
¼ cup water	*½ cup thinly sliced radishes*
2 tablespoons olive oil	*1 cup small broccoli florets*
1½ pound well-trimmed beef sirloin steak, 1 inch thick	*24 pea pods, blanched*
	4 teaspoons sesame seeds

1 In a small bowl, whisk together the soy sauce, vinegar, ginger, water, and oil.

2 Pour half of the mixture into a self-seal plastic bag. Cover the remaining mixture in a bowl and refrigerate it.

3 Place the steak in the self-seal plastic bag with the marinade, turning to coat. Seal the bag and marinate the meat in the refrigerator for 2 hours.

4 Preheat the broiler.

5 Remove the steak from the marinade and place the meat on a broiler pan. Broil the steak for 15 minutes (medium rare) or to desired doneness, turning once. Let the meat stand 5 minutes, and then carve it into thin slices.

6 Distribute the spinach leaves evenly onto 8 salad dishes. Top with the carrot, cucumber, and radish slices. Sprinkle the salads with the broccoli and place the pea pods on the salads.

7 Sprinkle the salads with the reserved dressing. Top with the steak slices and then sprinkle with the sesame seeds.

Per serving: *Calories: 245; Total fat: 13g; Saturated fat: 5g; Cholesterol: 62mg; Sodium: 468mg; Carbohydrates: 5g; Fiber: 2g; Sugar: 2g; Protein: 27g.*

Chapter 17

Slurpilicious Soups

. . . .

In This Chapter

▶ Singing soup's goodness

▶ Soups that'll stick to your ribs

▶ Lighter, healthier fare

▶ Standalone meals: Chili and chowders

. . . .

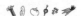
*W*hoever invented soups was a genius. What other food concoction allows you to dump almost anything into some water, cover it, and let it cook all by itself, and then call it a meal?

Soup is the ideal solution for gardeners. In late summer, when you have more vegetables than you know what to do with, when you can't even *give* away all that stuff hanging off vines and popping up through the ground, consider chopping up that yield and making a huge pot of soup. Soup is a cornucopia of nutrition and tastes.

No Glutens and Swimming with Flavor

As the old-time theme song from one of the large soup companies used to say about soup, MMMMM . . . MMMMM . . . GOOD! If you steam vegetables to serve as a side dish, the water used to steam them (which is overflowing with nutrients from these veggies) is poured down the drain. With soup, all the nutrients that these natural foods exude during cooking remain in the broth, and you just know that has to be healthy and good for you.

If soups have one drawback, it's that for the broths to be palatable, it seems like you have to dump in half the salt shaker. Still, you have options. The best option is to reduce the amount of salt used and use more herbs and spices for flavoring. Here are some tips for using herbs and spices:

- ✔ Fresh herbs are much more potent and impart more flavor than dried ones, so less is needed. But fresh herbs vary greatly in strength and the amount of flavor they exude.

- ✔ Dominant, strong flavors include cardamom, curry, ginger, hot peppers, black pepper, mustard, rosemary, cloves, and sage.

- ✔ Medium flavors are found in basil, celery seed, cumin, dill, fennel, tarragon, garlic, marjoram, mint, oregano, thyme, and turmeric.

- ✔ Then there are herbs that you can use by the bushelful. They add a very mild flavor, like parsley, chives, and chervil.

- ✔ Usually ¼ teaspoon of dried or powdered herbs equals ¾ to 1 teaspoon of fresh herbs that are cut or crumbled.

The recipes that follow will help you think beyond chicken noodle (albeit gluten-free noodle) soup. I don't mean to demean or berate chicken soup. At the first sign of a sniffle or sneeze, chances are you reach for chicken soup and hot tea. The medicinal effects of this soup are more than just an old wives' tale. Chicken soup has been prescribed for the common cold as far back as the ancient Egyptians.

If your soup is too thin for your liking, stir in a small amount of gluten-free instant potato flakes to thicken it up almost instantly. If it's too greasy, lay a few lettuce leaves on top of the broth to absorb the fat. And if you plan to freeze the soup, hold off adding any pasta to it until you thaw and reheat it, or the gluten-free pasta may get too soft and fall apart.

Broths and Hearty Soups

When you make rice or quinoa, using chicken broth instead of water infuses it with wonderful flavor. Use a small amount of broth instead of butter or oil to sauté vegetables. As for that take-home doggie bag from an Asian restaurant, adding a little broth is perfect for reheating a stir-fry. Instead of adding water to casseroles and roasts, use broth. Use broth as a base for gravies and au jus. Boil your gluten-free pasta in broth instead of water and taste what a difference it makes. Are you boiling chicken? Or boiling potatoes for a potato salad? Boiling them in chicken broth increases their flavor quotient. For added flavor and moisture, replace the water with broth when making your Thanksgiving stuffing (gluten-free, of course). Don't forget to use broth to baste the turkey. And the next time you make muffins, substitute chicken broth for the milk. Don't wrinkle up your face. Just try it!

Then there are the "meal-in-a-bowl" soups, the hearty soups that fill your kitchen with cozy and tantalizing aromas as they cook. Nutritionists believe that a hot, hearty soup satisfies hunger because it tends to be eaten slowly. Scientists claim that hearty soups fill you up because they are usually loaded with fiber, iron, potassium, lots of vitamins and minerals, and often are high in protein.

Spicy Chicken Soup

This soup is many things, but boring isn't one of them. You can adjust how hot this soup is by increasing or decreasing the amount of chili powder and hot pepper sauce you use. Just before serving, try stirring in ⅓ cup of gluten-free sour cream for variety; this addition adds even more flavor to the soup. Make plenty because your crew *will* want second helpings!

Preparation time: *10 minutes*

Cooking time: *35 minutes*

Yield: *6 servings*

1 medium onion, chopped	½ teaspoon pepper
2 cloves garlic, minced	2 teaspoons gluten-free Worcestershire sauce
¼ cup minced green pepper	½ teaspoon chili powder
2 tablespoons olive oil	1 teaspoon ground cumin
4-ounce can chopped green chilies, drained	¼ teaspoon hot pepper sauce
15-ounce can diced tomatoes	2 boneless, skinless chicken breasts, boiled until tender
Four 10.5-ounce cans gluten-free chicken broth	3 ounces processed cheese
¼ teaspoon salt	

1 In a large saucepan over medium-high heat, sauté the onion, garlic, and green pepper in oil until they're soft, stirring frequently.

2 Stir in the drained green chilies, tomatoes with their juice, broth, salt, pepper, Worcestershire sauce, chili powder, cumin, and hot pepper sauce. Cover the saucepan and simmer the soup for 20 minutes.

3 Cut the chicken into ½-inch cubes. Stir them into the soup and simmer for 5 minutes.

4 Stir the cheese into the soup, stirring until it's melted.

Per serving: Calories: 252; Total fat: 11g; Saturated fat: 3g; Cholesterol: 76mg; Sodium: 1,994mg; Carbohydrates: 9g; Fiber: 2g; Sugar: 6g; Protein: 28g.

Hearty Chicken Broth

There was a time when you could make this broth and then freeze it in ice cube trays to have handy to perk up rice, gravy, and so on. But alas, the ice cube tray is fast becoming a relic. However, you can still freeze small portions of this broth in some of the small plastic containers available. Leave the skin on some of the vegetables for added flavor and to add a bit of color to the clear broth.

Preparation time: *10 minutes*

Cooking time: *1½ hours*

Yield: *6 servings*

10 cups water	*2 ribs celery, cut in thirds*
1½ pounds chicken wings (about 6 wings)	*2 cloves garlic, cut in half*
4 thin-skinned potatoes, unpeeled, cut in quarters	*3 sprigs fresh parsley*
	½ teaspoon dried dill weed
1 medium onion, quartered	*1½ teaspoons salt*
8 fresh mushrooms	*5 peppercorns*
2 leeks, trimmed and cut into 4 sections	*1 bay leaf*
2 carrots, cut in large chunks	*1 clove*

1 Combine all the ingredients in a large stockpot.

2 Bring the water to a boil, and then reduce the heat and simmer, uncovered, for 1½ hours. (When the water begins to boil, don't skim the surface of the broth.)

3 Strain the soup into a large pot or bowl, removing all the solids. Let the broth cool.

4 Keep the broth refrigerated, covered, up to 3 days. Before reheating the broth, skim off and discard any congealed fat that has collected on top of the broth. You can also freeze the broth until you're ready to use it.

Tip: *After you strain the soup, pick out the potatoes, cut them up, and make a potato salad by adding green pepper, onion, salt, pepper, oregano, olive oil, and a dash of cider vinegar. You can also pick out the chicken wings, sprinkle them with salt, pepper, and lemon juice, and enjoy them either warm or cold.*

Per serving: *Calories: 238; Total fat: 8g; Saturated fat: 2g; Cholesterol: 38mg; Sodium: 685mg; Carbohydrates: 30g; Fiber: 4g; Sugar: 3g; Protein: 12g.*

Spaghetti and Meatball Soup

Have you ever known anyone to say "No, thank you" when offered spaghetti and meatballs? Kids from 3 to 103 will love this soup version of an all-time favorite combination. Serve it with a large tossed salad, and you have a complete dinner.

Preparation time: *20 minutes*

Cooking time: *20 minutes*

Yield: *4 servings*

4 teaspoons pesto sauce	*¼ teaspoon salt*
½ pound lean ground beef	*¼ teaspoon pepper*
½ onion, chopped	*⅔ cup spaghetti sauce*
1 clove garlic, minced	*Three 14.5-ounce cans gluten-free chicken broth*
½ cup carrots, sliced thin	
1 tablespoon olive oil	*¼ pound gluten-free spaghetti*
2 tablespoons chopped fresh parsley	*4 tablespoons grated Parmesan cheese*

1 Drain off the oil that has collected at the top of the pesto before measuring the pesto. Place the pesto in a medium bowl.

2 Add the ground beef to the bowl and mix it with the pesto until the ingredients are completely blended. Roll the mixture into tiny meatballs (no wider than a nickel). Set aside.

3 In a large saucepan, sauté the meatballs, onion, garlic and carrots in the oil, over medium-high heat, turning the meat frequently, until the vegetables are tender and the meat is cooked through.

4 Add the parsley, salt, pepper, and spaghetti sauce; bring to a boil over medium-high heat. Lower heat to medium-low, cover the pan, and gently simmer for 15 minutes.

5 In a medium saucepan, bring the broth to a boil. Break the spaghetti into fourths and add it to the broth. Cook the spaghetti over medium-high heat for 5 minutes, or just until the pasta is barely tender.

6 Add the spaghetti and broth to the meatball mixture and simmer for 3 minutes. Spoon the soup into bowls and sprinkle with the cheese.

Per serving: Calories: 253; Total fat: 10g; Saturated fat: 5g; Cholesterol: 53mg; Sodium: 2,091mg; Carbohydrates: 6g; Fiber: 7g; Sugar: 12g; Protein: 23g.

Lamb and Rice Soup

You've tried beef broth. You've tried chicken broth. Now try lamb broth. This isn't your ordinary soup! The egg-lemon sauce adds a whole new dimension to the taste sensation in the broth. Sautéing the vegetables first brings out their full flavor. Add the hot broth very slowly to the eggs to prevent curdling.

Tools: *Electric mixer*

Preparation time: *10 minutes*

Cooking time: *1¾ hours*

Yield: *6 servings*

1 tablespoon olive oil	2 gluten-free chicken bouillon cubes
¾ cup chopped celery	¾ teaspoon salt
1 onion, chopped	¼ teaspoon pepper
1½ pounds lamb bone-in shoulder steak	⅓ cup uncooked rice
8 cups water	3 eggs, at room temperature
2 tablespoons minced fresh parsley	3 tablespoons fresh lemon juice

1 In a large saucepan over medium heat, sauté the celery and onion in oil slowly, stirring often, until the vegetables are softened.

2 Add the lamb, water, parsley, and bouillon cubes.

3 Bring the liquid to a boil, and then lower the heat to medium-low, cover the pan, and simmer for 1½ hours until the lamb is very tender.

4 Remove the lamb and cut the meat into tiny pieces. Discard the bones and any fat. Add the lamb to the saucepan.

5 Stir in the salt, pepper, and rice. Cover the pan and simmer the soup for 15 minutes until the rice is tender.

6 In a large mixing bowl, use the electric mixer to whip the eggs for 3 minutes. Add the lemon juice.

7 Very gradually, drizzle the hot broth from the soup into the eggs, whipping the mixture on high to blend. (The easiest way to add the broth to the eggs is to tip the pan slightly so the broth comes to the top and then dip it out with a soup ladle.) When the bowl feels warm to the touch, lower the mixer speed to medium and continue slowly adding most of the broth from the saucepan.

8 Slowly pour the egg mixture back into the saucepan with the lamb, stirring constantly. Simmer the soup on low for 1 minute, stirring constantly. Serve immediately.

Per serving: *Calories: 231; Total fat: 12g; Saturated fat: 4g; Cholesterol: 154mg; Sodium: 655mg; Carbohydrates: 11g; Fiber: 1g; Sugar: 2g; Protein: 19g.*

Italian Beef Vegetable Soup

Nothing warms the tummy on a cold winter evening like a hot bowl of Beef Vegetable Soup. All that's missing are some warmed gluten-free rolls as an accompaniment. If you plan to freeze the soup, don't add the pasta because it may get mushy when you thaw it.

Preparation time: *15 minutes*

Cooking time: *35 minutes*

Yield: *10 servings*

¾ pound 90 percent lean ground beef

1 medium onion, chopped

1 teaspoon minced garlic

2 tablespoons olive oil

2 cups gluten-free beef broth

5 cups water

2 teaspoons gluten-free beef bouillon granules

14.5-ounce can diced tomatoes

8-ounce can kidney beans, undrained

½ small head cabbage, shredded

2 stalks celery, sliced thin

1 large carrot, sliced thin

1 small zucchini, cut into small cubes

2 tablespoons dried parsley flakes

¼ teaspoon pepper

1 teaspoon salt (add more salt to taste if needed)

1 teaspoon Italian seasoning

1½ cups uncooked gluten-free pasta (elbow macaroni, noodles, broken spaghetti, so on)

1 In a Dutch oven or large saucepan over medium-high heat, brown the beef, onion, and garlic in olive oil, breaking the meat up with a fork. Drain off the excess fat.

2 Stir in the remaining ingredients except the pasta. Heat to boiling.

3 Reduce the heat to medium-low. Cover and simmer the soup for 20 minutes.

4 Add the pasta and cook the soup 10 minutes more, or until the pasta is tender but not mushy.

Per serving: *Calories: 238; Total fat: 10g; Saturated fat: 3g; Cholesterol: 41mg; Sodium: 1,031mg; Carbohydrates: 20g; Fiber: 5g; Sugar: 3g; Protein: 18g.*

Meatless Marvels

Anyone who's ever been on a diet undoubtedly at some point has eaten cabbage soup. Although cabbage is certainly a healthy vegetable, don't neglect the other great options of vegetable soups available to you. Scientists are providing us with evidence that consuming a lot of vegetables and beans may reduce our stress levels, help fight cancer and heart disease, and fight free radicals. But aside from all this technical stuff, vegetable soups taste great!

ᕲ *Cream of Mushroom Soup*

Everyone on a gluten-free diet seems to be in search of a suitable substitute for con-densed cream of mushroom soup to use in casseroles. To convert this recipe to a con-densed version, add an additional ½ teaspoon cornstarch and use only 1 can of vegetable broth.

Tools: *Blender*

Preparation time: *20 minutes*

Cooking time: *10 minutes*

Yield: *4 servings*

2 tablespoons butter	1½ tablespoons cornstarch
1 small onion, chopped	2 tablespoons grated Parmesan cheese
1 clove garlic, chopped	1 teaspoon salt
1 celery stalk, sliced thin	½ teaspoon pepper
8-ounce can mushroom stems and pieces (reserve liquid)	1¼ cups half-and-half
Two 14.5-ounce cans gluten-free vegetable broth	2 tablespoons sherry

1 In a medium skillet, sauté the onion, garlic, celery, and mushrooms in the butter over medium heat until the onions are translucent and soft (about 6 minutes), stirring fre-quently.

2 Add 1½ cups of the broth and simmer until the vegetables are very soft (about 10 minutes).

3 In a medium bowl, stir the cornstarch into the remaining broth until smooth.

4 Put the vegetable mixture, the remainder of the broth, the cheese, salt, and pepper into a blender. Cover and puree. (Alternative method: You can blend the mixture with a wand blender until it's smooth.) Spoon the mixture into a medium saucepan.

5 Add the reserved mushroom liquid.

6 Heat the soup over medium heat, stirring constantly, until the mixture thickens.

7 Stir in the half-and-half and simmer until the soup is warmed. Do not allow the mixture to boil.

8 Remove the soup from the heat and stir in the sherry.

Per serving: *Calories: 234; Total fat: 15g; Saturated fat: 10g; Cholesterol: 45mg; Sodium: 1,157mg; Carbohydrates: 17g; Fiber: 2g; Sugar: 4g; Protein: 5g.*

☞ Three Bean Soup

Beans are high in carbs, but the good kind of carbs, the natural (not processed) carbs. They also are high in protein and fiber and contain almost no sodium or fat. Now how good is that? Using canned beans in this recipe cuts down on the preparation time of this soup without cutting down on taste. By mashing a few of the beans, the soup becomes thicker.

Preparation time: *10 minutes*

Cooking time: *1 hour*

Yield: *6 servings*

3 tablespoons olive oil

1 cup chopped onion

1 clove garlic, minced

1 cup chopped celery

1 cup chopped carrot

½ cup chopped green pepper

¼ cup fresh chopped parsley

15.5-ounce can navy beans, rinsed and drained

15.5-ounce can black beans, rinsed and drained

15.5-ounce can light kidney beans, rinsed and drained

1 bay leaf

1¼ teaspoon salt

¼ teaspoon pepper

8-ounce can tomato sauce

6 cups water

1 In a large saucepan, sauté the onion, garlic, celery, carrots, green pepper, and parsley in the oil over medium heat, stirring often, until the vegetables are soft.

2 Place ⅓ of the navy beans in a small bowl and mash them with the back of a fork.

3 Stir the mashed beans plus the remaining navy beans, black beans, kidney beans, bay leaf, salt, pepper, tomato sauce, and water into the saucepan. Stir to blend. Bring the ingredients to a boil, and then lower the heat and simmer, covered, for one hour. Remove the bay leaf before serving.

Per serving: *Calories: 277; Total fat: 8g; Saturated fat: 1g; Cholesterol: 0mg; Sodium: 1,452mg; Carbohydrates: 41g; Fiber: 14g; Sugar: 6g; Protein: 13g.*

⏺ Spinach Lentil Soup

This soup makes eating healthy fun and painless. You'll have to do a lot of searching to find a soup that is healthier for you and tastes better than this one. Adding a teeny amount of cider vinegar makes all the difference in the world in the taste of this creation. If the tomato sauce and salt are added too early, the lentils may not cook thoroughly.

Preparation time: *20 minutes*

Cooking time: *50 minutes*

Yield: *6 servings*

1 pound brown lentils	*2 bay leaves*
8 cups water	*10-ounce box chopped spinach, thawed*
2 tablespoons olive oil	*8 cups water*
½ cup chopped celery	*8-ounce can tomato sauce*
⅓ cup chopped carrots	*1¼ teaspoon salt*
1 large onion, chopped	*¼ teaspoon pepper*
1 clove garlic, minced	*2 teaspoons cider vinegar*
3 sprigs fresh parsley, chopped	

1 Place the lentils in a large saucepan and cover them with water. Cook the lentils on high until the water comes to a boil. Remove the pan from the heat and drain the lentils in a colander. Rinse them well under cold running water and drain again.

2 In the same saucepan, over medium heat, sauté the celery, carrots, onion, and garlic in the oil. Stir the mixture frequently until the vegetables are tender but not browned.

3 Add the lentils, parsley, bay leaves, spinach, and 8 cups of water. Bring the contents to a boil, skimming off any foam as needed.

4 Lower the heat, cover the pan, and simmer for 40 minutes, or until the lentils are very soft, adding more water if needed.

5 Stir in the tomato sauce, salt, pepper, and vinegar. Continue to simmer the soup for 10 minutes. Discard the bay leaves before serving.

Per serving: *Calories: 155; Total fat: 5g; Saturated fat: 1g; Cholesterol: 0mg; Sodium: 698mg; Carbohydrates: 22g; Fiber: 8g; Sugar: 5g; Protein: 8g.*

☞ Waist-Slimming Cabbage Soup

Make a large pot of this soup because it will keep in the refrigerator for several days. That's the bad news because now you don't have any excuse not to have it for lunch. It won't be as easy to say, "Oh, I just ran out of cabbage soup." The good news is that this is one terrific-tasting soup. Forget that it's healthy and just enjoy how good it is.

Preparation time: *15 minutes*

Cooking time: *1 hour*

Yield: *12 servings*

6 medium onions, chopped	*8 stalks celery, sliced thin*
2 cloves garlic, minced	*1 package gluten-free onion soup dry mix*
1 large green pepper, seeded and chopped	*½ teaspoon salt*
14.5-ounce can diced tomatoes with juice	*¼ teaspoon pepper*
1 medium head of cabbage, cored and chopped	*4 cups gluten-free chicken broth*
½ bunch parsley, chopped	*1 cup water*
3 large carrots, sliced thin	*2 bay leaves*

1 Place all the ingredients in a large saucepan.

2 Bring the ingredients to a rapid boil, and then reduce the heat, cover the pan, and let the soup simmer for 1 hour.

3 Discard the bay leaves before serving.

Per serving: *Calories: 78; Total fat: 2g; Saturated fat: 0g; Cholesterol: 0mg; Sodium: 540mg; Carbohydrates: 16g; Fiber: 5g; Sugar: 7g; Protein: 3g.*

Chili and Chowders: A More Filling Chow

Did you know (or even care) that the name *chowder* is French for "cauldron"? Chowders are soups that are thickened with milk. Although milk is good, using half-and-half is even better — it makes thicker and richer soups.

As for chili, each part of the country claims to have the best chili — whether it's Real Texas Chili, Authentic Cincinnati Chili, West Virginia's Real McCoy Chili, or California Turkey Chili (how can Turkey Chili be *real* chili?). Despite all these claims, the very best chili recipe doesn't come from any of these states or locales. The very best chili is the recipe for Unrivaled Chili below!

Unrivaled Chili

This chili is beyond mouth warming and tongue tingling. It borders on stomach-lining challenging. After an initial tasting, you can add more chili powder or a few drops of gluten-free hot pepper sauce if you like your tongue to blister and swell and your throat to be on fire. (We recommend that you taste this recipe first to be sure you want to add more hot stuff.) You can adorn your bowl with a dollop of sour cream, chopped green onions, cheddar cheese, or whatever you like. Serve this chili with gluten-free crackers, serve it over gluten-free pasta, or just eat it as is for the greatest bowl of chili you've ever tasted!

Preparation time: *10 minutes*

Cooking time: *20 minutes*

Yield: *6 servings*

1 tablespoon olive oil	15-ounce can kidney beans with liquid
1 pound 90 percent lean ground beef	15-ounce can black beans, rinsed and drained
½ medium green pepper, chopped	
1 medium onion, chopped	1½ teaspoons chili powder
1 rib celery, chopped	1 teaspoon cumin
2 cloves garlic, minced	¼ teaspoon cayenne pepper
8-ounce can tomato sauce	½ teaspoon salt
15-ounce can diced tomatoes	¼ teaspoon pepper
1½ cups water	¼ cup grated Parmesan cheese

1 In a large saucepan over medium-high heat, sauté the ground beef, green pepper, onion, celery, and garlic in the oil, breaking the meat up with a fork as it cooks.

2 Stir in the remaining ingredients except the cheese. Bring the ingredients to a boil, and then reduce the heat. Cover the pan and simmer, stirring occasionally, for 15 to 20 minutes, until the broth thickens.

3 Stir in the cheese until it's melted.

Per serving: *Calories: 329; Total fat: 10g; Saturated fat: 4g; Cholesterol: 49mg; Sodium: 1,039mg; Carbohydrates: 34g; Fiber: 10g; Sugar: 7g; Protein: 26g.*

Cheesy Corn Chowder

As *corny* as this may sound, some people have never tasted corn chowder. It's much tastier than cream of potato soup, and the cheese added to this soup makes it an instant hit with the family.

Preparation time: *10 minutes*

Cooking time: *20 minutes*

Yield: *4 servings*

4 strips bacon	1 teaspoon salt
1 tablespoon olive oil	⅛ teaspoon pepper
½ cup minced onions	¼ teaspoon dried oregano
¼ cup green pepper, minced	¼ teaspoon dried thyme
1 clove garlic, minced	1½ cups half-and-half
10-ounce box frozen corn, thawed	1 tablespoon cornstarch
2½ cups gluten-free chicken broth	¼ cup shredded sharp cheddar cheese

1 In a large saucepan, fry the bacon until it's crisp. Drain the bacon on paper toweling.

2 Add the oil, onion, green pepper, and garlic to the bacon drippings in the pan. Sauté the vegetables slowly for 5 minutes, until they're soft but not browned.

3 Add the corn, broth, salt, pepper, oregano, and thyme. Bring the mixture to a boil, and then reduce the heat. Cover and simmer for 2 minutes.

4 In a medium bowl, whisk together the half-and-half and cornstarch. Stir it into the corn mixture. Cook the soup over low heat, stirring constantly, until the mixture thickens slightly (about 6 minutes). Do not allow the mixture to boil. Crumble the bacon, and then stir in the bacon pieces and cheese until the cheese is completely melted.

Vary It! Some like it hot, and some don't. If you like spicy foods, add ⅛ teaspoon cayenne pepper to this chowder for extra pizzazz.

Per serving: *Calories: 305; Total fat: 20g; Saturated fat: 10g; Cholesterol: 50mg; Sodium: 1,211mg; Carbohydrates: 24g; Fiber: 2g; Sugar: 1g; Protein: 11g.*

Seafood Chowder

Although this chowder calls for clams and crabmeat, no one will be the wiser if you use scallops and shrimp or any combination of seafood you like.

Preparation time: *35 minutes, plus 1 hour resting time*

Cooking time: *35 minutes*

Yield: *6 servings*

½ teaspoon butter

2 slices bacon, minced

1 cup onion, minced

1 cup celery, chopped

Two 14.5-ounce cans gluten-free chicken broth

½ teaspoon dried thyme

¼ teaspoon salt

¼ teaspoon pepper

1 teaspoon dried parsley flakes

¼ teaspoon garlic powder

2 medium potatoes, boiled, peeled, and diced

2 cups broccoli florets, cut into small pieces

6.5-ounce can clams, liquid reserved

1½ tablespoons cornstarch

8-ounce bottle clam juice

1½ cups half-and-half

4.25-ounce can crabmeat

¼ pound fresh, shelled, cooked baby shrimp

½ cup sherry

½ cup grated Romano cheese

1 In a large saucepan, melt the butter, and then sauté the bacon bits over medium-high heat. When the bacon is crisp, add the celery and onion and cook, stirring frequently, until the vegetables are tender (about 5 minutes).

2 Add the broth; bring it to a boil.

3 Add the thyme, salt, pepper, parsley flakes, garlic powder, and potatoes. Stir in the broccoli and simmer until the broccoli is tender.

4 Drain the clams and set them aside, reserving the juice.

5 In a medium bowl, whisk the cornstarch into the reserved clam juice. Add the bottled clam juice. Stir the cornstarch mixture into the vegetable mixture and bring it to a boil. Reduce the heat. Stir in the half-and-half and simmer for 20 minutes.

6 Stir in the clams, shrimp, crabmeat, sherry, and cheese. Cook the chowder over low heat until the cheese is melted.

7 Set the chowder aside for 1 hour, covered, to allow the flavors to blend. Place the pan over low heat to slowly reheat. Do not allow the chowder to boil.

Per serving: Calories: 321; Total fat: 17g; Saturated fat: 9g; Cholesterol: 180mg; Sodium: 1,078mg; Carbohydrates: 25g; Fiber: 3g; Sugar: 4g; Protein: 18g.

Chapter 18

Stupendous Snacks

A s "into" nutrition as I am, I'm still a snacker. Pretty much all day long, I'm eating, so it's important to have handy, quick snacks, sans gluten, of course. Because we live in a society where snacks usually consist of crackers, cookies, or pretzels, it may seem at first as though gluten-free snacks would be hard to come by. But there's so much good news to convey about gluten-free snacking that the only problem is where to begin.

People today lead busy lifestyles, so we're usually grabbing snack foods to save time — so snacks-on-the-run are key. But snacking is more than just a time-saver. And while it sometimes has a bad rap, it turns out snacking may actually be *good* for you.

A study done throughout 12 European countries showed that people who eat more frequently are actually healthier than those who eat three square meals a day. (Hooray for snacking!) Some elderly people have poor appetites, so snacking more frequently enables them to get the nutrition they need. Snackers also tend to eat throughout the day (as opposed to throughout the evening), so their bodies have time to burn off the calories before bedtime.

And finally, the more you snack, the more your body has to work to digest all that food — and that uses up more energy. Aren't all the health experts telling us we should expend more energy? So eating must be good for us, and eating often must be better. Nibbling between meals lessens the hunger pangs, preventing gorging at mealtime. (Okay, okay, I know that *what* you're snacking on is an important consideration, but this is the *snack* chapter, not the weight-loss chapter.)

Now that I've made our case for snacking, let's get to it!

Snackin' Healthy

No matter what your age, you should be aware of a couple of rules when it comes to snacking. Know the ingredients in snacks you buy off the grocery shelf. For a general healthy rule, try to stay away from Olestra, artificial sweeteners, and anything hydrogenated (trans fats) or with MSG (those things don't have gluten in them; they're just bad for you).

When you read the list of ingredients, if a word has more than three syllables and is hard to pronounce, it's probably not good for you. Most likely it's a chemical additive and not something you should eat. You're better off sticking with natural ingredients.

If you're watching your weight, beware of bowls and bags. Mindlessly reaching into a large bag of chips or large bowl of popcorn usually ends up in overindulgence and tight jeans. On the other hand, if you have these snacks pre-portioned into snack-size self-seal bags or small serving plates, the degree of debauchery is limited to the amount of goodies you can squeeze into one little bag or onto one little plate.

One idea for snacking is to make your own gluten-free granola and trail mix. Have bags of cherries or grapes handy. Gluten-free crackers with cheese are always good. Keep a supply of gluten-free pretzels for the snack drawer. A single-serving container of gluten-free yogurt with fruit is a healthy alternative. You can find several brands of gluten-free tortilla chips in the grocery stores — add some salsa and you have a terrific snack. And it's always fun to munch on popcorn.

Cool Snacks for Chillin' Out

Everybody loves to snack, whether it's to curb the midafternoon grum-bellies, to eat something small to get you through the evening after an early dinner, or to make car trips or airline flights more pleasant. Snacking for people on a gluten-free diet, though, requires a bit more planning than for most people.

Some snacks require advance preparation because they need to be refrigerated or frozen. Let's dig into some of the options.

⬭ *South-of-the-Border Cheese Ball*

Most cheese balls are rolled in nuts. Nuts to that! This one has a covering in keeping with the flavoring of the cheese ball. You can make this quick-to-assemble appetizer a couple of days before company is expected and keep it wrapped in the refrigerator. Serve it with Homemade Tortilla Chips (you can find the recipe later in this chapter).

Tools: *Electric mixer*

Preparation time: *5 minutes*

Refrigeration time: *2 hours*

Cooking time: *None*

Yield: *8 servings*

8 ounces cream cheese, softened

2 tablespoons salsa

⅓ cup shredded Monterey Jack cheese

½ envelope gluten-free taco seasoning mix

⅓ cup crushed baked tortilla chips

Homemade Tortilla Chips (see recipe later in this chapter)

1 In a medium mixing bowl, use the mixer to blend together the cream cheese, salsa, Monterey Jack cheese, and seasoning mix until they're thoroughly blended (about 30 seconds).

2 Place the crushed chips on a piece of plastic wrap.

3 With a rubber spatula, scoop the cheese onto the crushed chips and smooth it into a ball. Roll the ball over the chips until it's covered with chips.

4 Wrap the cheese ball in a fresh piece of plastic wrap and refrigerate it for 2 hours until it's firm. Serve with Homemade Tortilla Chips.

Vary It! *If you like hot! then use hot salsa and hot taco seasoning in this recipe.*

Per serving: *Calories: 145; Total fat: 12g; Saturated fat: 7g; Cholesterol: 35mg; Sodium: 484mg; Carbohydrates: 5g; Fiber: 0g; Sugar: 1g; Protein: 4g.*

Tortilla Chips

Sure, you can buy a bag of gluten-free tortilla chips to serve with a cheese ball or chip dip, but they'll never measure up to these. Don't be so eager to eat them that you cut short the baking time; if you do, they won't be crisp.

Preparation time: *5 minutes*

Cooking time: *10 to 12 minutes*

Yield: *8 servings*

Nonstick cooking spray	*4 teaspoons olive oil*
Four 6-inch corn tortillas	*Salt for seasoning*

1 Preheat the oven to 400 degrees. Spray a baking sheet with cooking spray.

2 Lightly brush both sides of each tortilla with the olive oil.

3 With a clean pair of scissors, a knife, or a sharp pizza cutter, cut each tortilla into 8 wedges.

4 Place the wedges in a single layer on the baking sheet.

5 Sprinkle each wedge with a dash of salt.

6 Bake the tortilla wedges at 400 degrees for 10 to 12 minutes, or until the chips are crisp and light golden, turning the chips once halfway through baking.

7 Transfer the chips to paper towels and allow them to cool completely.

8 Store the unused portion at room temperature in an airtight container.

Vary It! *Tailor the chips to your liking by adding your favorite spices, like garlic powder, gluten-free barbecue seasoning, gluten-free Cajun seasoning, or gluten-free taco seasoning.*

Per serving: *Calories: 46; Total fat: 3g; Saturated fat: 0g; Cholesterol: 0mg; Sodium: 625mg; Carbohydrates: 5g; Fiber: 1g; Sugar: 0g; Protein: 1g.*

Almond Hummus

If you like hummus, you're going to love this. The almonds add a whole new depth to this popular snack. Spread this on gluten-free crackers or flatbread, or even on a sandwich topped with roasted red peppers, chopped kalamata olives, and crumbled feta cheese.

Tools: *Blender*

Preparation time: *10 minutes*

Refrigeration time: *3 hours*

Cooking time: *None*

Yield: *1½ cups*

Nonstick cooking spray	*2 tablespoons fresh chopped parsley*
¼ cup blanched slivered almonds	*¼ teaspoon salt*
15-ounce can garbanzo beans, rinsed and drained	*¼ teaspoon pepper*
	3 tablespoons fresh lemon juice
2 tablespoons olive oil	*¼ teaspoon gluten-free chicken bouillon granules*
½ teaspoon dried dill	
1 teaspoon cumin	*¼ cup water*

1 Over medium heat, sauté the almonds in a small skillet that has been sprayed with cooking spray. Stir frequently until the almonds are browned.

2 Place the almonds into a blender and puree until smooth. Then add the remaining ingredients, pureeing until smooth. You may need to scrape down the sides of the blender during this process. Depending on your personal taste, you may want to add more lemon juice.

3 Spoon the mixture into a serving bowl. Cover and refrigerate the hummus for several hours to allow the flavors to blend.

Per serving: Calories: 149; Total fat: 9g; Saturated fat: 1g; Cholesterol: 0mg; Sodium: 186mg; Carbohydrates: 14g; Fiber: 3g; Sugar: 3g; Protein: 6g.

☙ Pudding Pops

This recipe is so simple that older kids can make it themselves. Make these ahead and keep them frozen so you always have a handy snack on hand. You can spoon the pudding mixture into cupcake tins, individual molds, or even small paper cups.

Tools: *3-ounce paper cups, wooden sticks or plastic spoons*

Preparation time: *10 minutes*

Cooking time: *8 minutes*

Cooling time: *30 minutes*

Freezing time: *At least 2 hours*

Yield: *12 servings*

2½ cups 2 percent milk

3.4-ounce package cook-and-serve chocolate pudding mix

¼ cup sugar

¾ cup nondairy whipped topping, thawed

12 wooden sticks or plastic spoons

1 Pour the milk into a medium saucepan.

2 Stir in the pudding mix and sugar, and heat the ingredients, stirring constantly, until the mixture comes to a boil.

3 Lower the heat to medium and cook, stirring constantly, for 2 minutes.

4 Remove the pan from the heat and allow the pudding mixture to cool for 30 minutes, stirring several times.

5 Fold in the whipped topping.

6 Spoon the mixture into 12 molds, cupcake tins, or paper cups; insert the wooden sticks or plastic spoons into the center of the pops. Freeze until firm.

Per serving: *Calories: 87; Total fat: 2g; Saturated fat: 2g; Cholesterol: 4mg; Sodium: 67mg; Carbohydrates: 15g; Fiber: 0g; Sugar: 12g; Protein: 2g.*

☕ Caramel Milkshakes

Warning! This milkshake is definitely addictive! It takes moments to prepare and hours to forget. Kids who are old enough to use a blender can easily make this themselves. There's no way to even pretend this is a healthy snack, but once in a while it's worth the splurge.

Tools: *Blender*

Preparation time: *3 minutes*

Cooking time: *None*

Yield: *2 servings*

3 cups frozen vanilla yogurt

¾ cup milk

¼ teaspoon vanilla

1 teaspoon cinnamon

¼ cup caramel ice cream topping

1 Place all the ingredients in a blender.

2 Puree, with the lid on, for 20 seconds, or until smooth. Pour into 2 glasses.

Per serving: *Calories: 511; Total fat: 12g; Saturated fat: 8g; Cholesterol: 43mg; Sodium: 311mg; Carbohydrates: 91g; Fiber: 1g; Sugar: 84g; Protein: 11g.*

Fixing Salts and Sweets to Satisfy Your Munchies

Two hours after dinner, are you or a member of your family standing in front of the refrigerator, with the door wide open, trying to figure out what to eat next? Do you find yourself staring at the fridge for several minutes at a time? Don't get depressed; get determined. When you feel a snack attack coming on, you still have time to prepare a hot snack. Snacking definitely need not be dreary. You can make some of the selections in this section at the last minute, when the impulse hits. You can make others ahead and store them so your cache is always full.

☙ Honey Cinnamon Grahams

Whether you're making s'mores, a base for a cheesecake, or just snacking on these crackers, they are delicious. Watch the crackers closely in the oven. You want to bake them until the edges are just beginning to show signs of browning. Overbaking causes these crackers to get too hard. Should that happen, *don't* throw them away! Put them in a blender and puree them to use in a pie crust or as a base for a dessert.

Tools: *Electric mixer, rolling pin*

Preparation time: *10 minutes*

Cooking time: *9 to 11 minutes*

Yield: *24 crackers*

¾ cup gluten-free flour mixture	2 tablespoons honey
¼ cup coconut flour	⅓ cup brown sugar
½ teaspoon salt	1 teaspoon vanilla
½ teaspoon cinnamon	1 tablespoon milk
1 teaspoon baking powder	Nonstick cooking spray
¼ cup butter, softened	1 teaspoon cinnamon sugar

1 Preheat the oven to 325 degrees.

2 In a medium bowl, whisk together the flour mixture, coconut flour, salt, cinnamon, and baking powder.

3 In a large mixing bowl, use the mixer to whip together the butter, honey, sugar, vanilla, and milk.

4 Slowly add the dry ingredients to the butter mixture. Mix on medium speed until blended. (You may have to add a few more drops of milk if the dough won't hold together. The dough should be pliable.)

5 Lightly spray 2 baking sheets with the cooking spray.

6 On a sheet of plastic wrap, roll out the dough with a rolling pin to ¼-inch thick. Cut the dough into 2-inch squares and place the crackers on the prepared baking sheets.

7 Prick the top of each cracker several times with the tines of a fork.

8 Sprinkle the tops with cinnamon sugar.

9 Bake the crackers at 325 degrees for 9 to 11 minutes until the edges are barely beginning to brown. Remove the crackers to a wire rack to cool. Store in an airtight container.

Tip: *If you keep your coconut flour in the freezer, it may pack together. Take it out of the freezer the night before you plan to use it.*

Per serving: *Calories: 69; Total fat: 2g; Saturated fat: 1g; Cholesterol: 5mg; Sodium: 85mg; Carbohydrates: 14g; Fiber: 1g; Sugar: 8g; Protein: 0g.*

⌒ Trail Mix Bars

If you look at the ingredients for this snack and think, "Hmm, this looks *too* healthy for me!" don't be misled. Oh, it's healthy alright, but the honey and brown sugar definitely put these bars in the bet-you-can't-eat-just-one category. These bars hold for several days and are a far better alternative than packing cookies in lunchboxes.

Preparation time: 10 minutes

Cooking time: 10 minutes

Yield: 24 servings

½ cup sesame seeds	½ teaspoon cinnamon
½ cup sunflower seeds	2½ tablespoons butter
½ cup coconut	2 tablespoons honey
½ cup slivered almonds	2 tablespoons brown sugar
½ cup raisins	Nonstick cooking spray

1 In a small, dry skillet, heat the sesame seeds over medium heat, stirring often, until they're lightly browned. Place the browned seeds in a medium bowl. Repeat with the sunflower seeds, then the coconut, and then the almonds.

2 Stir the raisins and cinnamon into the seed mixture.

3 In a small saucepan, warm the butter, honey, and brown sugar over medium heat to softball stage, or 238 degrees on a candy thermometer. At this temperature, a small amount of this syrup dropped into cold water will form a soft, flexible ball. If you remove the ball from the water, it will flatten like a pancake after a few moments in your hand.

4 Pour the syrup over the seed mixture. Using a rubber spatula, blend the ingredients well to coat evenly.

5 Press the mix into a 9-inch-square pan that has been sprayed with cooking spray and let it cool slightly.

6 Cut the trail mixture into 24 pieces before the bars have completely cooled. Store the bars in an airtight container.

Vary It! In place of the raisins (or in addition to the raisins), you can use dried cranberries, cut-up dates, or dried apricots.

Per serving: Calories: 91; Total fat: 6g; Saturated fat: 2g; Cholesterol: 3mg; Sodium: 16mg; Carbohydrates: 8g; Fiber: 1g; Sugar: 6g; Protein: 2g.

♻ Macho Nachos

Gluten-free or gluttons for gluten, kids or adults, everyone loves these. They're almost embarrassingly easy to make. The beauty of this recipe is that you can make as many or as few as the occasion calls for.

Preparation time: *5 minutes*

Cooking time: *5 minutes*

Yield: *10 servings*

40 tortilla chips	*¼ cup shredded Monterey Jack cheese*
9-ounce can bean dip	*1 cup salsa*
1¼ cups shredded Colby cheese	

1 Preheat the oven to 400 degrees.

2 Lay the tortilla chips in a single layer on 2 nonstick baking sheets. (You don't need to grease the baking sheets.)

3 Spread each chip with bean dip (approximately 1 scant tablespoon per chip).

4 Sprinkle the cheese over the chips.

5 Bake the chips at 400 degrees for 7 to10 minutes, or until the cheese has melted.

6 Put the salsa in a bowl and serve it as a dip for the nachos.

Per serving: Calories: 142; Total fat: 8g; Saturated fat: 0g; Cholesterol: 18mg; Sodium: 441mg; Carbohydrates: 10g; Fiber: 1g; Sugar: 0g; Protein: 6g.

♻ Perky Popcorn

There are a lot of recipes for caramel corn, but they won't measure up to this one. Although kids of all ages love this, fair warning: If you have dentures or bridgework, you may find chewing this to be "denturally" challenging.

Tools: *Candy thermometer*

Preparation time: *20 minutes*

Cooking time: *35 minutes*

Yield: *10 cups*

2½ quarts (10 cups) popped popcorn

¾ cup pecan pieces

Nonstick cooking spray

1 cup brown sugar

½ cup water

¼ cup butter

¼ teaspoon salt

¼ cup light corn syrup

¼ teaspoon baking soda

1 Preheat the oven to 250 degrees.

2 Combine the popcorn and pecans in a large roasting pan that has been sprayed with cooking spray.

3 In a medium saucepan, stir together the brown sugar, water, butter, salt, and corn syrup.

4 Cook the syrup over medium heat, stirring occasionally with a wooden spoon, until the mixture comes to a full boil.

5 Insert a candy thermometer into the pan, making sure the bulb at the bottom doesn't touch the bottom of the saucepan.

6 Continue cooking the syrup until it reaches 238 degrees, soft-ball stage. (This will take 3 to 5 minutes.)

7 Remove the pan from the heat. Stir in the baking soda. The mixture will thicken immediately.

8 Pour the mixture over the popcorn and pecans, stirring until all the popcorn is coated.

9 Bake the popcorn at 250 degrees for 35 minutes, stirring every 10 minutes.

10 Remove the popcorn from the roasting pan and spread it out on wax paper to cool completely.

11 When the popcorn is cool, break it into pieces and store it in a tightly covered container.

Per serving: Calories: 235; Total fat: 11g; Saturated fat: 4g; Cholesterol: 12mg; Sodium: 137mg; Carbohydrates: 35g; Fiber: 2g; Sugar: 24g; Protein: 2g.

☕ Better Than S'mores!

Who doesn't love s'mores? Be sure to eat this snack as soon as it comes out of the pan (actually, let it cool just a tad so you don't burn your tongue). If you reheat this, the tortillas will become like leather. But freshly made, the tortillas are crisp and delicious. Have a napkin ready because these may be a little messy.

Preparation time: *5 minutes*

Cooking time: *4 minutes*

Yield: *8 servings*

Four 8-inch gluten-free flour tortillas	*1 banana*
¼ cup crunchy peanut butter	*½ cup semisweet chocolate pieces*
¼ cup marshmallow cream	*Nonstick cooking spray*

1 Spread 2 tortillas with the peanut butter.

2 Spread the marshmallow cream on top of the peanut butter, dividing evenly between the two tortillas.

3 Slice the banana fairly thin and place the slices on top of the marshmallow cream, dividing evenly between the two tortillas.

4 Sprinkle the bananas with the chocolate pieces.

5 Place the remaining two tortillas on top of each of the "sandwiches" and then cut each into 4 wedges.

6 Spray a nonstick skillet with cooking spray. Heat the pan for 45 seconds on high heat.

7 Place each tortilla "sandwich" in the pan and cook on high for 1 to 2 minutes until the bottom is lightly browned.

8 Spray the top of each "sandwich" with the cooking spray, and then turn them over and cook the second side until it's lightly browned. Serve warm.

Per serving: *Calories: 191; Total fat: 9g; Saturated fat: 3g; Cholesterol: 0mg; Sodium: 141mg; Carbohydrates: 26g; Fiber: 2g; Sugar: 19g; Protein: 4g.*

⌣ *Spicy Almonds*

Beware. This snack is definitely addicting. For added decadence, sprinkle the hot almonds with a ½ teaspoon of coarse salt as soon as they come out of the oven. When they have cooled, store them in an airtight container. They should keep for up to 3 weeks.

Preparation time: *15 minutes*

Cooking time: *15 minutes*

Yield: *3 cups*

¼ cup butter	*1 teaspoon coarse salt*
2 tablespoons gluten-free Worcestershire sauce	*1 teaspoon garlic powder*
	½ teaspoon cayenne pepper
2 tablespoons gluten-free soy sauce	*½ teaspoon sugar*
1 teaspoon cumin	*3 cups whole almonds*

1 Preheat the oven to 350 degrees.

2 Melt the butter in a medium saucepan.

3 Remove the pan from the heat and stir in the Worcestershire sauce, soy sauce, cumin, salt, garlic powder, pepper, and sugar.

4 Add the almonds and stir until they are evenly coated.

5 Transfer the mixture to a shallow baking sheet.

6 Bake the almonds at 350 degrees for 15 minutes, stirring once halfway through baking.

7 Let the almonds cool thoroughly before storing in an airtight container.

Per serving: Calories: 247; Total fat: 22g; Saturated fat: 4g; Cholesterol: 10mg; Sodium: 417mg; Carbohydrates: 8g; Fiber: 4g; Sugar: 2g; Protein: 8g.

☞ Cheesy Crisps

Take a cracker, crumble it all up, add one more thing to it, then make a new cracker out of it. That may not make a lot of sense, but it doesn't have to because the finished product is wonderful. The crackers we used in this recipe were Foods Alive Mexican Harvest Flax Crackers. You want to use a cracker that has spices and a touch of tangy flavor. These particular crackers have an advantage because they are made from flax seeds; you need a cracker with seeds for this recipe. To measure the 1½ cups of crackers, break the whole crackers into bits and squish them into a measuring cup.

Tools: *Food processor*

Preparation time: *7 minutes*

Cooking time: *30 minutes*

Yield: *36 crackers*

Nonstick cooking spray

1½ cups spiced flax crackers

1½ cups shredded sharp cheddar cheese

¼ cup water

1 Preheat the oven to 325 degrees. Spray a baking sheet with cooking spray.

2 Place the crackers in a food processor and grind them to a fine meal.

3 Add the cheese and water. Continue to process until the ingredients are well blended and a dough is formed.

4 Remove the dough and form it into a ball.

5 Place the dough between two sheets of plastic wrap and roll it out to ¼-inch thickness.

6 Transfer the dough to the prepared baking sheet.

7 Using a knife or pastry wheel, cut the dough into small squares or diamonds; don't separate or spread the pieces apart.

8 Bake the dough at 325 degrees for 30 minutes, or until the crackers are crisp and the edges are just beginning to brown.

9 Remove the crackers from the oven and let them set for 3 minutes. Then break or cut the crackers along the lines and remove them to a cooling rack.

Per cracker: *Calories: 24; Total fat: 2g; Saturated fat: 1g; Cholesterol: 5mg; Sodium: 37mg; Carbohydrates: 0g; Fiber: 0g; Sugar: 0g; Protein: 1g.*

Chapter 19

Decadent Desserts

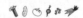
You've probably heard the saying "Life is short. Eat dessert first." Let's get real here and acknowledge that the most important food group is really dessert. Sure it's feasible to serve cheese and grapes for dessert, but that doesn't contain nearly the amount of sugar needed to satisfy a genuinely refined sweet tooth. Nor does it contain nearly enough calories to qualify as decadent. Dessert really should be an indulgence, something to anticipate, and something that you certainly don't have to be hungry to consume and thoroughly enjoy.

Desserts are a reflection of our society (this is the philosophical part of the book). Years ago, lime gelatin infused with crushed pineapple and miniature marshmallows constituted dessert. Today our tastes have become refined as we enjoy tiramisu, caramel turtle pecan cheesecake, and baklava sundaes (yeah, even if you're gluten-free!), just to name a few.

Why is dessert so important? Because dessert makes us happy. That's the good news. The bad news is that an odd phenomenon occurs when we consume too many desserts — our jeans shrink.

Let's contemplate this conundrum and look at the true problems. No one has totally ruined her health by consuming a bite of a luscious dessert. The real health culprits are the continual diet of high-fat foods, lack of exercise, and skipping meals, and then gorging.

Many desserts are made with fats (butters, shortening, oil). Using margarine as a butter substitute isn't the solution because margarine contains fat, too. If you're health conscious, when baking cakes, you often can replace half of the fat in a recipe with applesauce or use ¾ cup vegetable or olive oil for each cup of butter. Olive oil and vegetable oil are fats, but they are a far healthier choice compared to butter, shortening, or margarine.

Some decadent-tasting desserts are actually quite low in calories and fat. The Liqueur Cups in this chapter have only 166 calories per serving with just 5 grams of fat. The Chocolate Cranberry Cookies have 56 calories with 2 grams of fat. And all desserts have fewer calories when you only eat half a piece!

Pies and Cobblers You Can't Resist

Gluten-free pie crusts have been a challenge to many newly diagnosed celiacs. They needn't be. They can be easy to make, no matter how flaky you are. First, you don't even need a dough pie crust for many recipes. Crushed gluten-free cookies or nut crusts often work as a viable substitute.

For double-crust fruit pies, you can follow a few tricks for a successful gluten-free crust:

✔ Use ice-cold ingredients (butter or shortening, water or milk).

✔ Roll out the pastry between two sheets of plastic wrap (instead of wax paper), and sprinkle the plastic wrap with confectioners' sugar (instead of gluten-free flour mixture or cornstarch). Roll the dough thin. If the pie crust is too thick, it may not bake completely on the bottom.

✔ Moisten the edge of the bottom crust with water before placing the second crust on top. The moistened edge helps create a good seal after the two crusts are crimped together.

If you have any dough scraps left over, make a snack out of them — cut the dough into squares (or any shape you like), lightly butter them, sprinkle them with cinnamon sugar, and bake until they're golden.

The whole is worth more than the sum of its parts. If you look up the definition of *cobbler*, you'll find it described as "A deep-dish fruit pie with a top crust." That's it? This definition is missing the description of the aroma of the cobbler as it bakes and the scent drifts through the house. Nowhere in the definition does it describe how your heart begins to palpitate stronger as your fork cuts through the crisp crust, anticipating that first bite. Nor does it take into account the gratification and fulfillment you feel when that first bite of cobbler tantalizes your taste buds. The definition definitely does not do justice to the ever-popular cobbler.

Coconut Lemon Chiffon Pie

This is a very light dessert and perfect for summer entertaining. If you feel a real urge to exhibit domestic exuberance, you can toast the coconut before making the crust. This lends a different, almost nutty flavor to the crust as the heat releases the natural oils.

Preparation time: 5 minutes

Refrigeration time: 2 hours

Baking time: None

Yield: 12 servings

1½ cups shredded coconut

½ cup confectioners' sugar

3 tablespoons butter, melted

14-ounce can sweetened condensed milk

6-ounce can frozen lemonade, thawed

8 ounces (1 small container) nondairy whipped topping, thawed

3 tablespoons fudge ice cream topping

8 thin slices fresh lemon

1 In a medium bowl, stir together the coconut and sugar. Gradually stir in the melted butter. Press the mixture evenly over the bottom and sides of a lightly oiled 9-inch pie plate. Refrigerate the crust until it's firm (about 1 hour).

2 In a large bowl, stir together the condensed milk, lemonade, and whipped topping until no streaks remain. Spoon the filling into the chilled pie crust.

3 Spoon the ice cream topping into a small, microwave-safe bowl, and heat the topping in the microwave until it's fairly liquid, stirring frequently. Drizzle the topping over the filling.

4 Refrigerate the pie until the filling thickens, at least 1 hour. Before serving, put the lemon slices around the edge of the topping.

Vary It! *If chocolate isn't your most favorite thing in life (although how could it not be?), you can drizzle the top of the pie with whisked raspberry jam instead of the fudge topping.*

Per serving: Calories: 299; Total fat: 12g; Saturated fat: 9g; Cholesterol: 16mg; Sodium: 88mg; Carbohydrates: 45g; Fiber: 1g; Sugar: 40g; Protein: 3g.

Peanut Butter Custard Pie

This is unlike anything that has ever touched your palate before. *Divine* simply doesn't encompass the range of taste sensations that await you. If you're a fan of crunchiness, use extra-crunchy gluten-free peanut butter in place of creamy style. If you want to show off for guests, sprinkle a 1½-inch line of crushed peanuts around the edge after frosting the pie.

Tools: *Rolling pin, electric mixer*

Preparation time: *25 minutes*

Baking time: *10 minutes*

Refrigeration time: *4 hours*

Yield: *8 servings*

Nonstick cooking spray	*14-ounce can sweetened condensed milk*
7.2-ounce box gluten-free shortbread cookies	*3 egg yolks, lightly beaten*
¼ cup plus ½ cup creamy peanut butter	*2 tablespoons unsalted butter*
2 tablespoons plus 2¼ teaspoons cornstarch	*1 teaspoon vanilla*
1½ cups water	*½ of 11.75-ounce jar hot fudge sauce*

1 Preheat the oven to 375 degrees. Spray an 8-inch pie plate with cooking spray.

2 Break the cookies into a plastic self-seal bag. Use a rolling pin to crush the cookies until they're finely ground. Transfer the cookies to a medium bowl.

3 Add ¼ cup of peanut butter. Using a rubber spatula, mix the cookies and peanut butter until they're thoroughly blended.

4 Press the mixture onto the bottom and up sides of the prepared pie plate. The mixture will be sticky. Use the back of a wet spoon to help spread the crust, or dip your fingers in confectioners' sugar to spread the crust with your hands.

5 Bake the crust at 375 degrees for 10 minutes. Remove the crust from the oven and cool completely.

6 In a large mixing bowl, whisk all of the cornstarch into the water until it dissolves.

7 Stir in the condensed milk and egg yolks.

8 Add the remaining ½ cup of peanut butter, and use the mixer to whip the ingredients on low speed for 45 seconds.

9 Pour the mixture into a medium saucepan. Bring the mixture to a boil, stirring constantly with a whisk. Lower the heat to medium-high and continue cooking and stirring the mixture until it has thickened. Remove the mixture from the heat.

10 Stir in the butter and vanilla.

11 Cool the filling slightly before pouring it into the pie crust.

12 Warm the jar of hot fudge topping in the microwave (remove the lid first). Pour ½ of the jar onto the top of the pie and smooth it evenly over the top with the back of a spoon.

13 When the pie filling and topping are completely cooled, cover the pie and chill it for at least 4 hours.

Per serving: Calories: 605; Total fat: 33g; Saturated fat: 13g; Cholesterol: 48mg; Sodium: 214mg; Carbohydrates: 97g; Fiber: 3g; Sugar: 55g; Protein: 14g.

Posh Pineapple Pie

This pie is a must-serve in the summertime. It's lusciously sweet, yet light. Sprinkling the sugar on the top crust adds the perfect degree of crispness.

Preparation time: 15 minutes

Baking time: 30 minutes

Yield: 8 servings

¾ cup plus 2 teaspoons granulated sugar	1 teaspoon fresh lemon juice
1 tablespoon butter	Double recipe Double-Crust Olive Oil Pie Crust (see the following recipe)
3 tablespoons cornstarch	
¼ teaspoon cinnamon	1 egg white
20-ounce can crushed pineapple with juice	1 tablespoon water
2 tablespoons milk	2 teaspoons brown sugar

1 Preheat the oven to 425 degrees.

2 Prepare a double recipe of the Olive Oil Pie Crust as directed in the recipe that follows.

3 In a medium saucepan, stir together ¾ cup of granulated sugar, the butter, cornstarch, cinnamon, pineapple with juice, milk, and lemon juice.

4 Cook the mixture over medium heat, stirring constantly, until it thickens, and then continue to stir as the mixture boils for 1 more minute. Remove the pan from the heat and let the mixture cool slightly.

5 Pour the mixture into the prepared pie crust, and then cover it with the top crust. Cut slits in the top crust for air vents.

6 In a small bowl, whisk together the egg white and water. Brush it over the top of the pie.

7 Sprinkle the pie with 2 teaspoons of granulated sugar and the brown sugar.

8 Bake the pie at 425 degrees for 30 minutes, or until the crust is golden.

Per serving: Calories: 438; Total fat: 16g; Saturated fat: 3g; Cholesterol: 4mg; Sodium: 2mg; Carbohydrates: 39g; Fiber: 2g; Sugar: 36g; Protein: 1g.

Gluten-Free Pie Crust

When making a double-crust pie, double this recipe and follow the directions for the filling recipe.

Tools: *Rolling pin*

Preparation time: *15 minutes*

Baking time: *30 minutes*

Yield: *8 servings*

2 cups sifted gluten-free flour mixture

¼ cup sugar

½ teaspoon salt

½ cup corn oil

4 tablespoons ice-cold water

½ teaspoon vanilla

1 tablespoon confectioners' sugar

1 In a medium bowl, sift together the flour mixture, sugar, and salt.

2 In a small bowl, combine the oil, water, and vanilla.

3 Pour the liquid mixture into the center of the flour mixture. With a rubber spatula, stir the dough well until it holds together.

4 With your hands, knead the dough until it forms a smooth ball.

5 Sprinkle the confectioners' sugar onto a sheet of plastic wrap. Set the ball on the sugar and turn the dough to coat it. Cover it with a second sheet of plastic wrap.

6 With a rolling pin, roll out the dough into an 11-inch circle.

7 Place the dough in a greased 9-inch pie plate. Scallop the edges.

Per serving: Calories: 287; Total fat: 14g; Saturated fat: 2g; Cholesterol: 0mg; Sodium: 146mg; Carbohydrates: 39g; Fiber: 2g; Sugar: 7g; Protein: 0g.

Best-Ever Apple Cobbler

Whether you serve this warm from the oven or at room temperature and with or without ice cream, this sweet apple cobbler is delicious. For added decadence, drizzle the top of the warm pie with a sugar glaze (a mixture of sifted confectioners' sugar, vanilla, milk, and a dash of cinnamon).

Preparation time: *10 minutes*

Cooking time: *40 minutes*

Yield: *10 servings*

Nonstick cooking spray

7 cups peeled, thinly sliced Red or Golden Delicious apples (6 to 7 apples)

¼ cup plus 1/2 cup brown sugar

½ cup granulated sugar

2 tablespoons cornstarch

¼ teaspoon plus ¼ teaspoon salt

½ teaspoon plus ½ teaspoon cinnamon

¼ teaspoon nutmeg

2 teaspoons bottled lemon juice

½ cup gluten-free flour mixture

½ cup almond meal

1 cup chopped pecans

6 tablespoons butter, melted

1 Preheat the oven to 350 degrees. Spray a 10-inch pie plate with cooking spray.

2 Place the apple slices in a medium bowl. Stir in ¼ cup of brown sugar, the granulated sugar, cornstarch, ¼ teaspoon of salt, ½ teaspoon of cinnamon, the nutmeg, and lemon juice.

3 Spoon the mixture into the prepared pie plate.

4 In a small bowl, mix together with a fork the remaining ½ cup of brown sugar, ¼ teaspoon of salt, ½ teaspoon of cinnamon, the flour mixture, almond meal, and pecans. Stir in the butter until the mixture is evenly moistened. Crumble the mixture on top of the apples.

5 Bake the pie at 350 degrees for 40 minutes.

Tip: Pie plates vary in how many cups of filling they can hold. If you don't have a 10-inch pie plate, you can use a 9-x-9-inch pan or a deep-dish 9-inch pie plate.

Vary It! You can use canned gluten-free blueberry, cherry, or peach pie fillings in place of the apple pie filling.

Per serving: Calories: 345; Total fat: 18g; Saturated fat: 5g; Cholesterol: 18mg; Sodium: 173mg; Carbohydrates: 41g; Fiber: 3g; Sugar: 34g; Protein: 3g.

Crafting Cookies and Cakes from Scratch

Everyone loves cookies of all shapes, sizes, and flavors. Gluten-free cookies require just a bit more effort, but the results will be every bit as good as their wheat counterparts. When converting a wheat-based cookie recipe to gluten-free, you need to increase the leavening agent (usually gluten-free baking powder or baking soda) and the flavoring (add more vanilla or almond flavoring), and it's wise to add something that will add flavor; perhaps try toasted chopped nuts, chocolate pieces, toasted coconut, or dried fruits. You may want to substitute part of the liquid with juice, brewed coffee, or even a liqueur. When rolling out dough for cut-out cookies, sprinkle your rolling surface with confectioners' sugar instead of dusting it with gluten-free flour. (Using the flour mixture may make the cookies too dry.)

Gluten-free cookies don't stay fresh as long as wheat-based cookies, so you should either freeze them until they're needed, or sit down and eat every last one of them as soon as they're removed from the oven!

Here are a few tips for keeping your cookies at their best:

- ✔ If you made crispy cookies that are now several days old and are starting to lose their crunch, recrisp them by laying them on a baking sheet and heating them in a 300-degree oven for 3 to 4 minutes.

- ✔ If you made soft cookies that are now drying out, wrap a few in a damp paper towel and microwave them for a few seconds.

Many of the cookie issues regarding conversions apply to cakes as well. The alternative flours are heavier than wheat flour so they won't rise as much unless you add some extra stuff. As with cookies, you'll need to increase the amount of leavening and flavoring. It also helps to add an extra egg (both to help keep the cake moist and for leavening). Gluten-free pastries in general turn out better if you use whole milk rather than low-fat or skim milk. But because you're lucky enough to have this book, the recipes here already have all of those adjustments made.

To keep a layer cake in place on the cake plate, place a dab of frosting on the plate before placing the bottom layer. This holds the cake in place while you frost it. One more tip: If you plan to adorn your creation with shaved chocolate curls, white or milk chocolate makes better chocolate shavings because they're softer and curl more easily.

Chocolate Cranberry Cookies

If you've been dreaming of a cookie that will hold for more than one day and actually doesn't taste gluten-free, then your dreams have just been fulfilled. These stay moist and they freeze well.

Preparation time: *10 minutes*

Refrigeration time: *2 hours*

Cooking time: *12 minutes*

Yield: *54 cookies*

2 ounces (2 squares) unsweetened chocolate	*3 teaspoons baking powder*
¼ cup vegetable shortening or butter	*½ teaspoon salt*
1 cup granulated sugar	*½ cup semisweet chocolate chips*
2½ teaspoons vanilla	*½ cup dried cranberries*
2 eggs	*½ cup confectioners' sugar*
1 cup gluten-free flour mixture	*Nonstick cooking spray*
2 tablespoons cornstarch	

1 In a medium saucepan, melt the chocolate and shortening over medium-low heat, stirring occasionally.

2 Remove the pan from the heat and whisk in the sugar and vanilla. Whisk in the eggs, one at a time.

3 In a large bowl, sift together the flour mixture, baking powder, and salt.

4 Stir the chocolate mixture into the flour mixture with a rubber spatula. Stir in the chocolate chips and cranberries. Refrigerate the dough for 2 hours.

5 Preheat the oven to 350 degrees.

6 Roll the dough into 1-inch balls, and then roll the balls in the confectioners' sugar to coat. Place the dough balls 2 inches apart on the baking sheets that have been lightly sprayed with cooking spray. The cookies will spread during baking.

7 Bake the cookies at 350 degrees for 12 minutes. The cookies will be soft; let them rest on the baking sheets for 2 minutes before transferring them to a wire rack to cool.

Vary It! *Forgo rolling the cookies in the confectioners' sugar before baking, and when the cookies have cooled, frost them with a chocolate glaze instead.*

Per serving: *Calories: 56; Total fat: 2g; Saturated fat: 1g; Cholesterol: 8mg; Sodium: 52mg; Carbohydrates: 9g; Fiber: 0g; Sugar: 6g; Protein: 1g.*

Whoopie Pies

Whether you're a kid of 3 or 103, everyone loves Whoopie Pies! We used 6 sections of an 8-ounce dark chocolate candy bar (16 total sections in the bar) for this recipe. Make plenty of these, and then wrap them individually and freeze them so you'll always have a back-up snack on hand.

Tools: *Electric mixer*

Preparation time: *25 minutes*

Cooking time: *15 minutes*

Yield: *10 pies*

Nonstick cooking spray	*¾ teaspoon baking powder*
¼ cup butter, softened	*1 teaspoon baking soda*
⅔ cup brown sugar	*¼ teaspoon salt*
1 egg	*3 ounces (6 squares) dark chocolate, grated*
1 teaspoon vanilla	*½ cup whole milk*
2 tablespoons pure cocoa	*Whoopie Pie Filling (see the following recipe)*
1 cup gluten-free flour mixture	

1 Preheat the oven to 350 degrees. Lightly spray two baking sheets with cooking spray.

2 In a large mixing bowl, use the mixer to cream together the butter, brown sugar, egg, and vanilla. In another bowl, stir together the cocoa, flour mixture, baking powder, baking soda, and salt. Stir in the grated chocolate.

3 Add the dry ingredients alternately with milk to the butter mixture, beating until the mixture is smooth. The batter will become very thick.

4 Drop 2 tablespoons of batter onto the baking sheets. Using the back of a spoon that has been dipped in hot water, flatten the batter into a thin circle about 1½ inches in diameter. Repeat with the remaining dough. These cookies puff up but won't spread very much. You should have a total of 20 rounds.

5 Bake the dough at 350 degrees for 15 minutes, or until the rounds are firm to the touch. Cool the rounds on a wire rack.

6 Spread about 2 tablespoons of filling (see the following recipe) on half of the rounds, and then top the filling with the remaining rounds, pressing down gently to distribute the filling evenly.

Tip: In most recipes where chocolate is used as an ingredient, it lists 1 square of chocolate as being equal to 1 ounce. In this recipe, 2 squares of chocolate is equivalent to 1 ounce. The reason is that semisweet or unsweetened chocolate is found in the baking section of the grocery store, and each square equals 1 ounce. Dark chocolate, however, is not found in the baking section because it doesn't come packaged like the other baking chocolates. You have to buy a large, dark chocolate candy bar where each square is only ½ of an ounce. That's why this recipes lists "3 ounces (6 squares) dark chocolate," while the other recipes show 3 ounces as 3 squares.

Whoopie Pie Filling

½ cup butter, softened

¾ cup sifted confectioners' sugar

1 cup marshmallow cream

1 teaspoon vanilla

In a medium bowl, use the mixer to whip together all the ingredients until they're well blended.

Per serving: Calories: 369; Total fat: 18g; Saturated fat: 11g; Cholesterol: 60mg; Sodium: 346mg; Carbohydrates: 47g; Fiber: 9g; Sugar: 26g; Protein: 2g.

Nutty Biscotti

These are fantastic to keep on hand. They'll keep for several days in a plastic self-seal bag or in a covered plastic container. After the second baking, these "sticks" harden a bit, so be sure not to overbake them.

Tools: *Electric mixer*

Preparation time: *20 minutes*

Cooking time: *45 minutes*

Yield: *18 slices*

¾ cup blanched slivered almonds

1 tablespoon plus 2 tablespoons butter, softened

⅔ cup sugar

2 eggs

1 teaspoon vanilla

¼ teaspoon almond flavoring

1½ cups gluten-free flour mixture

1½ teaspoons baking powder

1 teaspoon baking soda

1 teaspoon instant coffee granules

⅛ teaspoon salt

½ teaspoon cinnamon

½ cup miniature semisweet chocolate chips

4 ounces (4 squares) semisweet chocolate

1 teaspoon corn oil

1 Preheat the oven to 350 degrees. Line a baking sheet with wax paper (or parchment paper).

2 In a small skillet, sauté the almonds in 1 tablespoon of butter until they're golden, stirring frequently. Remove them from the heat and let cool.

3 In a medium mixing bowl, use the mixer to whip together the remaining 2 tablespoons of butter, the sugar, and eggs on high speed until the mixture is thick and fluffy (about 2 minutes). Add the vanilla and almond flavorings.

4 In a small bowl, whisk together the flour mixture, baking powder, baking soda, coffee granules, salt, and cinnamon. Add the flour mixture to the egg mixture, beating just until the mixtures are thoroughly combined. Fold in the chocolate chips and almonds.

5 Transfer the dough to the prepared baking sheet. With damp hands, form the dough into a log about 14 inches long and 2 inches high. (The dough will be somewhat sticky to work with, but don't add more flour or your biscotti will turn out dry.)

6 Bake the dough at 350 degrees for 25 minutes, or until it just begins to brown on the outside and is firm to the touch.

7 Remove the log from the oven and let it cool for 10 minutes.

8 Gently slice the log into ½-inch slices. Stand the slices upright on a baking sheet. Bake them at 350 degrees for 20 minutes until they're firm (but *not* rock hard) and golden. Remove the biscotti from the oven and cool.

9 Cut the semisweet chocolate into small pieces and place it in a medium skillet with the oil. Heat the chocolate and oil very slowly over low heat, stirring often, until the chocolate has melted. (If the heat is too high, the chocolate will burn.)

10 Remove the skillet from the heat and dip the bottoms of the biscotti in the chocolate to coat. Set each piece on its side on a piece of wax paper to dry.

Vary It! If you want to live life on the wild side, soak some dried cranberries in Kahlua and then fold them into the batter when you add the chocolate chips and almonds.

Per serving: Calories: 190; Total fat: 9g; Saturated fat: 4g; Cholesterol: 29mg; Sodium: 138mg; Carbohydrates: 26g; Fiber: 2g; Sugar: 14g; Protein: 3g.

Chocolate Raspberry Bars

Bar cookies are perfect to take to picnics, to sprinkle with gluten-free colored sprinkles during the holidays, or to enjoy anytime. The melding of chocolate and raspberry has long been recognized as a deliciously delectable complementary combo, so indulge.

Tools: _Electric mixer_

Preparation time: _15 minutes_

Refrigeration time: _20 minutes_

Cooking time: _30 minutes_

Yield: _12 bars_

Nonstick cooking spray	⅛ teaspoon salt
½ cup softened butter	1 cup semisweet chocolate chips
¼ cup brown sugar	8-ounce can sweetened condensed milk
½ teaspoon cinnamon	⅓ cup raspberry preserves
¾ cup gluten-free flour mixture	⅓ cup coconut

1 Preheat the oven to 350 degrees. Spray a 9-x-9-inch baking dish with cooking spray.

2 In a large mixing bowl, use the mixer to whip the butter, brown sugar, and cinnamon together until they're creamy.

3 Whip in the flour mixture and salt.

4 Using the back of a spoon, smooth ⅔ of the mixture in the bottom of the prepared baking dish.

5 Bake the crust at 350 degrees for 12 minutes.

6 In a microwave-safe bowl, microwave the chocolate pieces and condensed milk for 1 minute; the chocolate should get soft and begin to melt. Stir the mixture to melt the remaining chocolate pieces. Spread the mixture over the partially baked crust. Refrigerate the baking dish for 20 minutes to set the chocolate layer.

7 Spread the preserves over the chocolate mixture.

8 Mix the coconut into the remaining flour mix, blending well. With your fingers, flatten out bits of dough and lay them on top of the preserves, partially covering the top of the chocolate mixture.

9 Using the back of a wet spoon, smooth out any lumps in the topping.

10 Bake the bars at 350 degrees for 30 minutes, or until the top crust is lightly browned. Cool the bars before cutting.

Tip: *When spreading the bottom crust in the pan, dip the spoon in very warm water to keep the dough pliable.*

Per serving: *Calories: 334; Total fat: 19g; Saturated fat: 11g; Cholesterol: 29mg; Sodium: 126mg; Carbohydrates: 37g; Fiber: 2g; Sugar: 34g; Protein: 9g.*

Chocolate Fleck Cake

Marie Antoinette had it right when she said, "Let them eat cake," and so you shall. This cake looks as good as it tastes. For a 9-inch round or square cake pan, cut the recipe in half. This frosted cake freezes very well. Bake it ahead to have on hand for unexpected company.

Tools: *Electric mixer*

Preparation time: *15 minutes*

Cooking time: *35 minutes*

Yield: *18 servings*

Nonstick cooking spray

1¾ cups gluten-free flour mixture

1 tablespoon baking powder

2 teaspoons baking soda

½ teaspoon salt

½ cup butter, softened

2 cups sugar

1 tablespoon vanilla

4 eggs

1 cup sour cream

3 ounces (3 squares) bittersweet chocolate, grated

¾ cup cold water

½ cup milk

Fudge Icing (see the following recipe)

1 Preheat the oven to 350 degrees. Spray a 9-x-13-inch baking dish with cooking spray.

2 Sift the flour mixture, baking powder, baking soda, and salt into a small bowl. Set aside.

3 In a large mixing bowl, use the mixer to cream the butter until it's fluffy.

4 Add the sugar and vanilla and continue whipping the ingredients until the sugar has been absorbed.

5 Whip in the eggs, one at a time.

6 Whip in the sour cream and grated chocolate.

7 Add the flour mixture alternately with the water and milk until the batter is well blended.

8 Spoon the batter into the prepared baking dish.

9 Bake the batter at 350 degrees for 35 minutes, or until a toothpick inserted in the center comes out clean.

10 Cool the cake completely on a wire rack before frosting.

Per serving, unfrosted: *Calories: 259; Total fat: 12g; Saturated fat: 7g; Cholesterol: 72mg; Sodium: 349mg; Carbohydrates: 37g; Fiber: 1g; Sugar: 23g; Protein: 3g.*

Fudge Icing

¼ cup butter

½ cup cocoa

2 teaspoons vanilla

3 cups sifted confectioners' sugar

1 Melt the butter in a medium saucepan. Remove it from the heat.

2 Using a spoon, stir in the cocoa and vanilla until the ingredients are blended.

3 Stir in the confectioner's sugar until it's blended and the frosting is smooth and spreadable.

Tip: *If the frosting is too thick, add a little milk. If it's too thin, add a little more confectioners' sugar.*

Per serving, frosting only: *Calories: 92; Total fat: 2g; Saturated fat: 1g; Cholesterol: 2mg; Sodium: 18mg; Carbohydrates: 20g; Fiber: 0g; Sugar: 19g; Protein: 0g.*

Caramel Cake

This is the cake you've been waiting to bake. Absolutely *no one* will know this is gluten-free! It's light and delicious. For a large family or for company, make a two-layer cake by doubling the ingredients and baking the batter in two 9-inch cake pans. Double the frosting recipe and use some as filling between the layers and to frost the top of the cake.

Tools: *Electric mixer*

Preparation time: *15 minutes*

Cooking time: *25 minutes*

Yield: *8 servings*

Nonstick cooking spray	*1 cup gluten-free flour mixture*
¼ cup plus ⅔ cup granulated sugar	*1¾ teaspoons baking powder*
2 tablespoons plus ¼ cup water	*¼ teaspoon salt*
¼ cup butter, softened	*½ cup milk*
2 eggs, at room temperature	*Caramel Fondant Frosting (see the following recipe)*
1 teaspoon vanilla	
1 tablespoon mayonnaise	

1 Preheat the oven to 350 degrees. Cut a piece of wax paper to fit the bottom of a 9-inch cake pan. Spray the cake pan with cooking spray, and then insert the wax paper and spray the top of the wax paper.

2 In a small stainless steel saucepan, stir together ¼ cup of sugar and 2 tablespoons of water. Over high heat and stirring constantly, cook the mixture until it's dark amber and the sugar has totally melted (about 4 minutes). Remove from the heat.

3 Very slowly, add the remaining ¼ cup of water, 1 tablespoon at a time. **Warning:** When you add the first 2 tablespoons, there will be a lot of splattering. Stand back so you don't get burned. Let the sizzling subside before adding the next tablespoon of water.

4 Return the pan to the heat. Using a whisk, stir the mixture for 30 seconds. Remove from the heat and let the syrup cool.

5 In a large mixing bowl, use the mixer to cream the butter. Add the remaining ⅔ cup of sugar and continue whipping until the ingredients are fluffy.

6 Add the eggs, one at a time, to the butter mixture, beating well after each addition.

7 Add the vanilla and mayonnaise.

8 Add the cooled sugar syrup, mixing well.

9 In a small bowl, sift together the flour mixture, baking powder, and salt. Add the dry ingredients to the butter mixture alternately with the milk. Use the mixer to whip the batter at medium speed until it's smooth.

10 Pour the batter into the prepared cake pan.

11 Bake the batter at 350 degrees for 25 minutes, or until a toothpick inserted in the center comes out clean.

12 Cool the cake in the pan for 10 minutes, and then invert it onto a cooling rack.

13 When the cake is cool, invert it onto a serving platter and frost it with the Caramel Fondant Frosting.

Tip: *The frosting will be fairly fluid when you spread it on the cake, but it thickens as it sets to form a smooth topping. After you pour the frosting over the top of the cake, use a spoon to spread it just over the edges of the cake so some of the frosting drips down the sides.*

Per serving, unfrosted: Calories: 243; Total fat: 8g; Saturated fat: 4g; Cholesterol: 70mg; Sodium: 258mg; Carbohydrates: 40g; Fiber: 1g; Sugar: 24g; Protein: 3g.

Caramel Fondant Frosting

Tools: *Electric mixer*

Preparation time: *10 minutes*

Cooking time: *15 minutes*

Yield: *Enough to frost a 9-inch single-layer cake*

1 cup brown sugar	*2 tablespoons butter*
⅓ cup half-and-half	*½ teaspoon vanilla*

1 In a small stainless steel saucepan, stir together the brown sugar and half-and-half.

2 Cook the ingredients over medium-low heat without stirring until the mixture reaches soft-ball stage, or 235 degrees on a candy thermometer (about 15 minutes). Remove from heat.

3 Stir in the butter until it has melted, and then let the mixture cool.

4 Transfer the mixture to a small mixing bowl. Stir in the vanilla.

5 Use the mixer to beat the mixture until it's of spreading consistency. (You can add a little half-and-half if the frosting becomes too thick).

Tip: *To cool frosting quickly, place the pan in a sink partially filled with cold water and stir the mixture until it cools.*

Per serving, frosting only: Calories: 143; Total fat: 4g; Saturated fat: 3g; Cholesterol: 11mg; Sodium: 35mg; Carbohydrates: 27g; Fiber: 0g; Sugar: 27g; Protein: 0g.

Surprising Guests with Fancy Finales

When you're preparing a meal for a really special occasion, you want to serve something that will earn ohhhs and ahhhs. The dessert recipes in this section will elicit all sorts of praise, but only after your guests get over their delight at all the trouble you went to for them. (Truthfully, some of these desserts are surprisingly easy, but no one needs to know that.)

The platter you use to serve the dessert makes a difference. Think about it. Doesn't pudding taste better when it's served in a champagne goblet rather than out of a plastic bowl? The extra effort you take to add finishing touches to both the platter and the dessert will enhance the total effect.

Decorate the plate, but also decorate the dessert. Picture a piece of cheese-cake served on its side on a chipped, everyday dish. Now picture that same piece of cheesecake set upon an attractive glass dish that has been drizzled with raspberry syrup and melted white chocolate or dusted with cocoa. Which presentation is more appealing? If you have a frosted cake, use a damp paper towel to pick up chopped nuts or coconut and adhere them to the side of the cake. If you're serving a chocolate cake, load the top with thickly shaved chocolate curls. Even before your guests taste the wonderful dessert, their sense of sight will appreciate the effort you went to and will stimulate their desire to consume your divine creation.

Strawberry Almond Torte

This ultimate version of strawberry shortcake is unlike any you've had before. This recipe calls for two 9-inch round cake pans to make a double-layer dessert, but you can also bake this cake in individual tart pans and then assemble individual strawberry shortcakes.

Tools: *Electric mixer*

Preparation time: *15 minutes*

Cooking time: *25 minutes*

Yield: *12 servings*

Nonstick cooking spray	*3 teaspoons baking powder*
2 cups gluten-free flour mixture	*½ cup plus ⅓ cup butter, softened*
½ teaspoon salt	*1¼ cups granulated sugar*
1 teaspoon baking soda	*4 eggs*

2 teaspoons vanilla

2 tablespoons mayonnaise

2 tablespoons orange juice

1 cup plus 1 to 2 tablespoons whole milk

4 ounces gluten-free almond paste

1 tablespoon amaretto (or milk)

1½ pints strawberries, sliced, sweetened with 1 tablespoon sugar

8-ounce container nondairy whipped topping, thawed

1 Preheat the oven to 350 degrees. Spray two 9-inch cake pans with cooking spray.

2 In a medium bowl, sift together the flour mixture, salt, baking soda, and baking powder. Set aside.

3 In a large mixing bowl, use the mixer to cream ½ cup of butter and the sugar together until they're fluffy. Add the eggs, one at a time, mixing well.

4 Blend in the vanilla, mayonnaise, and orange juice. (The mixture may look curdled.)

5 Slowly add the dry ingredients alternately with 1 cup of milk, blending well.

6 Spread the batter in the prepared pans. Bake the batter at 350 degrees for 25 minutes, or until a toothpick inserted in the center comes out clean. Cool the cakes completely before filling the layers.

7 Break the almond paste into small pieces and place it in a small mixing bowl. Use the mixer to whip together the almond paste and the remaining ⅓ cup of butter on low speed until the ingredients are blended.

8 Whip in the amaretto (or milk) and the remaining 1 to 2 tablespoons of milk until the paste mixture is of spreading consistency.

9 Place 1 cake layer on a serving dish. Spread the almond paste mixture over that layer. Top the paste with half of the whipped topping and then half of the strawberries.

10 Place the second cake layer on top of the first. Spread it with the remaining whipped topping, and arrange the remaining strawberries in an attractive pattern on top. Cover and refrigerate.

Per serving: Calories: 204; Total fat: 22g; Saturated fat: 13g; Cholesterol: 107mg; Sodium: 466mg; Carbohydrates: 59g; Fiber: 3g; Sugar: 31g; Protein: 5g.

No-Bake Lemon Squares

These most definitely are not the lemon squares you have eaten in the past. Sometimes when you're expecting company, you simply don't have enough time to make a complicated dessert, yet you want something delicious to serve. These squares take just minutes to put together. Be sure to allow for chilling time, both for the dessert and for yourself!

Tools: *Electric mixer*

Preparation time: *10 minutes*

Freezer time: *At least 3 hours*

Cooking time: *None*

Yield: *9 servings*

1⅔ cups gluten-free lemon cookie crumbs (about 12 cookies pureed in a blender)	1 can ready-to-spread lemon frosting
2 tablespoons granulated sugar	1 cup small-curd cottage cheese
3½ tablespoons butter, melted	1 cup sour cream

1 In a small bowl, use a fork to blend the cookie crumbs, sugar, and butter.

2 Pat the crumbs into a 9-inch square pan, reserving ¼ cup for the topping.

3 Put the frosting, cottage cheese, and sour cream into a large mixing bowl. Use the mixer to beat the ingredients on high until they're well blended.

4 Spoon the cream mixture on top of the crust.

5 Sprinkle the reserved crumbs on top of the cream mixture.

6 Cover the pan with foil and freeze for at least 3 hours. Remove the squares from the freezer 20 minutes before cutting and serving.

Tip: *Pamela's Lemon Shortbread Cookies are perfect for this recipe. There are 9 cookies in a 7.25 ounce box, so two boxes will be needed . . . and that will leave you with 6 extra cookies to snack on or pack in lunches.*

Vary It! *Not crazy about lemon? Use chocolate cookies for the base and gluten-free canned chocolate frosting in the mix.*

Per serving: *Calories: 456; Total fat: 27g; Saturated fat: 14g; Cholesterol: 47mg; Sodium: 308mg; Carbohydrates: 59g; Fiber: 1g; Sugar: 42g; Protein: 4g.*

Pumpkin Cheesecake

Using premade cookies as the base for this dessert saves you the time of making them from scratch, and you should be able to find excellent gluten-free, packaged gingersnap cookies on the market. You can add a simple garnish by putting dollops of sweetened whipped cream or gluten-free nondairy whipped topping around the edges, and then sprinkling the dollops lightly with cinnamon.

Tools: *9-inch springform pan, electric mixer*

Preparation time: *20 minutes*

Cooking time: *1 hour*

Yield: *9 servings*

1½ cups gingersnap crumbs (an 8-ounce package of gluten-free cookies pureed in a blender)

½ cup finely chopped pecans

½ cup melted butter

Two 8-ounce packages cream cheese, softened

½ cup plus ¼ cup granulated sugar

1 teaspoon vanilla

3 eggs

1 cup canned pumpkin

¾ teaspoon cinnamon

¼ teaspoon nutmeg

¼ teaspoon ginger

1 Preheat the oven to 350 degrees.

2 In a small bowl, mix together the gingersnap crumbs, pecans, and butter with a fork. Press the crust mixture onto the bottom and 1½ inch up the sides of a 9-inch springform pan. Bake the crust at 350 degrees for 10 minutes. When the crust is finished baking, turn the oven temperature down to 325 degrees.

3 In a large mixing bowl, use the mixer to whip together the cream cheese, ½ cup of sugar, and vanilla until they're well blended.

4 Add the eggs, one at a time, until they're blended into the batter.

5 Reserve 1 cup of the batter and set it aside.

6 To the remaining batter in the bowl, add the remaining ¼ cup of sugar, pumpkin, cinnamon, nutmeg, and ginger. Using the mixer, blend well.

7 Spoon the batters alternately on top of the crust. Using a knife, cut through the batter to marbleize.

8 Bake the batter at 325 degrees for 1 hour, or until the top of the cheesecake is dry and the edges are just beginning to brown.

9 Run a knife around the edge of pan, and then let the cake cool completely.

10 When the cheesecake is thoroughly cooled, remove the side of the pan and transfer the cake to a serving dish. Cover and refrigerate.

Tip: *Make sure the cheesecake cools completely before refrigerating it to avoid the top from cracking or getting weepy (where moisture condenses on top of the cheesecake).*

Per serving: *Calories: 454; Total fat: 36g; Saturated fat: 19g; Cholesterol: 155mg; Sodium: 316mg; Carbohydrates: 29g; Fiber: 2g; Sugar: 26g; Protein: 7g.*

Liqueur Cups with Mocha Raspberries

In case the title of the recipe didn't give it away, this piece of work is impressive. Instead of making your own chocolate cups, you can pick up a package of one of several excellent commercial gluten-free chocolate cups on the market.

Tools: *Double boiler, new ½-inch pastry brush, 16 small fluted paper or foil baking cups*

Preparation time: *20 minutes*

Refrigeration time: *60 minutes*

Cooking time: *None*

Yield: *16 servings*

16 chocolate-covered espresso beans	*½ cup whole milk*
16 fresh raspberries	*3 tablespoons amaretto*
1 teaspoon corn oil	*3 tablespoons crème de cacao*
1 cup semisweet chocolate chips, divided	*8-ounce container nondairy whipped topping, thawed*
32 large marshmallows	

1 Insert an espresso bean in the center of each raspberry.

2 Melt ⅓ cup of chocolate chips with the oil in the top of a double boiler over barely simmering water (do not allow the water to boil or to touch the bottom of the top pan).

3 Roll the stuffed raspberries lightly in the chocolate and set them on wax paper to dry.

4 Melt ⅓ cup of chocolate chips in a double boiler over barely simmering water (do not allow the water to boil or to touch the bottom of the top pan). Dip a new, clean, dry ½-inch pastry brush in the melted chocolate. Brush the chocolate on the bottom and insides of the baking cups, approximately ⅛ inch thick, pushing the chocolate into the ridges and smoothing as much as possible. Place the papers or foil cups into muffin pan cups. Chill until the chocolate has set.

5 Carefully peel off the paper or foil; set the chocolate cups aside.

6 In a medium saucepan, combine the marshmallows, the remaining ⅓ cup of chocolate chips, and the milk. Stir constantly over low heat until the chocolate melts and the ingredients are combined. Refrigerate the filling for a few minutes until it thickens.

7 Stir in the amaretto and crème de cacao.

8 Fold in the whipped topping.

9 Carefully spoon the mixture into the chocolate cups. Place a mocha raspberry on top of each dessert. Refrigerate until serving time.

Per serving: *Calories: 166; Total fat: 5g; Saturated fat: 4g; Cholesterol: 1mg; Sodium: 15mg; Carbohydrates: 22g; Fiber: 1g; Sugar: 16g ; Protein: 1g.*

Part IV
The Part of Tens

"I think you're overreacting, but yes, I'll find out if your opponent's boxing gloves are gluten-free."

In this part . . .

Every *For Dummies* books concludes with top-ten lists, and this one is no exception. You'll find one chapter with suggestions for gluten-free comfort foods, and another with ideas for cooking gluten-free with the kids.

Chapter 20

Ten Easy-to-Prepare Comfort Foods

In This Chapter

▶ KISS: Keep It Simple, Silly

▶ Warming you from the inside out

*Y*ou know what comfort foods are — they're the foods you turn to when you're stressed, sad, depressed, happy, or looking for some nostalgic association with memories of the past. But we all know what comfort food *really* means. It means carbs, and I'm not talking about the kind of carbs you get from a pile of broccoli. It means *gluten,* and you know it!

Comfort foods are foods like biscuits, breads, cinnamon rolls, donuts, bagels . . . all the stuff that's off-limits when you're gluten-free. Without those foods to turn to, you may feel stranded, deprived, and restricted, singing, "I can't get no (uh) sa-tis-FAC-tion . . ."

Nope. No singing, no crying, no feeling like you can't have those old family faves. I have some ideas for satisfying those urges while staying 100 percent gluten-free. I'll warn you, though, they're not necessarily calorically correct, so don't come cryin' to me when your jeans don't fit anymore.

Get Your Kicks with an Easy Mix

Fine. I know this is a cookbook. I know you, being a cookbook reader, *love* to search for hard-to-find, ridiculously expensive ingredients. I know you even don't mind measuring, and that you have the patience to let something rise. You might even know what "proofing" is.

Well at the risk of offending those of you Real Cooks, I'm not that. Not any of it. If I want to satisfy my craving for brownies, cookies, cakes, breads, and other wumfy comfy foods, I turn to my favorite mix. Add to it a couple of eggs, a swish of oil, a glob or two of water or milk, and I stick it in the oven, patting myself on the back like I'm Danna Krocker. And you know what? No one knows the difference!

Mom's Old-Fashioned Meatloaf

Nothing says "comfort" like Mom's meatloaf. Just take ground beef (or turkey if you're watching your weight), and add some onion, basil (or any other spices you'd like), a couple of eggs, and some gluten-free crackers or bread crumbs. It really doesn't matter how much of anything you use, so don't sweat it. Using your hands, glob it all together until it's a big ball of — well, raw meatloaf. Stuff (proper cooks might use the term *press*) it into a pan — a bread-loaf pan works well — and bake it at 325 degrees for 45 minutes to an hour. You'll know when it's done when the juices that rise to the top are no longer red — and when the crowd just can't wait any longer.

No Woes with Nachos

It's simple to make great nachos — you start by dumping a pile of chips on a microwaveable or oven-safe plate and topping them with cheese. But from there, you really should think outside the typical-nacho-toppin's box and get creative. Add some veggies (so you can call it nutritious) — maybe sliced zucchini or yellow squash — tomatoes, jalapenos, cooked hamburger or ham slices, chunks of turkey, maybe even anchovies. Okay, I heard a collective groan of "EWWWWs" out there, but I personally love 'em, so give me a break. Leave them off yours if you want to be a party pooper. Throw the whole mess in the microwave or oven until the cheese melts, and you have yourself some nachos. Remember to top them with guacamole!

Potato Salad with a Past

Whether it was part of the family picnics, or a Saturday night staple, potato salad definitely makes it into the comfort food compartment. Start with (please tell me you can guess what I'm going to say next) potatoes. Yes! You guessed it! Potatoes! Just peel them, and then cook them for a really long time — until they're mushy-to-taste (some people like 'em chunky and crunchy). Then drain and mush 'em up. At this point, you can add pretty much anything you want and call it potato salad. Mayo, sour cream, hard-boiled eggs, onion, sweet pickles or relish (ick), salt, pepper, spices . . . you get the idea. Remember to refrigerate it if it has dairy products in it.

Heavenly Homemade Veggie Soup (Go Ahead and Add the Pasta!)

Soup is, by definition, a potpourri of yummy stuff all melded together in a big hodge-podge of warmth and flavor. Cooking-wise, soup is my kind of recipe rebel — for the most part, no matter what you throw in there, you can't go wrong. Shopping-wise, it's easier yet: A quick stop in the meat aisle (or skip it if you're vegetarian), and another in the produce aisle, a quick grab of premade chicken or beef stock, and you're outta there. Throw everything into a slow cooker or Dutch oven, and let it cook slowly, adding spices and extra water or a little wine as you'd like. About five minutes before you want to eat, add some gluten-free pasta, if you'd like. By the time you serve it, it should be just right.

Hey Puddin', How'd Ya Get So Sweet?

Puddings are easy to make, using basic ingredients including milk, sugar, eggs, fruits, and spices — as well as some kind of thickener such as gluten-free flour (you may want to use rice or tapioca). Break out your most romantic spices, add a little fruit (canned blueberries are nice), a teaspoon or so of vanilla, and whip in a touch of cream. Cook the pudding slowly on the stove in a double boiler, or maybe in a water bath in the oven. Take your time, though. Puddings need to cook slowly to prevent curdling, and the family will appreciate the scents that linger longer. Make lots, however, because pudding is just as good cold as it is warm.

Chow Down New England Style!

Lots of things about clam chowder entitle it to bear the designation of a comfort food. It may bring back memories of celebrating the New Year with warm, creamy white soup topped with paprika or nutmeg. Or maybe you've visited or lived in New England, retaining nostalgic thoughts of the misty New England coastline, the seafood, frosty winters, shrimp boats, and of course, New England clam chowder!

The problem with most clam chowders is that the recipes call for flour — but just a tablespoon or so. I figure, why bother? And, more important, what's the point? If you must, use a gluten-free flour to thicken, but note that purists prefer their chowder un-thickened with plenty of crisp bacon, onion, new potatoes, and thyme — and lots of fat, fresh-from-the-ocean clams! Not being a purist *or* a Real Cook, I use canned minced clams. Serve with some crunchy gluten-free crackers or bread you've made from a recipe in this book.

Quick and Simple "Mac-a-Cheese"

Few foods soothe the soul like creamy, gooey macaroni and cheese. Whipping up a gluten-free version is quick and easy. There are all types of gluten-free pastas available — some are made from corn, others from rice or brown rice, and they come in all shapes and sizes. Best of all, they taste like the real deal! They're widely available these days, and even regular grocery stores often carry them. Pick a pasta shape and taste you like, and cook it *al dente* (my Real Cook friends tell me this means "so it's not cooked all the way"). Add your favorite kind of cheese (Velveeta works well and has even less fat and calories than cheddar!), and let it melt. If you want a thinner consistency, add a little milk and butter. Then dig in and enjoy the "mac-a-cheese" satisfaction.

Chase Away the Winter Blahs with a Big Bowl of Chili

There are a bazillion ways to make chili, but no matter how you make it, chili always gives you that warm-you-from-the-inside comfort-food feeling. My personal favorite is black-bean chili, with or without meat. If I add meat, I usually use ground turkey. Brown the meat first (I usually sauté some veggies with the meat), and then just start adding ingredients. For this version, I use lots of black beans (hence the clever name "black bean chili"), some diced chilies, diced tomatoes, and the secrets to success: brown sugar and honey. I realize that some like it thicker than others — to thin it out you can add some chicken or beef stock, and then just let it simmer for hours. You can serve it over brown rice, or if you like Ohio-style chili, you can serve it over pasta with onions and cheese sprinkled on top.

Cheeseburgers in Paradise

Cheeseburgers *are* paradise, no matter where you are when you eat 'em. You can try to find edible gluten-free hamburger buns, but I'll warn you that they're tough to find, and they cost a fortune. Instead, consider wrapping your burger in a crispy lettuce leaf (I like them chilled). Even most restaurants will serve them that way, but be careful that they don't just give you a burger that they've plucked the bun off of, because the burger will be glutenated with bun crumbs.

Chapter 21

Ten Ideas for Cooking Gluten-Free with the Kids

In This Chapter
▶ Letting your little helpers give you a hand
▶ Sneaking in some food facts
▶ Serving meals in creative settings

Parents of young children have this June Cleaver fantasy of cooking with kids. Everyone is wearing aprons (matching and homemade, of course). The kids are standing on their stepstools (that they made with Dad in the garage that morning) and politely taking turns measuring and pouring without so much as a drop spilled on the counter. Half an hour later, a beautiful creation is passed around and hailed as holy, while the children, bursting with pride, sample their creations.

In reality, kids don't care whether the electric mixer is still on when they pull it out of the batter. Nor do they realize that it's important to hold the cracked egg over the bowl *before* breaking it open (but they *do* know that Mommy grumbles a lot when she cleans eggs off the kitchen floor). They're about as careful at measuring as I am (not very), and although their hand-eye coordination for video games is exceptional, they can't seem to pour an ingredient *into* a bowl. And as for politely taking turns — yeah, a mom can dream.

But ya know what? It's still fun. *Really* fun. And although little helpers are sometimes far from helpful, getting in the kitchen and cooking something is a part of life that no child should miss. Furthermore, learning to cook is educational and will encourage them to eat more nutritiously than if they become accustomed to turning to processed snack foods.

So don your apron, dig up a makeshift stepstool or two, and keep the broom and mop handy. It's time to get cookin' with the kids!

Have a Lasagna Night

Lasagna is a cinch. You can buy several varieties of gluten-free lasagna noodles in health food stores. Personally, I like the type that doesn't have to be cooked first, because — well, I've already admitted that patience isn't my greatest strength, and using noodles that don't have to be cooked first allows me to skip a step. It also prevents me from cooking them too long and ending up with mush. If you use the kind of lasagna noodles that don't have to be cooked first, be sure to make sure the dry noodles are touching sauce so they become tender while they cook. Then just layer with your favorite ingredients like you would a "regular" lasagna, bake, and voilá! It's lasagna night!

Use Cooking to Teach Ingredient Insights

One of the best ways to know whether a prepared food is gluten-free (at a restaurant, for instance) is to know how it's usually prepared. For example, if you know that meatloaf generally has bread crumbs in it, you know that at a restaurant, social event, friend's house, or market, the meatloaf available to the general public is probably off-limits. One of the valuable lessons kids pick up when cooking with you is what ingredients generally go into what prepared foods. They also start to understand how to make choices, substitutions, and other decisions that are crucial for a gluten-free lifestyle.

Jazz Up Meals with Colorful Vegetables

The healthiest meal is one with a rainbow of colors. Prepare a healthy supply of veggies, such as red, yellow, and green peppers, tomatoes, cucumbers, radishes, and carrots, and keep them in the refrigerator. Before serving, slice the veggies thinly — or cut them into different shapes (pointy triangles, twists, comb shapes, or whatever you can think of).

Throw a Homemade Pizza Party

Nothing is more fun to make together (albeit messy, messy, messy) than pizza. Everyone can make theirs the way they like it, so you can turn it into a pizza party and let everyone have it their way. Use a premade gluten-free crust, or make one from the recipe in Chapter 10. Then set out a bunch of veggies, remembering to incorporate lots of color, and whatever meats the kids like (or use the leftover meatloaf from Chapter 20's recipe). Smear the crust with a little spaghetti sauce, and then let the kids add the toppings they like. Top with some grated cheese if you want, and then bake the pizzas at 325 degrees until the cheese starts to melt (about 8 to 10 minutes), and enjoy the smell as it fills the house with that pizza-to-perfection aroma.

Try Some Herbalicious Preparations

People think children like things plain — and they do — but they also like a little excitement in their foods. As you're teaching them to cook, make sure to introduce them to herbs, which add flavor and nutrients and are *always* gluten-free. Let the kids pick out some fresh herbs from the store, or better yet, grow your own in a windowsill herb garden. Pinch off a leaf every now and then, squeeze it or rub it, and let the kids enjoy the different herbal fragrances. Let them suggest recipes that would be good with the various herbs. Here are some ideas: homemade tomato basil soup, Minty Juleps (using lemonade, Sprite, or whatever you happen to have on hand), spaghetti, salads, and omelets.

Make It Fancy Schmancy

I know I'm all about simplicity, but everyone enjoys dressing up from time to time. And what better reason to pull out the fancy duds than for an elegant dinner that the kids plan. Don't worry, you may think they'll plan an all-dessert-day (okay, those are fun, too!), but they won't. They know what's good, and they'll probably come up with some great ideas. Use your best tableware and silverware, and make sure that good conversation is part of the meal. Maybe play some soft music in the background. Have everyone dress up! Try to have one of these elegant evenings once a month or so.

Have Fun with Food Facts

It's never too early to teach children about good nutrition. Take time while you're cooking with your kids to talk to them about why they need to eat lots of protein (it helps their muscles grow) and explain which foods are good sources of protein. Remind them that fruits and veggies are important for lots of reasons, and have them think of healthy snacks and meals. The more they get involved with the decision-making process, the more impact it will have on their food choices in the future.

Make Candy

You know those cute candied fruit and flowers that decorate cakes, cookies, and other treats? They're really not that hard to make! And kids love making them — just watch out for curious little fingers wanting to dip into hot syrup! Start by making sugar syrup (also called *simple syrup*) by mixing sugar and water over low heat until it turns clear — then boil it for a minute or two longer. You can make the syrup as sweet and thick as you want by adding extra sugar. I'm really not much for measuring, but if you want a starting point, try three parts water to one part sugar for thin syrup, and then keep adding sugar to make it thicker. After you have the syrup the consistency you want, dip the fruit or flowers in it. Set them on wax paper while the syrup cools and hardens.

Emphasize Breakfast by Making It Fun

Everyone knows breakfast is the most important meal of the day, so how do you get kids to eat in the morning? It's all about the fun! Try making funny-face pancakes — just mix an egg, a little apple juice, some butter, and gluten-free baking mix (sorry, I don't measure — you *know* the consistency you're looking for!). You might want to add a little cinnamon or nutmeg for a twist. Whisk it all together, and pour the batter into a lightly oiled frying pan — make "ears" if you want — and then let the kids decorate the pancakes with powdered sugar and maple syrup. They can use fruit chunks or slices for the eyes; mouths can be made from oranges (go ahead and leave the rind on — it's edible *and* healthy!).

Picnic in the Playroom

Picnics are a blast, but sometimes the weather just doesn't permit. That's okay. A picnic is still a picnic as long as some of the important elements are there: eating with your fingers, sitting on a blanket on the ground, and maybe even gluten-free s'mores! The important thing is to anticipate the fun of a picnic, no matter where it is. Plan special foods to eat with your fingers, like hot dogs, deviled eggs, chicken bites, and fruit chunks.

Oh, and about those s'mores. They're really easy to make gluten-free style. Just take your favorite cookie (some companies do make gluten-free "graham" crackers) and use it for the outside. Roast your marshmallows — sure, do it over the stove if you want, but be careful — then put part of a chocolate bar in the middle and squish it all together. Now *that's* a picnic!

Index

• *N* •